# LeeWards *Illustrated Library of*

# *Arts and Crafts*

**FULLER & DEES**
TIMES MIRROR

New York • Los Angeles • Montgomery

## FULLER AND DEES

**PRESIDENT**
James Lueck

**PROJECT EDITORS**
Pat Warner
Nell McInnish

## THOMAS A. CHACHARON & ASSOCIATES AND SYNTHEGRAPHICS CORPORATION

**EXECUTIVE EDITOR**
Richard G. Young

**CONSULTING EDITORS**
Thomas A. Chacharon
Sidney Lewis

**PROJECT EDITOR**
Bonnie Oberman

**ART DIRECTOR**
Will Gallagher

**PICTURE EDITOR**
Holly Harrington

**ASSOCIATE PICTURE EDITOR**
Barbara Metzger

**LAYOUT STAFF**
John Mahoney
Deloras Nicholas
Joseph Petek

**COPY RECORDERS**
Nancy Bonfield
Linda Noel

**ASSIGNMENT PHOTOGRAPHY**
Larry Gregory
Wayne Lennenbach

**ILLUSTRATIONS**

Joanna Adamski-Koperska
Victor Brecher
Joe Chmura
John Draves
Ken Hirte
Margalit Matso
Will Norman
Joe Petek
Gabriel
David Meyer

## LEE WARDS

**CONSULTANTS**
Ward Beck
Ken Bieschke

## CONTRIBUTING AUTHORS

**Lucille Bealmer** (Batik)
Instructor in Art Education
Art Department
Northern Illinois University

**Dorothea A. Bilder** (Silk Screen)
Assistant Professor
Art Department
Northern Illinois University

**Barbara W. Eshback** (Color in Crafts)
Instructor, Lecturer
Troy, New York

**Dennis A. Grabowski** (Macrame')
Instructor of Art
Niles High School
Skokie, Illinois

**Charles A. Guerin** (Relief Printing)
Teaching Assistant
Northern Illinois University

**Lily D. Klump** (Felt Craft)
Author of handicraft books

**David McKay** (Co-author Mask Making)
Associate Professor and Director of Graduate Art Program
Northern Illinois University

**Elizabeth McKay** (Co-author Mask Making)
Chairman of Art Department
Elgin High School
Elgin, Illinois

**Miriam W. Meyer** (Terrariums)
Author, Illustrator of published works on plants and wildflowers

**Beverly J. Plummer** (Crafting with Gourds)
Author of books and articles on folklore, folk music, and crafts

**Anita Schlossberg** (Needlepoint)
Vice-President and Crafts Coordinator
Marita Enterprises
Boston, Massachusetts

©FULLER & DEES MCMLXXIV
3734 Atlanta Highway, Montgomery, Alabama 36109
Library of Congress Cataloging in Publication Data
Main entry under title:

**The Illustrated Library of Creative Arts and Crafts**

1. Handicraft.
TT157.I43          745.5          74-22068
Complete Set ISBN 0-87197-076-7
Volume I ISBN 0-87197-077-5

# Introduction

**The Illustrated Library of Creative Arts and Crafts** is designed for the beginner interested in becoming involved in crafts. Because of the renewed interest in creative handicrafts, this series describes more than forty different types of crafts — all contained in a single source. These volumes could not cover all possible crafts, so the articles are limited to those of current popularity and to those which involve a minimum of expense.

Each article is divided into six main categories. The **Historical Introduction** describes the origin and development of the craft, its spread through various cultures, as well as famous people who have been associated with the craft. The **Common Terms** section defines terms, items, or names as they relate to the individual craft. **Basic Equipment and Supplies** lists the tools and materials needed. The section under **Basic Procedures** provides start-to-finish procedures for handicraft projects. Each article also contains three to five projects based on the supplies and procedures discussed. **For Additional Reading** lists other references for those who wish to increase their knowledge of a particular craft.

**The Illustrated Library of Creative Arts and Crafts** is intended not only to inspire the budding craftsman, but to provide new ideas, techniques and whole new areas of creative handicrafts for the experienced craftsman to explore. The fun-to-do projects in this comprehensive series will be a source of enjoyment and relaxation for the entire family.

# *Table Of Contents*

A very old Oriental process, silk screen printing techiniques are widely used by artists and craftsmen alike.

Because of its soft, nonwoven texture, felt is an excellent material for gift and bazaar items, toys, and wearing apparel.

Relief Printing offers today's craftsman a simple, effective handprinting method.

For centuries, masks have been used in religious ceremonies, for entertainment, as well as "just for fun" projects.

Once the province of Victorian parlors, these gardens-under-glass are not only beautiful and decorative, but make delightful family projects.

# Macramé

**The ancient art of knotting has been revived as a popular and intriguing twentieth-century craft.**

Many people tend to think of macramé as a relatively new craft. However, like several other currently popular crafts, the fascinating art of knotting is an extremely old activity in which there has been a renewed interest in recent years.

Knotting and the decorative intertwining of knots can be found in headdresses, yokes of robes, fringes, shawls, and other articles of clothing from some of the earliest civilizations. Ancient Egyptian and Assyrian friezes and paintings contain examples of this technique. African tribal masks include excellent samples of this early craft, as does the knotted armor used in Africa during the Middle Ages. The headmen of the Marquesas Islands in Polynesia used macramé techniques to create body ornaments that were decorated with shells and other objects from the sea. Further examples of macramé and weaving are to be found in the basketry of the North American Indians.

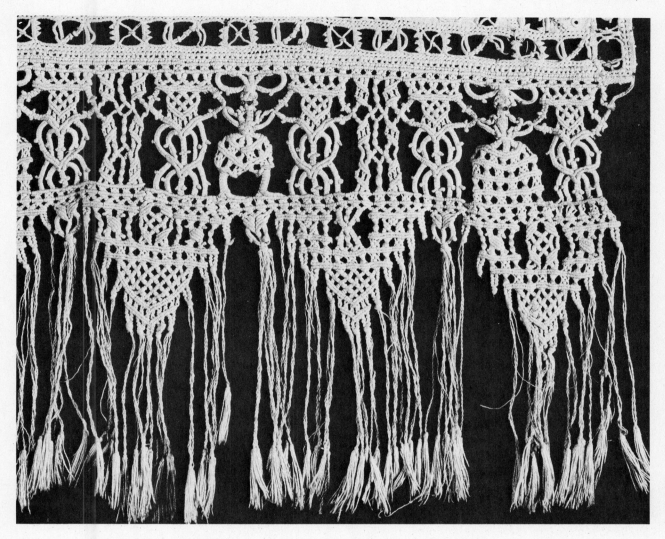

**Figure 2. Sixteenth- and seventeenth-century Italian lacemakers utilized macramé to create intricate designs. In this piece of seventeenth-century macramé lace from Italy, figures of men and women are formed by using Horizontal and Diagonal Clove Hitch Knots. (Courtesy, The Art Institute of Chicago.)**

The spread of macramé throughout Europe by the Crusaders and by the gradually increasing mobility of people is a most interesting study. Macramé was introduced to the Spaniards by the Moors during their long military occupation of Spain. Using needles and small hooked tools to work lace patterns, the traditional Spanish lace mantilla was made in this way.

Italian lacemakers of the sixteenth and seventeenth centuries were skilled at *punto gropo* or *groposi* (knotted point), with which they created

**Figure 1. Macrame hanging planters have become extremely popular with the increase in indoor gardening. (Courtesy, The Macrame Workshop, Chicago; photo, Bill Arsenault.)**

delicate and intricate patterns at the unwoven ends of a piece of fabric. Lace was also made as a separate material and attached to a fabric, as on liturgical linens and ecclesiastical vestments.

During the seventeenth and eighteenth centuries, the making of lace was frequently undertaken by English court ladies. Indeed, the Victorian period was responsible for a flurry of macramé activity. Not only did these ladies make such personal articles as parasols, handkerchiefs, small purses, collars, pin cushions, and watch pockets, the overly decorated interiors of drawing rooms and parlors were embellished with such macramé creations as mantelpieces, pillow covers, window draperies, bell pulls, and light shades.

Knotting has always been popular with seamen; sailors in the British Royal Navy used it extensively to decorate their ships. Bell covers, sea chest covers, table cloths, bunk pockets, and picture frames were just a few of the items produced by these men during their off-duty hours at sea. Often these pieces of handwork were used as gifts when the sailors went ashore, helping to spread the craft of macramé to such places as the South Seas, the China coast, India, and the Americas. "Square Knotting" and "McNamara's Lace" were two of the terms used by the sailors to describe their work. In fact, the term macramé did not come into use until the nineteenth century. It comes from *madrama*, a Turkish word that means "towel" or "napkin", and the Arabic word *migramah*, which refers to an embroidered veil.

Because of the machine-manufactured styles and the emphasis of the modern, streamlined look during the 1920's and 1930's macramé lost its popularity during the early part of this century. Now, with the attention being given to crafts and the value being placed on handmade objects, macramé has again become a popular craft that provides much satisfaction and enjoyment for those who undertake it.

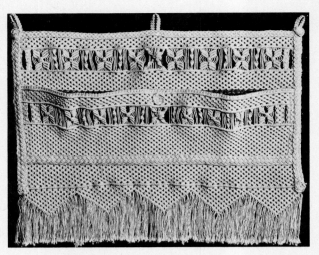

*Figure 4. Alternating Square Knots and Diagonal Clove Hitches are knotted with white seine twine to form a sailor's bunk pocket. The bunk pocket is used to store personal items in the crowded quarters of a ship. (Courtesy, Costume and Textile Study Collection, School of Home Economics, University of Washington.)*

## Common Terms Used In Macramé

**Alternating Knots:** horizontal rows of knots that also form a pattern of knots on the diagonal.

**Clove Hitch:** a horizontal, diagonal, or vertical knot in which the working thread loops twice around one or more core threads.

**Core Threads** (cords): the center cords that have a knot tied over them.

**Holding Cord:** a beginning cord that has additional cords fed onto it, generally by means of a Lark's Head knot.

**Knotting Board:** a board on which the working threads are pinned or taped.

**Knotting Cords:** also called "working cords," those cords or threads that are tied over a core thread.

**Negative Area:** those parts of a macramé design that are open or unknotted.

**Positive Area:** those parts of a macramé design that are filled with knots.

**Sampler:** a small piece of macramé that illustrates how knots are tied.

**Sennit:** a series of knots, usually Square knots, tied and repeated to produce a chain.

**Spiral Knot:** one-half of a Square knot; uses the

*Figure 3. Knotting has been used extensively by sailors for both utilitarian and decorative purposes. A variety of knots is handsomely displayed on this nineteenth-century sailor's sampler. (Courtesy, The Mariners Museum of Newport News, Virgina.)*

same beginning cord and spirals around its core threads.

**Square Knot:** a flat knot made by tying two working cords over two or more core threads.

**Working Thread:** see Knotting Cord.

## Basic Equipment And Supplies

Many people feel it is necessary to invest in sophisticated tools before they can seriously begin to work on a craft project. This is almost impossible with macramé because the tools one needs are likely to be items that one already owns. For those materials that must be purchased, however, hardware stores, craft shops, knitting suppliers, upholstery supply stores, and rope companies are all excellent sources for supplies. The yellow pages of the telephone directory are helpful in locating a special kind of material: check under rope, yarn, string, etc. A local hobby shop may have just what is needed, although the material might be recommended for something other than macramé. Common sense, buying and tying various cords, and evaluating results are the best way to determine which materials are best suited for one's purposes.

The following is a list of items that may be useful when undertaking almost any macramé project:

1. A padded surface. This refers to the knotting board; it may be styrofoam block, a clip board with a heavy piece of cardboard attached to it, a piece of insulation board or homosote, a polyurethane foam pad, or a cork board.

2. Pins or tacks. These help to keep the tension constant on the holding cord and to mark pattern distances on the macramé object.

3. Scissors.

4. Rubber bands. These will hold long macramé cords that have been wound into a bundle.

5. Crochet hook (or a bent paper clip). A hook of some sort is often needed to pull or force a cord through a bead or complicated knot.

6. Rug or tapestry needle. Either of these serves as a handy tool for weaving in loose ends or finishing off the end of an object.

7. Cord. This is the one item used in macramé that has the greatest variation in selection.

Using common sense and maintaining an inquisitive attitude is essential when determining what kind of cord is best. Generally, any kind of cord will do when beginning to learn the basic knots. It would be more advantageous, however, to use a thick cotton cord as the knots will be more clearly visible. When selecting macramé cord, avoid a smooth, slick cord because it cannot hold a tight knot. Many synthetic cords, for example, are difficult to knot because they relax and loosen after they have been tied. Also unsatisfactory for knotting is soft yarn. Because the yarn stretches as it is pulled, it is very difficult to maintain a good definition of knots. These two hints should not restrict one who is searching for suitable materials, nor should one cease experimenting with different kinds of cording. Once work has begun, however, individual sensitivity will determine the right material for a particular object.

## Basic Procedures

Using macramé to create an object is not at all difficult once a person understands and knows how to employ certain essential procedures. As a first step, proper measurement of the working cords will not only make the work more enjoyable but also easier to finish.

### MEASURING MACRAMÉ CORDS

To avoid having to add to cords that have become too short to work with, it is important to begin with the proper length of material. To do this, the final length of the finished piece should be estimated and multiplied by four. Therefore, if the desired finished product is to be a two-foot long wall hanging, the cords used should be approximately eight feet long. This amount of material will then accommodate any knot chosen.

The number of cords needed can be estimated by use of the following method: Lay short pieces of cord next to each other until their width is equal to one inch. For example, if five cords laid side by side measure one inch wide, then a wall hanging that is going to be 12 inches wide will require 60 vertical cords. However, since some kind of starting knot must be used to attach a vertical cord to the holding cord, two verticals or knotting cords will be made from each length of cord that is cut. Thus, only 30 cords have to be cut instead of 60, but the cords should be eight times the length of the proposed piece. Then, when each cord is folded in half and tied to the holding cord, the result will be the proper number of verticals at four times the length of the final piece.

Consider, for example, a piece that is to be 12 inches wide and two feet long. When laid next to each other, there are five cords in one inch. Therefore, 30 lengths of cord, each 16 feet long, are cut. The cords are then folded in half and tied to the holding cord, thereby resulting in 60 verticals that are eight feet long.

Obviously, some knots will require more cord than other knots. One such knot is the Clove Hitch: both the core of the Clove Hitch knot as well as the working or knotting thread of the Vertical Clove Hitch need extra cord. For this reason, it is recommended that an extra long cord be fed into the macramé in addition to the regular number of verticals.

In finishing an object, one may wish to eliminate the ends of the verticals. These ends should not be cut too short; rather, they should contain a generous two inches of cord. Then the ends should be carefully woven back into the final knots on the back of the finished piece. The ends may also become fringe that gently brings the macramé to completion.

## BASIC MACRAMÉ KNOTS

A knot is produced by intertwining two cords with each other and fixing their tension. In macramé there are certain knots that are considered basic because (1) the procedures used to tie them are closely related, (2) the patterns they create are quite similar, and (3) the purpose they serve is fundamental to the creation of a knotted object.

### Lark's Head

When starting a piece of work, the Lark's Head Knot is useful for fixing the working threads in a beginning position. The following procedures are those used for tying a Lark's Head Knot:

**1.** Cut a holding cord and pin or tie it to a knotting board.

**2.** Cut a group of four cords 24 inches long.

**3.** Fold one of the cords in half making a loop. Place the loop *under* the horizontal holding cord so that the loop is pointing down.

**4.** Reach through the loop and draw the ends of the cord down through the loop.

**5.** Pull the cord ends and tighten the Lark's Head Knot.

**6.** Use the Lark's Head Knot to tie the remaining cords to the holding cord in order to prepare for tying additional macramé knots.

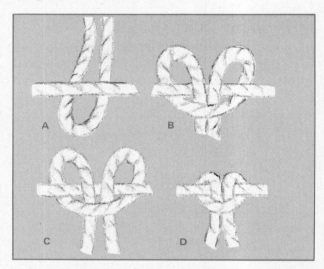

*Figure 5. The Larks Head Knot is tied by placing a looped cord under the horizontal holding cord as shown in (a); the ends of the cord are drawn down through the loop (b) and tightened (c) to form the final knot (d).*

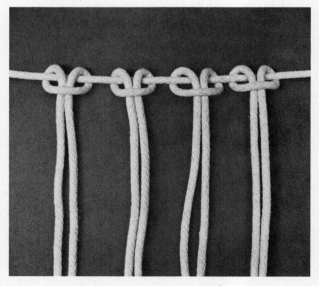

*Figure 6. To begin a piece of macramé, working cords are fastened to a holding cord with Larks Head Knots. (Linda Parker.)*

## The Clove Hitch—Horizontal

The Clove Hitch (also referred to as the Double Half Hitch) is an important knot because learning how to tie it provides basic information for tying a variety of other knots. When knotted repeatedly in rows, the Clove Hitch can serve as a solid knotted surface or as a decorative band of relief knots between open areas of a macramé object. Moreover, because the Clove Hitch functions as a linear knot similar to a single line in a drawing, an entire surface of these knots can be created in a horizontal, diagonal, or vertical pattern.

To tie the Horizontal Clove Hitch, one must begin with a holding cord to which a group of vertical cords has been attached with the Lark's Head Knot. Then, working left to right, proceed as follows:

**1.** Using the first vertical thread as the horizontal core, place it on top of the remaining vertical cords. The horizontal core can also be a new thread of sufficient length that is laid across the vertical threads. The core can be pinned or taped in place.

**2.** The next "working" vertical thread should be brought from under the horizontal core, looped over the top of the core, and then dropped down behind the core and pulled to the *left* of its starting point.

**3.** The knot should be tightened to the left.

**4.** Repeat the same procedure in order to tie the second half of the knot.

**5.** The knot is again tightened to the left.

In order to pack the row of Clove Hitches under the row of Lark's Head Knots, one must be sure that there is no slack between the Lark's Head Knot and the first Clove Hitch Knot. Making sure that the first knot is tight prevents any unsightly gapping between the rows of Clove Hitches. Use the thumbnail to push the Clove Hitches together;

**Figure 7. To begin the Horizontal Clove Hitch, the first vertical cord on the left is placed horizontally across the top of the remaining vertical cords (a) to form a horizontal core. The second vertical thread is looped over the top of the horizontal core, dropped down behind the core, and pulled to the left (b); the procedure is repeated with the same vertical strand (c) to form the second part of the knot. The finished knot is pushed to the left, and the process is continued with each successive vertical cord (d) until the row has been completed. To form a second row, the horizontal core used in the first row is pulled back across the vertical cords (e). The vertical thread on the right is looped over the horizontal core, and the same procedure is simply followed in reverse (f).**

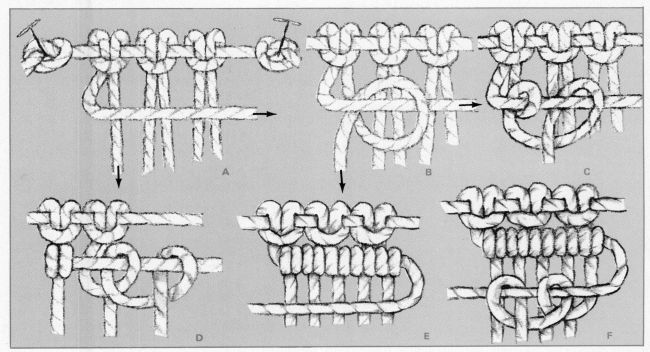

this will contribute to the neatness of the work. A complete Clove Hitch Knot has a single vertical thread dropping down from between the two loops that form the knot.

In tying the horizontal Clove Hitch or its diagonal and vertical variations, the following rules are important: (1) The core thread, which is not a "working" thread, does not move; it always remains in a consistent directional position. (2) The core thread always lays on top of the working thread. That is, at the start of a new knot, the core should be on top and the working thread underneath.

After completing a row of Clove Hitches by working left to right, one then works right to left as follows:

**1.** Continue to use the same core thread, moving it so that it is pinned or taped to the left of the vertical knotting threads.

**2.** Using the vertical thread at the far right from under the horizontal core, loop it over the top of the core. Next, drop it down behind the core and pull it to the right of its starting point.

**3.** Tighten the knot and remove any gap between the original row of knots and this one, which is the first knot in the second row.

**4.** Repeat the procedure in order to tie the second half of the Clove Hitch. Be sure to keep checking for any gapping or inconsistencies in the tightness of the knotting.

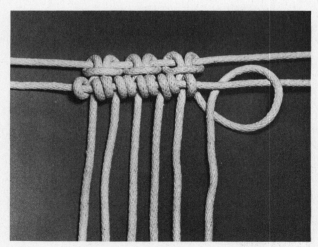

*Figure 8. Learning to tie the Clove Hitch Knot is an essential lesson in macramé. Once mastered, the versatile knot may be used to create a variety of interesting patterns. (Linda Parker.)*

## The Clove Hitch—Diagonal

The steps for knotting the Diagonal Clove Hitch from left to right and from right to left are the same as those used for knotting the Horizontal Clove Hitch. But in order to tie diagonal knots, the core thread is held, pinned, or taped at an angle.

To tie an X with Diagonal Clove Hitches, it is recommended that a top row of Horizontal Clove Hitches be tied over a horizontal core that is a new thread rather than an existing vertical thread. (See Step 1 in the procedure for tying the Horizontal Clove Hitch.) This not only improves the symmetry of the knotted surface; the two ends of the new core thread also become the diagonals of

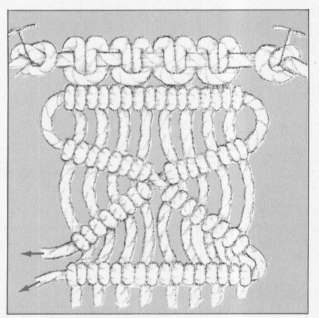

*Figure 9. The Diagonal Clove Hitch, a variation of the Horizontal Clove Hitch, is created by placing the core thread on an angle and tying Clove Hitch Knots along the diagonal core. The resulting pattern will depend upon the selection and placement of the core thread.*

the X. One of the diagonal threads can then become the bottom of Horizontal Clove Hitches unless the X pattern is continued, in which case the diagonals continue to criss-cross the length of the macramé.

The Clove Hitch Knot can also be given a curved direction by carefully controlling the core thread to follow a curve. It is possible to work in any direction as long as the direction is carefully planned and the core thread is guided properly. Pinning the core thread or marking a curve or an angle on a sheet of paper and laying it under the macramé might prove helpful with more complicated directional Clove Hitch Knots.

## The Clove Hitch—Vertical

The Vertical Clove Hitch is basically the same knot as the Horizontal and Diagonal Clove Hitches. However, there are certain major differences between the working thread and the core thread: (1) The working or knotting thread is the horizontal thread and is always behind the core. (2) The core thread is the vertical thread and is always on top of the working thread.

To tie the Vertical Clove Hitch, it is best to begin by using the Lark's Head Knot to attach a series of not less than four cords approximately 18 inches long to a holding cord. Then a row of Horizontal Clove Hitches should be tied from *right to left*, using a new core thread that also measures 18 inches and that has a beginning tail of about two inches at the right end of the core. After this has been done, the Vertical Clove Hitch is tied from left to right as follows:

**1.** Start with the left end of the horizontal core by laying it under the first vertical thread. Note that the horizontal core has now become the ''worker.''

**2.** Loop the working thread over the vertical core, then feed it behind the core and up through the loop.

**3.** Tighten the knot by holding the vertical core taut and pulling the working thread in an upward direction.

**4.** To tie the second half of the knot, bring the working thread again in front of the vertical core. Then feed it behind the core and up through the loop.

**5.** Tighten this second knot by again holding the vertical core and pulling the working thread in an upward direction. After completing the first Vertical Clove Hitch, it will appear as two beads, one on top of the other.

Continue the rest of the knotting, always placing the vertical core on top of the horizontal knotting working thread.

After the first row of Vertical Clove Hitch knots is tied from left to right, the next row proceeds from right to left. Once again, the working thread is placed behind the vertical core.

**1.** Bring the horizontal working thread over the vertical core, then feed it behind the core and up through the loop.

*Figure 10. To form a row of Vertical Clove Hitches, the horizontal core changes its role and becomes the working thread. The knot is started by placing the horizontal working thread under the first vertical thread, now serving as the vertical core. The working thread is looped over the vertical core, fed behind the core, and pulled through the loop to form the first half of the knot. To tie the second half of the knot, the working thread is again brought in front of the vertical core, fed behind the core through the loop (a), and tightened by pulling the working thread in an upward direction. The procedure is continued on each consecutive vertical thread (b) until the row has been completed. The second row is formed in the same manner starting from the opposite direction (c).*

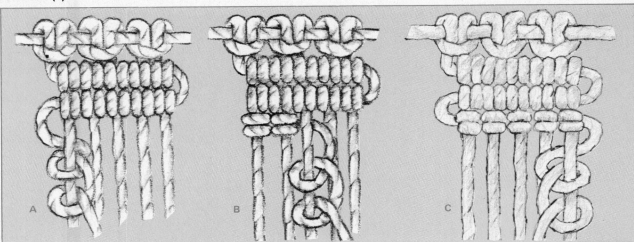

**2.** Tighten the first loop.

**3.** Again bring the working thread in front of the vertical core, then feed it behind the core and up through the loop.

**4.** Tighten the second knot.

In order to pack even rows of Vertical Clove Hitch Knots that lay solidly next to each other, be sure to remove the gap between the rows of knots by tightly tying the first half of a new knot. This will create a more solid surface.

When tied in a number of rows, the Vertical Clove Hitch will resemble the Horizontal Clove Hitch. Using the two knots next to each other can provide a very handsome surface and also impart great strength and stiffness to macramé. By increasing or decreasing the tightness of these knots, a concave/convex form can be created. Practice and experimentation will illustrate the many patterns, shapes, and dimensional forms that can be achieved with the Clove Hitch Knot.

### The Square Knot and the Alternating Square Knot

Of the many knots used in macramé, the two that are most important and most basic are the Clove Hitch Knot and the Square Knot. All other knots are either variations of these two or use parts of them. Hence, understanding these knots and being able to tie them is essential in learning the art of macramé.

Begin the Square Knot with a holding cord to which a group of vertical cords has been attached by the Lark's Head Knot. Use six vertical cords that are approximately 24 inches long; divided in half, this will give 12 verticals measuring about 12 inches each.

The Square Knot is tied with four verticals. It is, therefore, always easiest to work with a multiple of four when tying Square Knots. Follow these steps:

**1.** Using the first four vertical threads, allow the two middle threads to become the core or non-working cores.

**2.** Lay the *left* outside vertical over the two center cores.

**3.** Lay the *right* outside vertical over the "tail" or end of the left cord.

**4.** Pass the right vertical under the center cores and up through the loop made by the left cord.

**5.** Pull the two cords tight. This is the first half of the Square Knot.

**6.** To tie the second half of the knot, lay the *right* cord over the center core of threads.

**7.** Next place the left cord on top of the tail of the right cord.

**8.** Pass the left cord under the center core of threads and up through the loop made by the right cord.

*Figure 11. Using four vertical cords attached to a holding cord by a Larks Head Knot, a Square Knot is tied by placing the left outside vertical cord across the two center cords and bringing the right vertical cord over the end of the left cord (a). The right vertical cord is placed under the center cores and passed through the loop made by the left cord to form the first half of the knot (b). To complete the knot, the procedure is reversed by placing the right cord over the two center core threads, bringing the left cord over the end of the right cord and passing the left cord under the two center strands and up through the loop made by the right cord (c).*

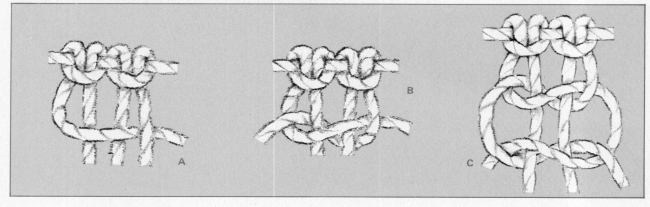

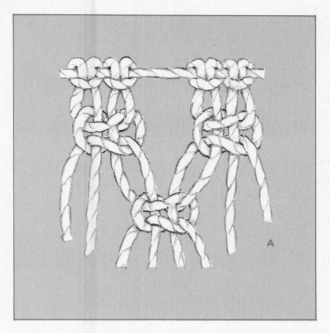 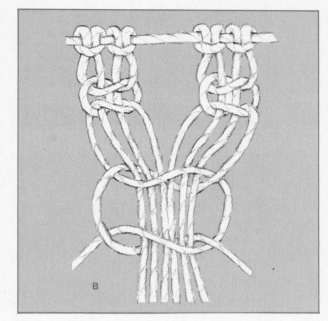

*Figure 12. To create an Alternating Square Knot pattern, Square Knots are tied along the first row beginning with the strand on the far left and continuing across the entire row. In the second row the first two cords are dropped, and a Square Knot is tied with the next four cords (a). The size of negative or open spaces between knots is increased in an Alternating Square Knot pattern by tying a Square Knot over six threads that are fed into the core of the knot and passed through the two outside vertical cords (b).*

**9.** Pull the cords tight in order to complete the Square Knot.

**10.** Using the next groups of four verticals each, tie two more Square Knots, following Steps 1 through 9.

**11.** For the second row of Square Knots, do not use the first two vertical cords. Instead, begin the first knot in the second row by using the third through the sixth verticals. Two Square Knots will be tied in the second row, leaving two verticals at the beginning and two at the end.

**12.** Tie the third row of Square Knots exactly as the first.

Note that the first half of the Square Knot begins by using the left vertical, and then the right vertical is used to complete the second half. Always alternate the cords in tying the Square Knot. If in tying a sennit (a chain) of Square Knots, one forgets with which cord to continue knotting, careful examination of the last knot tied and location of the cord that comes from underneath the vertical loop formed by the Square Knot will indicate the beginning cord for the next knot.

Furthermore, it should be noted that *two or more threads may be used as a core* for any of the macramé knots. For example, if in tying a pattern of Alternating Square Knots, one wants to increase the size of the negative or open spaces between the knots, a group of six threads can be fed into the core and up through two outside verticals to tie over them. Or the four center threads may be used as a core and the knot tied with the two left and two right verticals. Either of these will in-

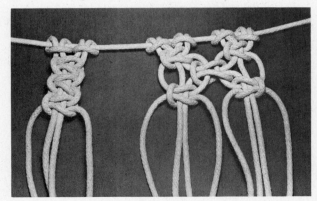

*Figure 13. Four cords are used to form a Square Knot. The knots may be tied in a series to create a sennit of Square Knots (left), or two or more groups of knots may be alternated (right) to form a more open design. (Linda Parker.)*

crease the size of the negative opening as well as the size of the knot itself.

The Square Knot, as well as the pattern that is created by alternating the Square Knot to form a surface or fabric has been demonstrated above. In creating a surface of Square Knots, the number of Square Knots that are tied over the core threads may be varied. For example, a horizontal row of four Square Knots over each core might be alternated with a horizontal row of one Square Knot over each core. This will increase the size of the negative opening between the Alternating Square Knots and give a varied light and dark pattern to the surface of knots.

Additional threads also may be fed into the core of any of the Clove Hitch Knots. These additional cores will increase the diameter of the Clove Hitch Knots and create a surface with a higher relief.

### The Spiral Half Knot

A sennit is a series of knots tied around core threads to produce a single chain. The Spiral Half Knot is most effective when used in this manner; it can also be used in an alternating pattern. A series of Spiral Half Knot sennits—all twisting in the same direction—makes a very attractive decorative area. However, a group of at least six knots should be tied on each core in order to use the spiral to its greatest advantage. Review the instructions for tying the Alternating Square Knot if unsure of how to create the alternating pattern of knots. Tie the Spiral Half Knot in the following manner.

**1.** Begin by feeding two 18-inch long cords onto a holding cord by using the Lark's Head Knot.

**2.** Lay the *left* outside vertical over the two center cores.

**3.** Lay the *right* outside vertical over the "tail" or end of the left cord.

**4.** Pass the right vertical under the center cores and up through the loop made by the left cord.

**5.** Pull the two cords tight. This completes the first Spiral Half Knot.

**6.** To tie the next knot, use the *left* cord again and follow Steps 2 through 5.

When tying the Spiral Half Knot, the series of

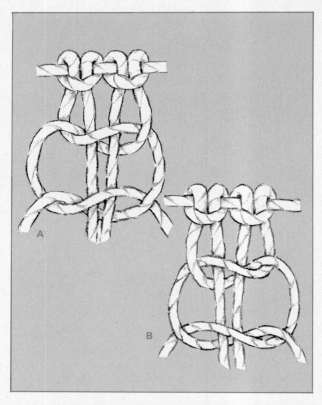

*Figure 14. The Spiral Half Knot is tied by laying the left vertical thread over the two center cores, placing the right vertical cord over the end of the left vertical cord, and passing the right vertical cord under the center cores up through the loop made by the left cord (a). A series or sennit of these knots will create a spiral to the right; to create a spiral to the left, the same knot should be tied in reverse (b).*

knots should always begin from the same side of the core threads. As a result of always using the left vertical thread, the knots will spiral to the left.

## OTHER VARIETIES OF KNOTS

The following short descriptions and diagrams will serve as a reference for a variety of knots that can be used in place of the basic macramé knots or as decorative emphasis for areas in macramé objects.

### The Half Hitch Sennit

This makes a most attractive sennit and is very simple to do. Refer to the beginning steps of the Vertical Clove Hitch for specific directions.

Using four cords—two as a core and two as outside cords to tie with—will make an interesting sennit. Experiment also with doubling and tripling the Half Hitches over the core.

## The Alternating Lark's Head Sennit

Using four cords, two of which are core threads and two as working/tying threads, alternate the Lark's Head Knot as shown in the diagram.

Each of the sennits can also be used to knot or create an interlocking surface. Begin the surface by tying the first knot with the left vertical; before tying with the right vertical, feed it into the loop of the sennit next to it. In this way the series of sennits are locked together.

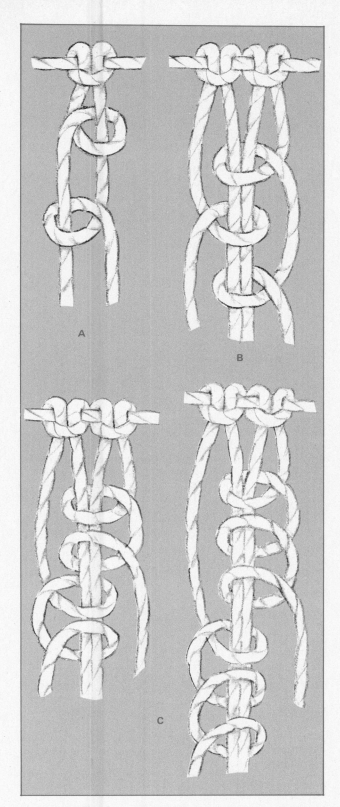

Figure 15. A Half Hitch is simply the first half of a Vertical Clove Hitch. To form a sennit of Half Hitches, two cords may be alternated with one another (a), alternated around two or more core threads (b), or doubled and tripled over several core threads (c).

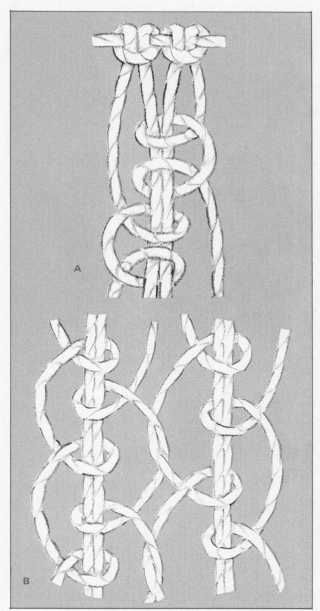

Figure 16. Larks Head Knots are tied alternately around two core threads to form an alternating Larks Head sennit (a). The pattern may be varied by interlocking several groups of sennits (b).

## The Overhand Knot

This is the same simple knot that is tied at the end of one's sewing thread. Its use is a practical one: to hold beads in place, to keep threads from unraveling, or to add texture to an otherwise empty area. It can also be tied into another knot of the same type and alternated with series of cords to create a fish net fabric.

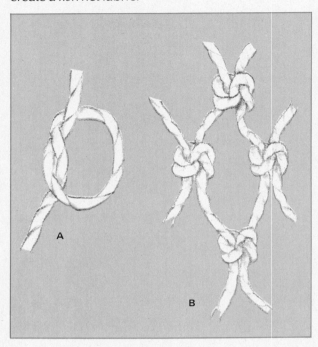

*Figure 17. The simple Overhand Knot, used to hold beads in place and to tie the endings of cords, is made by forming a loop and pulling one of the ends through the loop(a). To create a fish net pattern, the Overhand Knot is tied alternately on a series of cords (b).*

## The Overhand Wrap Knot

This knot is made the same as the Overhand Knot, except that one end of the cord continues to wrap around the loop of the Overhand Knot. When the end has been wrapped through the loop several times, the knot should be pulled gently, but tightly. To enlarge the knot, the number of wrappings around the original loop should be increased.

## The Chinese Crown Knot

This woven knot is a good one to practice before beginning to tie some of the more complicated woven knots that follow. It is more effective when tied with more than one cord or when heavy cords are being used for the macramé piece.

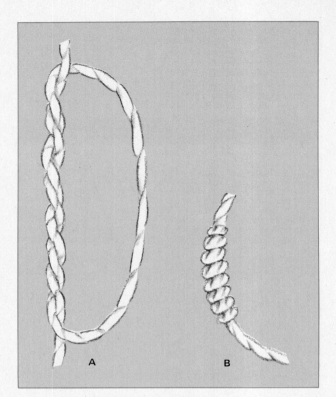

*Figure 18. By tying an Overhand Knot and continuing to wrap the end of the cord around the loop, a new variation, the Overhand Wrap Knot, is formed (a). The knot is tightened by gently pulling the knot together (b). The size of the knot will depend upon the number of wrappings.*

*Figure 19. One cord is woven around another to form a Chinese Crown Knot. The left cord is twisted as shown in the diagram, and the right cord is wound around the left cord in the direction indicated by the arrows.*

## The Josephine Knot

The Josephine Knot is tied as follows:

**1.** Begin by laying the *left* vertical under itself to form a loop.

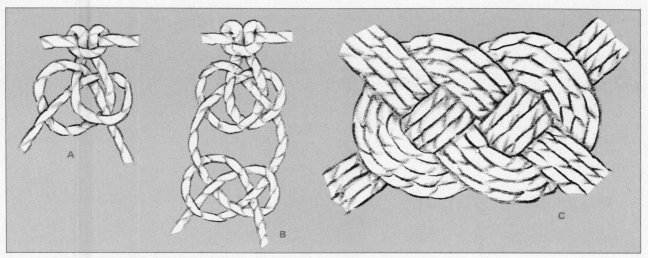

*Figure 20. The Josephine Knit is tied by looping the left vertical cord under itself, placing the right vertical cord over the loop, (b); and weaving the cord through the loop, and under the left cord's tail (a). To enable a series of knots to lie flat, the second knot in a sennit should be tied in reverse (b); to add texture and variety to the knot, four cords may be used in tying the knot (c).*

**2.** Lay the right vertical over the loop, feed it under the left cord's tail, and continue weaving it over, under, over, under, and out of the knot.

**3.** Gradually tighten the knot.

**4.** Begin the next Josephine Knot using the *right* cord. This alternating of beginning cords is done so that the sennit of knots lays flat. If the Josephine is always tied starting with the same cord, the sennit of knots has a tendency to twist.

*Figure 21. The Josephine Knot may be tied loosely or tightly with two, four, or any multiple number of cords. The Josephine Knot shown above is tied tightly with four cords. (Linda Parker.)*

To increase the size and weight of the Josephine Knot, experiment in tying the knot by using four cords instead of two. This will also add greater interest to the woven quality of the Josephine Knot.

## The Monkey's Fist

This knot (also called the Man Knot or the Turk's Head) takes some patience to master; persistence, however, will be rewarded. It can be used as an ending for a long fringe at the bottom of a macramé wall hanging, it can be added to the surface of an object, or it can be used as a button.

To form the Monkey's Fist, cords should be wrapped around the fingers. For making the first several practice knots, it is recommended that a heavy cord be used. This will make it easier to see and understand how the Monkey's Fist is tied.

**1.** Wrap the cord vertically around the fingers four times.

**2.** Wrap the cord horizontally four times around the vertical bundle, going from front to back.

**3.** Remove the bundle from the fingers and wrap through the large loops firmly around the center of the cords. Do this four times.

**4.** To tighten the original loops of cord, begin with the original end of the cord and gently trace it through the series of loops until the firm ending

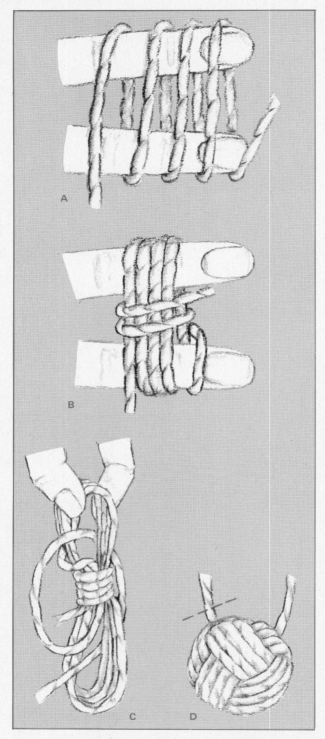

*Figure 22. The Monkey's Fist has the appearance of a woven ball. To begin the knot, a cord is wrapped vertically around two pencil-like objects four times (a). Starting from the front, the cord is then wrapped horizontally around the vertical bundle four times (b) and the bundle is removed from the fingers. To finish the knot, the end of the cord is wrapped through the large loops four times (c) and pulled gently to tighten the knot until a ball is formed.*

is inside the knot. Then gradually tighten the loops, pulling them firmly until a ball of woven/knotted cord is formed.

**5.** The final end of the cord may be clipped because it is held firmly on the inside of the knot.

## Design And Macramé

After having mastered the tying of several macramé knots and having worked some simple projects, designing and creating one's own pieces can prove to be very rewarding. In thinking through details, however, some of the following recommendations should be considered.

A project should be thought of as a complete object, with an idea of how the finished piece will look—not just how some individual areas will be designed. A simple sketch is often helpful, especially on graph paper (although the vertical and horizontal lines should not become a deterrent to

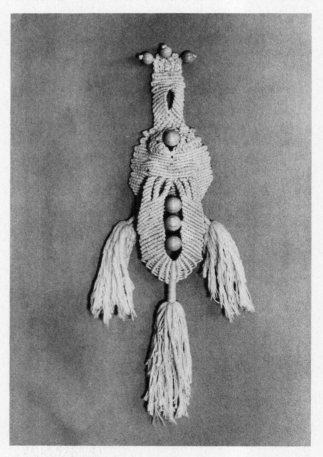

*Figure 23. Horizontal Half Hitches are packed tightly together in a macramé sculpture titled "She" by Dennis Grabowski. The tension on the core threads causes the surface to warp, creating a three-dimensional effect. (Linda Parker.)*

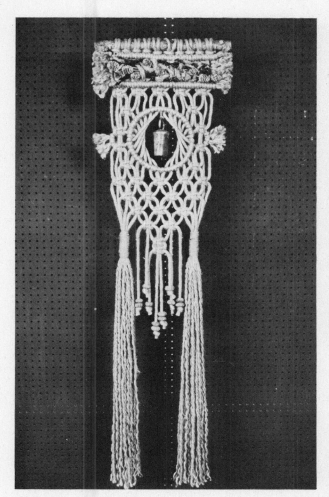

Figure 25. A large hanging planter composed of Alternalting Square Knots provides an attractive setting for a series of plants. (Courtesy, The Macramé Workshop, Chicago; photo, Bill Arsenault.)

Figure 24. The basic Square Knot is alternated to form the main body of this macramé hanging. Beads, pine cones, and a bell are incorporated in the hanging for decorative purposes. (Courtesy, The Macramé Workshop, Chicago; photo, Bill Arsenault.)

diagonal or other patterns). Since each knot creates a different textural surface, special attention should be given to combining knots that will complement each other. It is very easy to overwork a design by using too many different knots rather than carefully selecting a few. Large areas of a single kind of knot will produce a much stronger design than small areas of various knots. Simplicity used in knotting and designing will more often than not produce an object of visual and aesthetic merit.

The design of the positive (full) and negative (open) areas of a macramé piece must also be given some thought. Different knots will create a denser fabric or surface than others. A finished project should be perceived as having different tones. Imagine, for example, using white, gray,

Figure 26. Horizontal and Diagonal Clove Hitch Knots are combined with Alternating Square Knots and some wrapping to create a contemporary macrame hanging. (Courtesy, The Macramé Workshop; photo, Bill Arsenault.)

*Figure 27. Long strands of dyed red jute are suspended from a macrame sculpture composed of Alternating Square Knots. The sculpture, "Red Forest," by Claire Zeisler is 98 inches high and 88 inches wide. (Collection, First National Bank of Chicago; photo, Bill Arsenault.)*

and black. White areas would be very open and use a minimum of knots, perhaps just vertical cords with an occasional Overhand Knot. The gray areas would contain slightly more knotting—a series of sennits or some loose weaving of the threads. Finally, the black areas would be of dense or heavy knotting. Solid knots, such as the Alternating Square Knot, a group of Josephine Knots, or the Horizontal and Vertical Half Hitch, are ideal for a black area. Balancing the white, gray, and black areas could be worked out in a sketch with different knots assigned to different tones.

Color is another important aspect of designing. Because of the wide range of dyed cord that is available, it is tempting to let color overpower a piece. Color should help to bring emphasis to a design, not overwhelm it. Color should also help to define knots, not confuse them. Experimentation is essential to see how color can enhance one's work and emphasize certain knots.

There is certainly no reason to avoid looking at as many examples of macramé as possible, whether in shops, books, magazines, or museums. This is an excellent way to learn to translate textures and tones into knots and to begin working on a design of one's own.

## THREE-DIMENSIONAL MACRAMÉ

Macramé need not be limited to flat objects; because of the tension created in tying the knots, it is possible to produce a self-supporting structure. Designing such an object takes special thought, especially as to which knots will lend the greatest amount of strength to the finished piece.

Knotting a hanging macramé is a much easier task than making a standing structure. Wire, thin strips of wood or metal that are flexible enough to bend and hold a shape, or forms that are cast in a particular shape can be used. Embroidery hoops, bamboo rings, metal rings, and collars are all excellent items for this purpose.

Lastly, the possibility of knotting a relief on a macramé surface should not be overlooked. Feeding more cords into and around existing knots provides the necessary additional threads to create a surface on which to design reliefs.

## Projects You Can Do

For both of the belts shown in the illustrations, a three-ply cord ⅛ inch thick was used. Cotton is the easiest cord with which to work.

### OPEN LOOP BELT

This belt is made of interlocking sennits of Square Knots. It is self-locking by feeding the fringed ending through the two beginning loops of the belt. The Square Knot sennits may be alternated with Spiral Half Knot sennits.

The belt is begun by cutting four cords eight times longer than the intended waist measurement. The four cords are then interlocked at their midpoint. A series of eight Square Knots is knotted with each group of four cords.

Next, one of the core threads is pulled, forcing the Square Knots into an arc. The other core thread

*Figure 28. After cutting the four cords for the first project, the Open Loop Belt, the cords are interlocked at their midpoint.*

*Figure 29. The second project, the Solid Square Knot Belt, will require a buckle. An interlocking buckle similar to the one shown in the diagram is suggested.*

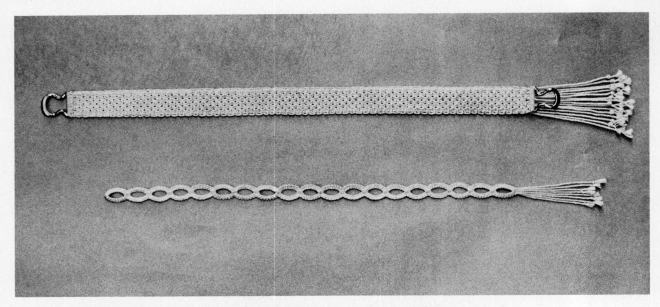

*Figure 30. Both the Open Loop Belt (left) and the Solid Square Knot Belt are composed of Square Knots. Directions for making these belts are given in the "Projects" section. (Linda Parker.)*

should not be pulled—the extra bulk of this second core allows the arc to be relaxed on its outside edge. The two sennits are joined by using two cords from each and tying two Square Knots. Then eight more Square Knots are tied and one of the cores is pulled to create the arc. This procedure is continued until enough loops have been knotted and formed to reach around the waist. The fringe is finished with Overhand Wrap Knots.

## SOLID SQUARE KNOT BELT

A very handsome belt can be made by using only Square Knots. Three-ply, ⅛ inch thick cord is suggested, as is an interlocking buckle (see diagram).

Onto the left side of the buckle are fed an even number of cords (eight or ten should be enough) that are eight times longer than one's waist measurement. This length should be a multiple of four.

As the Square Knots are made, an even tension should be achieved and none of the cords should gap or be loose. Tying the knots firmly creates a solid and regular alternating knotted surface. The design of the belt can be varied by knotting solid or diagonal patterns of Clove Hitch Knots: When the desired length of the belt is reached, a Lark's Head Knot should be tied with every other cord onto the right side of the buckle. Two of these

cords should be used to tie an Overhand Knot on the back side of the belt to keep the Lark's Head from untying. Overhand Knots or Overhand Wrap Knots will keep the final ends from unraveling.

## THREE-DIMENSIONAL BELL HANGING

This project requires three metal or wooden rings of different sizes. One ring should be three inches in diameter and two rings four inches in diameter. One of the four-inch rings establishes the circumference of the hanging. A four-inch ring has a circumference of 13 inches. First the cord has to be measured to determine how many pieces are needed per inch (three-ply cord, ⅛ inch thick requires eight cords per inch). Eight cords times 13 inches equal 104 cords. These will be folded in half to make two vertical knotting threads per cut cord. Therefore, 52 lengths of cord will be needed and should be cut into 10-foot lengths. Ultimately, the hanging will be approximately two feet long. All of the cords should be attached to the three-inch ring by using a Lark's Head Knot. Next, the verticals should be tied to the first four-inch ring, using a Horizontal Clove Hitch and placing the ring in a horizontal position. (The ring acts as the core for the Clove Hitch Knots.) A three-inch drop should be allowed for between the top ring and second ring.

The project should be hung so that it is easier to

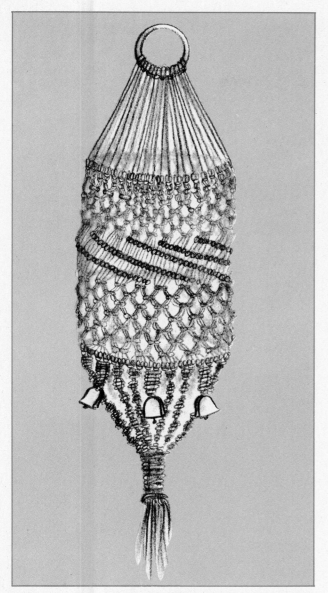

*Figure 31. To complete the final project, the Three-dimensional Bell Hanging, a mastery of the Horizontal Clove Hitch Knot and the Alternating Square Knot is required.*

work on and the ring should be hanging evenly. One begins by tying Square Knots around one of the four-inch rings, thus beginning a cylinder of alternating Square Knots. Depending on one's imagination, bands of different knots can be introduced that will make a more attractive hanging, but one should not get too involved with designing this section. Knotting is continued until a cylinder eight to ten inches long is completed.

Next, Horizontal Clove Hitch Knots are attached to the other four-inch ring. Then, using vertical cords, several bells with a variety of sounds are

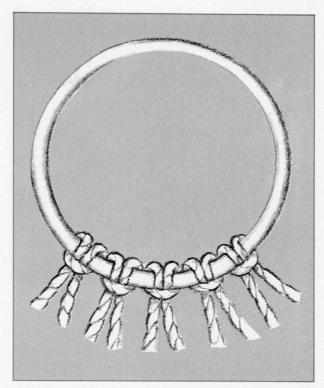

*Figure 32. To begin the Three-dimensional Bell Hanging, cords are fastened to the three-inch ring by using Larks Head Knots.*

tied on. After the bells are attached, the vertical cords are grouped and a sennit of Spiral Knots is tied between every two bells. The sennits should be at least five inches long. Finally, the ends of the sennits are pulled together and additional cord is used to wrap a two-inch section of the ends to make a large tassel. The latter is finished by untwisting the cords so that each ply is separated. By grasping the tassel and shaking the hanging, one can enjoy the sound of a macramé bell hanging.

## For Additional Reading

Andes, Eugene, **Far Beyond the Fringe: Three-Dimensional Knotting Techniques Using Macramé and Nautical Ropework,** Van Nostrand, 1973.

Graumont, Raoul, and Hensel, John, **Encyclopedia of Knots and Fancy Rope Work,** Cornell Maritime Press, 1970.

Harvey, Virginia I. **Macramé: The Art of Creative Knotting,** Van Nostrand, 1967.

Meilach, Dona Z. **Macramé: Creative Design in Knotting,** Crown, 1972.

Phillips, Mary Walder, **Step-by-Step Macramé,** Golden Press, 1970.

Short, Eirian, **Introducing Macramé,** Watson-Guptill, 1970.

# Needlepoint

**A highly personalized and functional craft, needlepoint offers a challenge in its design and satisfaction in its completion.**

Thousands of years ago, embroidery was used mainly to reinforce fabrics and to make them more durable. The stitches were laid over the woven materials without much thought given to design. Inevitably, however, the decorative possibilities occurred to some artistic minds, for embroidered canvas garments have been found in Egyptian tombs, indicating the decorative use of embroidery as early as 1500 B.C. Indeed, ancient Egyptian embroideries contained many of the stitches still being used today.

Figure 2. This New England needlepoint on line dates back to the late seventeenth century. Domestic needlepoint patterns were common to the colonists who wished to show off their knowledge of stitches. (Courtesy, The Henry du Pont Winterthur Museum.)

For many centuries, the particular embroidery craft known as needlepoint was closely associated with the church and with nobility. Inspired by old tapestries, nuns carefully stitched ecclesiastical designs and taught this ancient art to ladies of nobility. The early crusaders brought many beautiful embroideries to England from the East, most of which were donated to the church to compensate for the crusaders' pillaging of temples and palaces on their journeys.

As the result of efforts by English ladies to develop new stitches and refine the craft, by the twelfth and thirteenth centuries needlepoint had sur-

*Figure 1. The basic Continental stitch was used to create the contemporary needlepoint design shown on the opposite page. (Courtesy, Maria del Carmen Garza.)*

passed all other forms of embroidery as aristocratic art.

Furthermore, guilds were established about this time and apprentices were skillfully trained to satisfy the increasing demand for needlepoint articles. English work was preferred to any other because of its superior workmanship and quality. The needlepoint pieces of this period usually depicted recorded history or told a story.

By the seventeenth century, laws were repealed that had prevented peasants and the middle classes from wearing silks and embroideries as well as particular colors. Emphasis then became more centered on domestic and ceremonial articles. Ladies stitched samplers to demonstrate their knowledge of stitches and patterns; the pieces were considered valuable and were willed

*Figure 3. This sixteenth century velvet embroidery hanging was the work of Elizabeth, Countess of Shrewsbury. Such needlepoint panels were used as curtains or coverlets. Elizabeth's needlepoint was well known for its symbolic design and fine workmanship. (Courtesy, Victoria and Albert Museum.)*

*Figure 4. The "Boare" emblem, a detail from Figure 3, was worked in the Tent stitch. This stitch is traditional and still popular in needlepoint work. (Courtesy, Victoria and Albert Museum.)*

to relatives and friends. Usually, the samplers measured approximately 9 by 36 inches and included 15 or 20 stitches that are still popular today. Many of these early samplers are on display at the Victoria and Albert Museum in London.

Floral needlepoint designs became popular during the eighteenth century as did *Bargello*, a kind of canvas embroidery that originated in Italy. Early settlers brought European designs to America and combined them with Indian patterns. This activity, however, was limited to wealthier women with more leisure time. Martha Washington, for example, had great talent for embroidery and her ten chair seats, made in one year at the age of 69, can be seen today at Mount Vernon. The average household, however, was occupied with spinning, dyeing, weaving, and handsewing the clothing and furnishings that were necessary for daily existence.

By the end of the eighteenth century, finishing schools included needlepoint in their curriculum, and the work gained in popularity as an enjoyable pastime. The first printed and colored patterns were produced in Germany and became known as Berlin work. By the twentieth century, Berlin

work came to be known as canvas with a stitched center. Floral centers were preworked and women filled in the background, usually in a dark color such as red, green, maroon, or black. World War I forced a change of the name to zephyr work, but still the craft was limited to following printed patterns or background work.

Needlepoint in America has recently experienced a transition, and while many women still enjoy the traditional methods, more and more are exercising their individuality to produce artistic work that reflects individual tastes and characteristics. Men have also become fascinated with needlepoint and many proclaim its value as a therapeutic and useful hobby.

Needlepoint is durable. It will outlast most other decorative materials. Used as upholstery, it almost never need to be replaced. An infinite variety of items may be created with this craft, including such projects as pictures, chair seats, purses, pillows, vests, bedroom slippers, doorstops, coasters, screens, rugs, wall hangings, and book covers.

## Common Terms Used In Needlepoint

**Bargello:** a needlepoint variation of short and long stitches running in a straight line on the canvas. A different color or shade is used for each line of stitching, and designs are formed as the groups of colors or shades are repeated.

**Basketweave or Tent Stitch:** used for background work, the Basketweave starts in the upper right-hand corner and proceeds from that point to cover the canvas diagonally in ever increasing rows. It provides a back padding and looks like basketweave on the back side.

**Canvas:** heavily sized fabric over which stitches are made; woven with single or double threads, it has open holes which are called *mesh.*

**Continental Stitch:** especially desirable for upholstery and rugs, this stitch serves as padding and saves wear on the needlepoint.

**Diagonal Stitch:** worked from one corner to the diagonally opposing corner, this stitch does not pull the canvas out of shape.

**Grospoint:** the stitch that is most commonly used in needlepoint.

**Half-Cross Stitch:** worked vertically or horizontally, this stitch provides no back padding and is thus suitable only for pictures or articles that will not be subject to wear.

**Mesh:** the open holes woven in the canvas; the size or gauge of the canvas—*i.e.*, the high count or low count—is determined by the number of threads woven per inch.

**Mono:** a canvas woven with single horizontal and vertical threads; usually white, such canvas is suitable for Diagonal, Continental, Basketweave, or Bargello stitches.

**Needlepoint:** counted embroidery stitches worked with a needle over the threads of a canvas and providing decorative stitching on an even count mesh foundation.

**Penelope:** a double-thread canvas woven with two horizontal and vertical threads.

**Persian:** loosely twisted and easily separated yarn available in strands or skeins of two-ply yarn.

**Petitpoint:** the term used to describe a stitch worked on a very small mesh canvas; most useful when close attention to detail must be observed.

**Ply:** the number of strands constituting the thickness of yarn.

**Quickpoint:** the term used to describe the largest of all needlepoint stitches; suitable for rugs or wall hangings.

**Rug Yarn:** usually two-ply, this is a thick, bulky, and tightly twisted yarn used for quickpoint.

**Tapestry Needle:** a blunt pointed needle, usually short and ranging in size from number 24 to number 14 (even numbers only).

**Tapestry Yarn:** processed to be fade-proof, this is a tightly twisted, smooth, four-ply yarn.

**Trame:** a basting stitch sewn across the mesh to indicate design and change of color.

## Basic Equipment And Supplies

The materials described below are readily available in yarn or craft shops. The art-needlework sections of large department stores are also a good source for supplies. This craft has become so popular that boutiques specializing in needlepoint abound in most large cities. These, however, generally specialize in hand-painted canvases or original design that are more expensive than the mass-produced items.

### CANVAS

There are two types of needlepoint canvas, single mesh (mono) and double mesh (penelope). The former has single, evenly spaced threads running in both directions, crosswise and lengthwise. Double-mesh canvas is woven with double threads instead of single, leaving evenly spaced square meshes for the needle to work through. Canvas is available by the yard and numbered according to the holes per inch or mesh.

Any stitch method may be used on double-thread or single-thread canvas with the exception of the Half-Cross Stitch, which cannot be worked on a single-thread canvas. If necessary, it is possible to

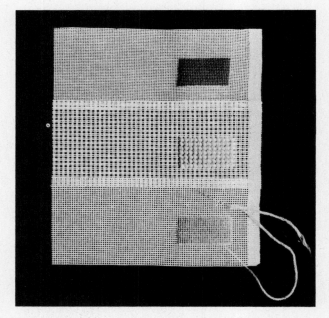

*Figure 5. Samples of the Continental stitch are shown (from top to bottom) on 14-count mono canvas with Persian yarn, 5-count penelope canvas with acrylic rug yarn, and 10-count mono canvas with tapestry yarn.*

separate the threads on penelope canvas so that a petitpoint stitch can be worked.

Choose a strong canvas, somewhat stiff, with an even weave and free of knots.

## YARN

Wool is the most commonly used material for making needlepoint items, but unusual effects can be achieved using silk or cotton floss for finer stitches. Wool strands should have a long, smooth fiber with a fairly loose twist. Hand knitting yarns, spun with a short fiber, are not satisfactory.

### Persian or Crewel

This wool comes in an abundance of colors and shadings. Its strands may be easily separated for work on high-count mesh or combined for low count.

### Tapestry

This is four-ply wool, usually fade proof, for covering ten-mesh canvas. It had previously been produced in limited colors, but with the increasing popularity of this craft, most producers of tapestry have expanded their lines to include new, bright shades as well as the traditional ones.

### Rug

This heavy two-ply yarn used for quickpoint can be cotton, wool, or acrilan.

In general, one can use one strand of three-ply persian wool on canvas number 18 to 22; two strands of persian wool on number 14 to number 16 mesh canvas; and one strand of tapestry wool or all three strands of persian wool on number 10 to number 12 mesh canvas. For larger mesh canvas, use rug yarn or two or more strands of tapestry wool. It is important to experiment with the wool in relation to the canvas to be sure the canvas will be covered but not crowded.

## NEEDLES

A blunt-pointed tapestry needle is always used in needlepoint work. Needles range in size from fine to the large rug needle. They are numbered 24 to 14, even numbers only. The higher the needle

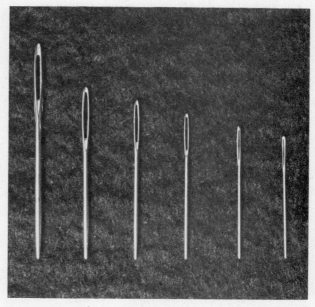

*Figure 6. Tapestry needles used for needlepoint may be chosen from a selection numbered from 14 to 24. The larger the number, the smaller the needle.*

number, the higher the number of mesh on which it will be used. The most popular size mesh, number 10, requires a number 18 needle. The canvas threads should not be moved when the threaded needle is pushed through the canvas. All tapestry needles have elongated eyes to facilitate threading. It is wise to have several needles, not only because one may get misplaced, but also by threading several needles at once, one can work in an uninterrupted fashion. Plastic pill bottles make excellent containers for different sizes of needles.

## FRAMES

Needlepoint can be held in the hand and taken along when traveling or visiting. However, for intricate designs many people prefer to use a frame. The frame also serves to keep the shape of the piece straight. Lap frames as well as floor frames are available. Never use a hoop; it will pull the work out of shape.

## ACRYLIC PAINT MARKERS

These are available in packages of primary colors and are used to paint an original design on the canvas. They must be waterproof so that the color will not bleed when dampened. Experiment with a trial piece of canvas and the paints to make sure there is no problem.

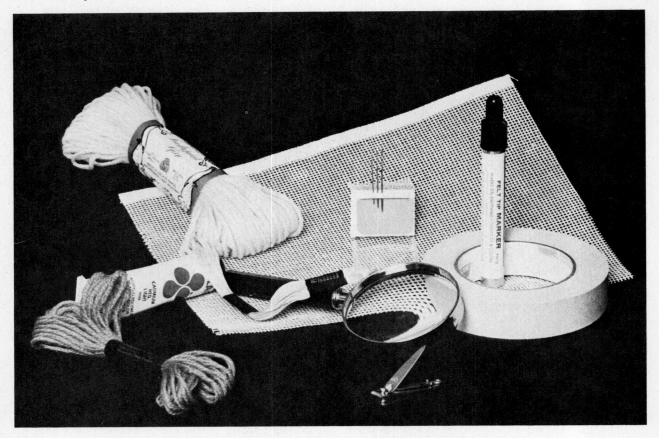

*Figure 7. The supplies for needlepoint include yarn, canvas, acrylic paint, needles, magnifying glass, nail clippers, waterproof marker, and masking tape.*

## MAGNIFYING GLASS

If working on very fine canvas or doing the petit-point stitch, it is helpful to see the stitches as clearly as possible. One way of doing this is with a magnifying glass. Needless to say, it is necessary to use a type which leaves the hands free to work. There is a type available that fits on the head with an adjustable band. Another is suspended from the neck and allows one to look through it to the work beneath. Using a magnifying glass is optional, of course.

## SMALL CLIPPERS OR NAIL CLIPPERS

These are for cutting the yarn close to the canvas when a strand is finished.

## Basic Procedures

It is not only quite simple to learn how to needlepoint, but preparation for both learning and doing projects is minimal. Once the basic techniques are learned, this craft may become habit forming. The work is fun, the results are lovely, and an infinite variety of items may be created.

## PREPARING THE CANVAS

The amount of canvas necessary obviously depends on the project being done. If covering a piece of furniture, allow two inches more of unworked canvas than the piece measures on each side. This will be needed in the upholstering. Mark with a felt-tipped pen or a basting stitch the border around the area to be covered with needlepoint.

If making a pillow, the amount of canvas worked will vary with the type of pillow form. If it is foam rubber, the finished needlepoint should measure exactly the same as the form. If the form is filled with kapok, feathers, shredded foam, or a similar material, the finished pillow should be about one inch larger all around so that the form will fit well into the corners.

If the canvas does not have a selvage edge on the sides, tape them with masking tape to prevent unraveling.

## PREPARING THE YARN

Cut the yarn in 24-inch lengths to avoid its wearing thin when pulled through the canvas. If using a heavy yarn, such as rug yarn, a longer length may be used. Keep the double part of the yarn short so that it will not wear when pulled through the canvas.

To estimate the amount of yarn needed, measure off four 18-inch strands of the selected wool. Work a 1-inch-square sample on the canvas in a chosen stitch. When finished, measure any wool that is left in the needle and add that amount to any strands left over. Subtract that amount from the 72-inch total of the original strands. The result yields the amount of yarn to be used per square inch.

Now measure the length and width of the entire area to be covered. Multiply this by the above quarter-inch figure. Divide the results by 36 to get the yardage. This procedure must be followed for each color. Remember that it is always better to buy too much wool than too little.

## DESIGNING NEEDLEPOINT

For those who are creative, it is possible to paint directly on the canvas with acrylic paint and then embroider over the design with wool in any variety of desired stitches and color tones. However, for others it is a simple matter to transfer to canvas any design, from a wallpaper pattern to a picture from a magazine. Of course, after transferring a design, one chooses the colors to be used.

After selecting a design, decide on the size for the finished product. The importance of this cannot be over-emphasized. Whether it be a particular picture frame, handbag frame, pillow, or seat cover, it is much easier to alter the design on the canvas than to adjust the item after the needlepoint has been completed.

Use translucent graph paper, available at art supply stores, for transferring a design. Center a sheet of graph paper on top of the design and secure it with tape. Using a soft pencil, trace the design square by square, following the outline of the

*Figure 8. Traditional floral patterns are shown in a piece of Berlin work (above) and an Austrian canvas (below).*

picture. All curved lines must follow, in step fashion, the square marking of the graph paper. Each square of the paper symbolizes a stitch on the canvas so it is easiest to use the same size graph paper as canvas, that is, graph paper 10-to-the-inch for number 10 canvas. Remove the paper and proceed to plan colors. Block in the colors in order to see the design on the paper.

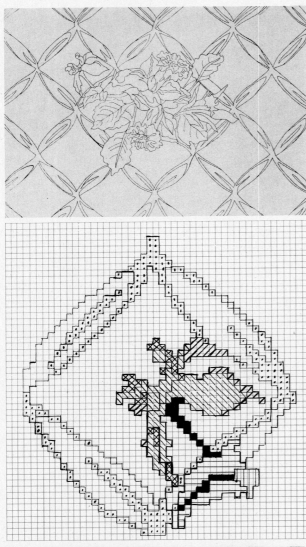

*Figure 9. To plan an original needlepoint design, a sketch (top) should be drawn on tracing paper and then blocked out on graph paper (center). With the canvas over the graph paper, the design may be painted on the appropriate areas of mesh. (Courtesy, NeedleMania, Chicago; original design by Nancy Boyar.)*

The size of the mesh used determines the size of the finished piece. The easiest way to reduce a design is to prepare it on large graph paper, and then stitch the design on a finer mesh canvas. To enlarge a design, have the picture enlarged any size up to four times the size of the original at a photocopy or blueprint shop.

To transfer the design to canvas, first measure the design. Allowing two inches on each side for blocking and finishing, cut the canvas and tape the edges. Then place the canvas over the graph paper and, using an acrylic paint, draw the outline on the canvas. If it is difficult to see, work on a glass table with a light shining from below, or tape the canvas and the paper to a window exposed to bright sunlight.

## THREADING THE NEEDLE

To thread the needle easily, loop the yarn around the needle. Grasp it very tightly between thumb and index finger and pull it firmly over the needle. Then with the other hand, push the eye of the needle over the doubled yarn.

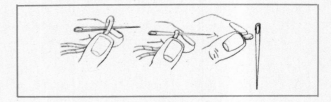

## LEARNING THE BASIC STITCHES

Follow the diagrams below to learn the basic stitches. If left-handed, turn the illustrations upside down.

### Half-Cross Stitch

Start at upper left-hand corner of canvas. Bring needle out to front of canvas at the point that will be the bottom of the first stitch. The needle is in

vertical position when making this stitch. Always work from left to right and turn the work around for the return row.

## Continental Stitch

Start at upper right corner and work across to left. Bring needle out to front of canvas at the point that will be the bottom of the first stitch. The needle goes under two meshes of canvas diagonally. Always work from right to left and turn work around for the return row.

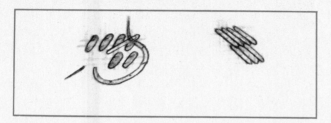

## Basketweave Stitch

Start at upper right corner and bring the needle up through the canvas at point A, down through B, and out through C. Then put the needle in at D and out through E. Then needle in at F and out through G. Start next row in at H and out through I. This Completes four stitches. Stitch number 5 goes from I back to A. Complete the stitches to number 10 on the diagram in numerical order to finish the diagonal row. Stitch number 11 starts the next row upward.

After starting a row going up, the needle is horizontal for each stitch and goes under two meshes of canvas. The needle slants diagonally to begin a new row down as in the first stitch. Going down, the needle is always vertical as in stitch number 2, and goes under two meshes of canvas.

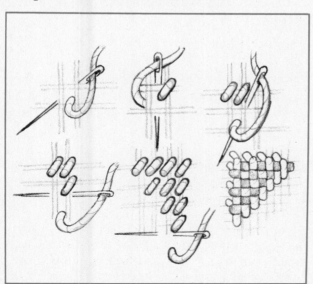

Again, if left-handed, turn the diagram upside down and start at the lower left-hand corner instead of the upper right. Work from left to right instead of right to left.

This stitch looks complicated, but actually is not. It is well worth mastering because it gives a thick, highly durable, and smooth finish to any background.

## Diagonal Stitch

This is quite similar to the basketweave when completed. Beginning at the right-hand side, stitch diagonally up one, cross horizontally under two, and stitch diagonally up one again. Work all rows in one direction only. Unlike the Basketweave, all stitches are worked horizontally across the back.

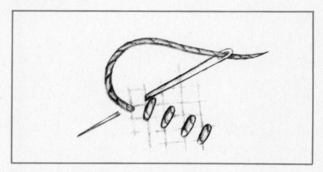

## Bargello Stitch

This stitch is worked vertically rather than diagonally and usually is worked over the same number of meshes throughout one piece of needlepoint. Colors are usually worked in numerous shades, progressing from light to dark or vice versa. Most patterns are built upon the first row of stitches. Because Bargello lends itself to geometric designs and works rapidly, it is a popular form of needlepoint today.

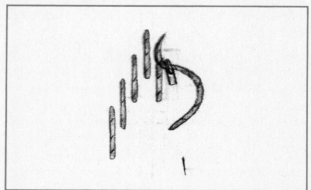

*Figure 10. Bargello, or the flame stitch, may be used to create a variety of patterns.*

## CLEANING AND BLOCKING

If the work needs a little freshening before it is finished or mounted, brush the surface with a clean cloth dipped in carbon tetrachloride or another cleaning fluid. Heavily soiled pieces have been known to launder well in a wool-wash solution. However, the yarn must be colorfast. Many people add a measure of salt or vinegar to the solution to prevent bleeding. Roll the piece in turkish towels to remove as much moisture as possible.

If the piece does not need washing, roll it in a very damp turkish towel and leave overnight. Place the canvas wrong side up on a soft wood board that is larger than the finished needlepoint. Pat the canvas into the proper shape. It must be exactly fitted to the desired measurements and its corners square before beginning to tack it to the wood. It may be helpful to have the board marked off in inch squares.

Using aluminum, rustproof tacks, start by placing a tack in the center of the top of the unworked canvas. Then pull the canvas tightly and place a tack in the center of the bottom. Now pull out the sides and place a tack in the center of each side. Place tacks at regular intervals along the edges of the canvas. It may be necessary to re-position the tacks frequently to work the canvas into the proper shape. Allow the canvas to dry thoroughly

—at least 24 hours—before removing it from the board. Do not trim the canvas until it has been blocked.

If the piece is not to be secured to a piece of furniture or a picture frame, it is best to size it so that it will always retain its blocked shape. To do this, spread a very thin coat of glue, preferably rabbit-skin glue in thin solution, on the canvas with a pastry brush. Scrape off the excess with a knife. Allow the coat of glue to dry and remove the canvas from the board.

## FURTHER SUGGESTIONS

Following are some helpful hints to make a finished product professional looking.

### Starting and Ending Yarn Lengths

Do not tie knots in the yarn. To start, hold about two inches of the first strand of yarn on the back of the canvas. Work a couple of stitches over this end to fasten it securely. When about two inches of yarn are left at the end of a strand, use the needle to run the end under the stitches on the wrong side of your embroidery to secure the yarn. Cut the end of the yarn close to the canvas, so there will not be any ends to tangle and catch in the yarns. To start successive pieces of yarn, run about two inches of yarn under the stitches previously made on the back of the canvas to anchor

*Figure 11. Basic needlepoint stitches include the Basketweave (left), the Diagonal (right), and the Scotch (below).*

the end. Do not start and stop at the same place in each row because this creates a ridge on the canvas.

### Eliminating Twists in Yarn

A strand of yarn tends to twist as its is worked. To correct this, hold the canvas in one hand and dangle the yarn and needle until the yarn becomes untwisted.

### Twisting the Yarn

Certain stitches will cause the yarn to untwist. To correct this, turn the needle between thumb and forefinger in the direction of the twist.

### Ripping Out Errors

Do not use scissors because they may cut the canvas. Unthread the the needle and slide it under the last stitch. Pull out the yarn. Repeat until the wrong stitches are completely removed. End off the yarn. Do not reuse the ripped out yarn.

## Projects You Can Do

The best way to learn needlepoint is to do it. The first two projects described below are not complicated and when finished will represent knowledge of five basic stitches. For the third project, it

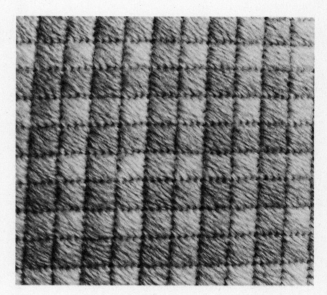

is suggested that a kit be used. The fourth project calls for a creative background with an already worked design. Do whichever is most appealing.

### COASTERS

To make a set of four needlepoint coasters, each with a different design and different stitch, the following materials are needed: (1) an 8-inch length of 30- or 36-width number 10 canvas; (2) two skeins of tapestry wool of *contrasting* colors; (3) two number 17 tapestry needles; (4) four four-inch squares of felt; (5) masking tape; and (6) Elmer's or Sobo glue.

Cut the canvas into four eight-inch squares and tape the sides with masking tape. Mark off a four-inch square in the center. The first square will combine the Half-Cross and the Continental Stitches (two stitches may therefore be learned at once and the difference between them will be apparent only to the most experienced and critical eye). Since the pattern is done in a checkerboard or a variation thereof, work the two stitches in any arrangement desired. Start with the Half-Cross Stitch and begin at the top left-hand corner of the canvas. Remember never to use a knot. Do not pull each stitch too tightly because excessive tension will pull the canvas out of shape. Each stitch should have a plump and consistent appearance.

Having stitched the first row from left to right, turn the work upside down and begin the second row of the Half-Cross Stitch square. Complete the first square of the design; if the Half-Cross Stitch has been mastered, do the next square in the Continental Stitch. When changing colors or coming to the end of a thread, pull the yarn to the back of the work and run about one inch through the back of the worked stitches to secure it. Trim the remaining thread closely with clippers or small scissors. The thread may be run through the back of the stitches in order to move from one completed block to one yet to be worked.

Having mastered these two stitches, do the three remaining coasters in the Basketweave, Diagonal, and Bargello stitches.

After the squares have been sized and dried, apply glue around the edges, covering the outer threads of the design as well as the bordering mesh of the canvas. Cut out the coaster one-half inch from stitching and fold under the unworked canvas. If the corners are too bulky, cut diagonally into the corner and glue one side under the other. Spread glue lightly on the coaster and the felt and press together. Weigh down with a heavy book until dry.

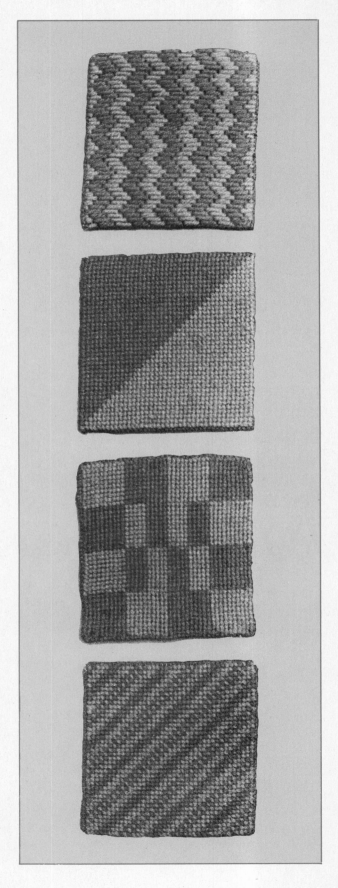

*Figure 12. Coasters are an easy and useful way to practice basic needlepoint stitches. From top to bottom they include the Bargello stitch, the Basketweave stitch, a combination of the Half-Cross and Continental stitches , and the Diagonal stitch.*

*Figure 13. These decorative letters may be easily transferred to a canvas by using the method described under ''Designing Needlepoint'' in this article.*

*Figure 14. Colonial girls learned the alphabet and embroidery by stitching samplers.*

## MONOGRAMMED PIN CUSHION

Monograms may be used to personalize any needlepoint projects that one undertakes. In the accompanying illustration, each square indicates one stitch. In working the letters, the size will vary according to the size mesh being used. The cushion shown here was done on number 13 mesh with two strands of Persian yarn.

The materials needed for this project are: (1) a nine-inch square of number 10, 12, or 13 canvas (this will make a six-inch cushion, but if a different size is desired, cut the canvas three inches wider and 3 inches longer than the desired finished size of the cushion); (2) one 40-yard skein of Persian yarn for background; (3) two yards each of five different colors for the monogram; and (4) one-quarter yard of any suitable fabric for the backing.

Tape the edges of the canvas, then fold it in half lengthwise and in half again widthwise. This will mark the center of the canvas. Place the center stitch of the monogram on this spot. Following the

*Figure 15. The initial on this pincushion adds a personal touch. Refer to Figure 13 in this article to design your own monogrammed pincushion.*

graph, complete the monogram. Work the background in the Basketweave or Continental Stitch, leaving 1½-inch borders.

Block the finished square. Cut fabric for backing in a nine-inch square. Placing right sides together, stitch three sides of the cushion together. Clip the corners and trim the edges. Turn to right side and push out the corners with the eraser end of a pencil. Insert stuffing and sew the open side with a blind stitch. The cushion should be stuffed until it is very firm.

## TOTE BAG

The tote bag illustrated is available in a kit, complete with painted canvas, necessary yarns, needle, and instructions for working and finishing. There are literally hundreds of designs on the market today. You will find that a kit packaged with just enough yarn of each color is a most economical way of starting painted needlepoint unless one does original designing.

There are a few suggestions to follow in doing this project. There is usually a row of small boxes painted on one side of the canvas showing the different colors used in the piece. Place an inch of the matching thread next to the painted color. This will be an invaluable reference to indicate

the change of color. When working, do areas of one color in rows as much as possible. Single or scattered stitches are best filled in later. In most instances, it is wiser to work the design before the background. Sometimes it is necessary to make a decision about which color to use if the paint overlaps or is not clearly marked.

Most painted pieces will be worked on mono canvas. The Half-Cross Stitch cannot be worked on this canvas, but either the Continental or Basketweave stitches will work well. It is best to work from the center of the design out, unrolling the unworked portion as the work progresses.

*Figure 16. A tote bag worked in needlepoint is a practical project as well as an attractive handbag. (Courtesy, Spinnerin Yarn Company.)*

Figure 17. There is a wide range of kits available for needlepoint. Projects include coverings for upholstery (a) and tennis rackets (b), belts (c), decorations (d), and glass cases (e). A canvas may even be the background for a clock (f). (Courtesy, LeeWards, top and bottom; Spinnerin Yarn Company, center.)

*Figure 18. Experimenting with design and color brings a modern touch to this decorative piece of needlepoint. (Courtesy, The Schlossberg Collection.)*

*Figure 19. The Continental stitch is used in this multi-colored still life. A checkerboard foreground and an interesting background add an extra dimension to the preworked design. (Courtesy, The Schlossberg Collection.)*

## PAIR OF PICTURES

This project uses needlepoint with already worked designs. These are available in great abundance at most needlework stores and departments. The designs have been worked by hand by skilled craftsmen, the great majority of whom come from Madeira, Taiwan, Austria, and, most recently, China. These are usually of a more traditional design than the painted pieces. However, it is not difficult to give a modern touch to a traditional look. Instead of working the background in all one color, one can experiment with a variety of alternatives.

The pictures illustrate the effect achieved by varying the background colors and designs. If a dramatic effect is not preferable, work with soft tones of one color. Use a variety of stitches; there are hundreds more that have not been described here. Indeed, if needlepoint fascinates you, as it does so many people today, additional information is available in a great variety of books and publications.

## For Additional Reading

Cook, Inman, and Pierce, Daren, **Pleasures of Needlepoint,** Universal, 1972.

Gilmore, Betty, **The Needlepoint Primer,** Chilton, 1973.

Handley, Hope, **Fun with Needlepoint,** Scribner, 1972.

Lightbody, Donna M., **Introducing Needlepoint,** Lothrop, Lee and Shepard, 1973.

Walzer, Mary M., **Handbook of Needlepoint Stitches,** Van Nostrand Reinhold, 1971.

Williams, Elsa S., **Bargello Embroidery,** Van Nostrand Reinhold, 1967.

# Batik

**Batik, an ancient craft newly revived, results in the creation of beautiful and decorative fabrics through the use of resist substances and dyes.**

Throughout civilization, mankind has been interested in self-adornment. One manifestation of this interest is fabric decoration, which has played a significant part in the history of various peoples. Wall paintings and tablets have told the story of cloth dyeing and embellishment. Indeed, archaeological evidence of this craft dates as far back as 5000 years.

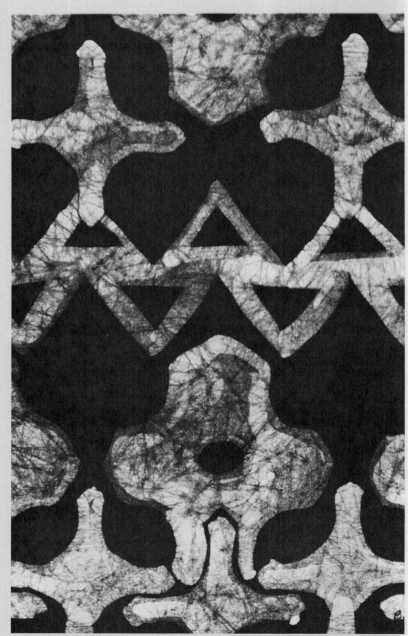

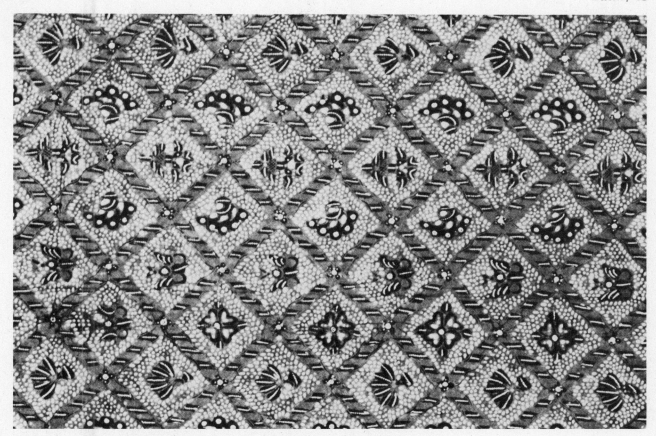

Figure 2. Archaeological evidence indicates that the ancient art of batik was widespread among various cultures throughout the world. This traditional Indonesian batik illustrates the skill achieved by early craftsmen. (Collection, Mr. and Mrs. Edward Holcomb.)

Although the discoverers or originators of the batik process remain unknown, fragments of decorated fabrics which have been resist dyed have been found in many places in the world. In Roman writings, wax, flour paste, clay resists, and dyeing have been described in historical accounts. It is assumed that the techniques were brought to Egypt from India, because tools and blocks for fabric decoration dating from 3000 B. C. have been found in India. And it was trade with India which also introduced wax resists to Indonesia and Java, where the world's finest batiks are still produced. (In Javanese, *tik* means light dots or points against a darker background.)

Ancient and highly prized decorated fabrics are

Figure 1. The batik process utilizes wax resists and dyes to print designs on cloth. Stencils were used to create the unusual patterns shown on the cotton batiste fabric (opposite).

also attributed to China and Japan, while African history shows that the first decorated textiles were probably painted with fingers, sticks, twigs, or simple brushes; designs were printed with resist pastes and dyed on cloth. Pre-Hispanic Peruvians also used hand stamps, stencils, and rollers to print designs on cloth, while dyes were painted. Many fabric fragments found have been dyed in one color.

Batik has been defined as writing with wax, writing with light against dark, or writing with little bits or little dots. The art is called writing because of the tool, called a *tjanting*, which is used in the application of hot wax to cloth. A tjanting is a pen-shaped tool with a brass or copper receptacle for holding hot wax and a spout for its application. The wax is drawn on the cloth and the cloth is then dyed, the original color of the cloth being retained only under the wax.

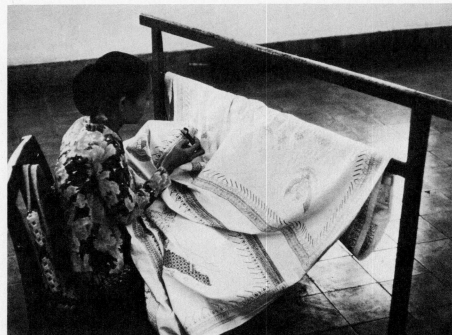

Figure 3. A Javanese batik artist (left) applies wax with a tjanting, the traditional tool of batik. (Photo, courtesy of Alice Holcomb.) Historically, batik was used for self-adornment as well as decorative purposes. The silk scarf from India (below, left) and the dress from Malaysia demonstrate the versatility of this craft. (Silk scarf from the collection of Dr. and Mrs. Jack Arends; dress from the collection of Mr. and Mrs. Edward Holcomb.)

Batik is a fabric-dyeing process in which a resist substance is applied to the cloth wherever color is to be reserved. Waxes, resins, and starch pastes can be used as resists. Decorative design patterns are produced through use of resists and dyes on cloth and paper.

Recently, artists and craftsmen have been reviving several of these techniques. In Java, the old traditional methods are still used; however, there and elsewhere in the world, new ideas and processes are being tried. Presently, there are hundreds of craftsmen working and experimenting with batik.

Contemporary methods and inexpensive materials are available to all who are eager to learn. The idea of painting designs on cloth with waxes and immersing the cloth into dyes to create images is, indeed, like magic.

# Common Terms Used In Batik

**Acid Dyes:** a group of dyes for silk and woolens requiring acetic acid as an assistant.

**Assistant:** a chemical that allows dye to work with fabric.

**Batik:** a process of fabric decoration in which waxes, resins, and flour pastes are used as resists on cloth before dyeing.

**Cold Dyeing:** a process of coloring fabric in a dye solution of about 100° Fahrenheit.

**Crackle:** thin web-like lines caused by cracking wax in fabric before dyeing.

**Direct Dyes:** that group of dyes with an affinity for cotton, linen, and viscose rayon.

**Dye Bath:** the liquid containing dyestuff, assistants, and water in which cloth is immersed and colored.

**Dye Paste:** a thick mixture in which dyestuffs, assistants, chemicals, and thickening agent are combined and used for painting and printing on cloth.

**Dyes and Dyestuffs:** chemicals that can be put into solution and become basically transparent liquids for coloring cloth.

**Fastness:** the ability of a dye on cloth to retain its intensity and depth of color after being subjected to washing, boiling, sun, and light.

**Fiber Reactive Dyes:** a fairly new group of dyes, invented in 1956 in England. These work in a cool water solution with salt and washing soda assistants and react with cotton, linen, and silk fibers.

**Finishing:** the completion process that includes the washing, rinsing, drying, and ironing of a decorated fabric.

**Fixation:** the process by which dye color is set in fabric.

**Ground Color:** the original color of cloth before dyeing.

**Hot Dyeing:** the process of dyeing cloth in a color bath that has been heated to 140° Fahrenheit or higher.

**Household Dyes:** a combination of several groups of dyestuffs that can be used for natural and synthetic fabrics.

**Immersion Dyeing:** the process of placing a fabric into a solution of dyes for coloring fibers.

**Mercerizing Process:** the treatment of cotton with caustic soda to increase its affinity for dyes; mercerized cottons should not be washed before dyeing.

**Overdyeing:** the process of dyeing color over color.

**Paste (To Paste):** the mixing of dyestuff with a small amount of cold water before dissolving in hot water prior to dyeing cloth.

**Repeat:** a unit of design used repeatedly in the decoration of a single fabric.

**Resist:** the process of applying a substance for the purpose of keeping an area of cloth free from dyes.

**Salt:** common or plain salt (sodium chloride) used as a chemical assistant for fabric dyeing; it is not mixed with iodine as is iodized salt.

**Sizing:** the stiffener applied to a fabric to give it body.

**Solvent:** the liquid used to dissolve the remainder of waxes in fabric.

**Stamping:** a method of creating designs on fabric by pressing objects or blocks into a substance and onto cloth.

**Steaming:** the process for setting colors in fabric through moist heat.

**Stencil:** a thin paper, film, or metal cut or perforated to allow a design to form on the surface underneath when resists or dye pastes are applied.

**Synthetic Fibers:** man-made fibers produced through chemical synthesis.

**Thickener:** a gel-like substance made with starch or gum and added to dyes for direct application to cloth.

**Viscose Rayon:** a manufactured fiber that can be dyed with the same dyes used for linen and cotton.

**Washing Soda:** a chemical substance used as a fixing agent that causes a reaction between fiber reactive dyes and fabric.

**Wet Out:** the dampening of fabric with water before immersing in a dye.

## Basic Equipment And Supplies

The materials used for batik are readily available in most communities. Many of the materials and supplies can be purchased in grocery, drug, variety, department, and hardware stores. Some equipment is available in the home. The following is a basic list: (1) an appliance for heating wax, such as an electric skillet, fryer, hot plate, or double boiler; (2) a table or other large working surface; and (3) a frame (stretcher, embroidery hoop, or other type of frame used to hold cloth).

Basic supplies include: (1) fabric (about three yards of 100% cotton—especially muslin—is excellent for the beginner); (2) wax (one to two pounds of paraffin and some beeswax, available in grocery stores and candle shops, among others); (3) household or fiber reactive dyes (the former are available in drug and variety stores and the latter can be bought from batik craft suppliers) of the following colors: lemon yellow, yellow, scarlet, magenta red, blue, and turquoise—brown and black are optional; (4) cleaning fluid; (5) contact paper; and (6) common salt, soap, and vinegar.

### TOOLS AND OBJECTS

1. **Brushes.** One wide bristle brush, one narrow bristle brush, and one pointed brush for application of waxes and dyes. Natural bristle brushes of various widths can be purchased at hardware stores or artist supply shops. Flat paint brushes in one-half inch, one-inch and three-inch widths are adequate for most surface application in batik work. One tapered brush or flat brush with bristles cut diagonally could be used for small areas. Japanese bamboo brushes, which are pointed, can be used for application of wax in fine details.

2. **Tjanting.** A *tjanting* is a drawing tool for holding hot wax and is used for designing line

**Figure 4.** *A wide assortment of tools (left) may be used to create intersting batik patterns. After drawing the design with a crayon, a pencil, or charcoal, wax is applied to the design with a tjanting or a brush. Designs may also be applied to the fabric with woodblocks, metal stamps, or cookie cutters. Both household and fiber-reactive dyes (right) provide the batik artist with a variety of colors.*

patterns; available at craft shops handling batik supplies.

3. Stamps and blocks used for printing designs with hot wax on fabric. Such objects include cookie cutters, metal tools, or cardboard tubes.

## OTHER EQUIPMENT AND SUPPLIES

In addition to the basic items already mentioned, other equipment supplies needed are: (1) rubber gloves; (2) an electric iron; (3) large plastic or enamel dishpans (pans should be large enough to immerse fabric in dyebath); (4) measuring spoons and cups; (5) wooden spoons, dowels, or paint sticks for stirring dyes; (6) jars, preferably with wide mouths; (7) scissors; (8) cardboard scraps to be used for making printing blocks; (9) newspaper; (10) plastic bags and plastic wrap; and (11) crayons, pencil, charcoal, or ball-point pen for drawing design on fabric.

*Figure 5. Many of the basic supplies for batik are found in the household. The equipment shown here includes washing soda, soap flakes, an iron, spray starch, salt, dish pans, paper towels, an appliance for heating wax, measuring cups and spoons, rubber gloves, newspapers, and fabric.*

# Basic Procedures

The batik process is basically a resist method of producing images and designs on cloth or paper: designs are planned, the cloth is washed, hot wax is applied to it, and the cloth is dyed. The areas covered with wax resist the dyes and remain the color of the cloth. Unwaxed areas are the dyed color. Batiks can be planned for one-, two-, or three-color sequences—some designers use as many as 20 colors. After the last dye application, the wax is removed and the cloth is finished.

Batik is fun and satisfying but the process is a time-consuming one that requires patience on the part of the beginner. Designs need to be drawn carefully so the eventual placement of waxes and dyes is clear.

## FABRIC

Very fine, 100% cottons are best for batik. Because most new fabrics are treated with sizing, preparation of the cloth requires washing, preshrinking, rinsing, and pressing. A thin starch solution or spray starch will help in pressing fabric smooth and in keeping the hot wax from spreading into the fabric.

The exciting part of doing batiks lies in the production of original designs. Beginners should try to create design ideas which might be derived from nature or man-made environments; from people and animals; or from geometric and free shapes. Design patterns can, of course, be drawn repeatedly on the fabric.

The design should be drawn on the fabric with crayon, pencil, charcoal, or ball-point pen. When drawing on paper, the artist usually draws dark lines and shapes against a light background. However, in drawing a design for a batik, the dots, lines, and shapes are drawn in wax and remain light against a dark (dyed) background. The hot wax drawing should penetrate the cloth. This is done by having the cloth stretched tightly on a frame, stretcher, or embroidery hoop.

### Stretching or Holding the Fabric

The cloth should be stretched tightly so that waxing tools can glide freely, allowing the hot wax to penetrate easily.

Stretch the cloth evenly on a frame, tacking it at corners—the position of the fabric being waxed can be changed as often as necessary. Keeping the fabric free of the working surface is advantageous and the stretcher frame permits this both for waxing and for painting dyes onto the cloth. Some craftsmen also like to have fabric on a frame when using a stamping process. Regular batik frames are available at batik supply stores.

There are some things about stretching the fabric which should be kept in mind. Large frames are cumbersome and heavy, a definite disadvantage. Tacking of lightweight cotton or silk may leave marks on the cloth, so some artists pin fabric to a chair and hold cloth stretched tightly in one hand while waxing with brush or tjanting with the other hand. One might also place bricks, rocks, or other weighted objects on the end of the cloth and hold the section to be waxed tightly in one hand. Some artists let the fabric lie flat on waxed paper or foil that has been placed on the working surface; after the waxing, the fabric is gently pulled away from the surface.

## WAX

Paraffin, the most inexpensive wax for batik, produces a crackle or vein-like webbing in the design pattern. Because using paraffin alone can result in the wax not clinging to or penetrating the cloth, a small portion of beeswax should be combined with the paraffin. Beeswax may be more difficult to obtain. Some art supply companies sell a batik wax which is a combination of beeswax and paraffin—an ideal wax contains equal amounts of each. A cake wax, product #2305, much like beeswax but less expensive, is produced by Mobil Oil Company. Other petroleum companies have similar products.

### Applying Hot Wax

The simplest way to apply wax to the fabric is with a brush while the wax is hot. A double boiler or a saucepan set in a pan of water can be used for melting wax, either on the stove or on a hot plate. If using a can of wax, place it in a pan with three or four inches of water that is heated at a low boil. Never place a can of wax directly on the burner.

When the wax reaches a temperature of about 240° Fahrenheit, it can be brushed on the fabric.

The temperature is correct if the wax goes through the cloth and looks quite clear. If the wax is not hot enough, it only coats the fabric and is opaque. When this happens the fabric should be rewaxed with hot wax in the same areas on the under side. Wax is too hot when it starts to smoke. The wax pot should never be left unattended and baking soda should be kept handy to smother a flame. *Never* use water on or near hot wax. The table on which fabric is to be waxed should be heavily covered with newspaper and should be within reach of the hot wax.

The brush is immersed in the hot wax and should be allowed to heat up a bit. When picking up the hot wax on the brush, wipe the excess wax against the edge of the pan to prevent any dripping. Apply the wax to the design on the area of fabric that is to be kept free of dye.

Large areas that are to be waxed should be outlined with a small brush first. Then the larger space inside the outline can be filled in with a wider brush. Apply the wax by brushing in towards the middle of the space from the outline.

### Decorative Processes

Design outlines should be kept open and free of wax. The wax can be applied about one-eighth to one-fourth inch from the lines. To prevent wax from spreading over the line, water can be painted on the outline. This wets the cloth and

*Figure 6. The most common method of applying hot wax to a design is with a brush. Broad areas may be quickly and easily covered. The fabric should be raised to allow the wax to penetrate the cloth.*

resists the wax. When the outlines of the design are consistently kept free of waxing, subsequent dyeing will create dark lines around the shapes and patterns of the batik fabric.

Brushes should be cared for between waxings. While they should not be left to cool and harden in the wax, they do not need to be cleaned each time they are used. When placed in hot wax for a few minutes, wax-coated brushes will soften and can be used again for waxing.

For centuries, as mentioned earlier, the Javanese have used a tool called a tjanting for wax writing in dots and lines. Using a tjanting is optional for the beginner—as with any other new skill, it requires practice. It is held very much like a pencil, and hot wax is picked up in the brass or copper cup and permitted to flow through the spout, thus creating a delicate linear drawing. To prevent accidental drippings of hot wax, always hold a piece of cloth or a padded paper under the tjanting when carrying it to the work surface from the stove or burner. Covering areas of designs not to be waxed with newspaper is always helpful. Designs created with the tjanting have identifiable characteristics. The fabric, penetrated just as it is with brush work, usually has fine patterns of swirls, spirals, dots, and lines.

The simplest, most inexpensive stamping tools can be made from cardboard or the cardboard tubing which comes inside paper towel rolls. Cut

the tubing or cardboard in about two-inch lengths. Fold and shape into a block or form in a lengthwise direction, with the ends retaining the cut surface. The block can be bound tightly with tape. Both ends of the block must be flat and can be used for stamping hot wax onto the cloth.

The contemporary batik artist also can devise many metal stamps for designing fabric. The hardware and kitchenware departments of stores contain hundreds of such items. All kinds and shapes of cookie and doughnut cutters, and such kitchen tools as apple cutters, potato mashers, canape cutters, patty shell makers, etc., can be used. Metal tools, nuts, bolts, washers, pipes, and boxes are among other objects found in the hardware store that are excellent. Other objects might include metal parts of toys, corks, or cans which can be cut, bent, and shaped. Imagination is very important in visualizing how a variety of objects can become tools for batik designs. It is important to keep experimenting.

Because metals are excellent conductors of heat, small metal objects such as cutters should be glued on wood or pressed into cork, the latter to be used as handles. Small sections of dowel rods attached to the metal objects also work effectively.

*Figure 7. With practice, the tjanting (below left) may be used to apply wax for linear designs. Imaginative patterns are easily stamped by dipping printing blocks (right) into hot wax.*

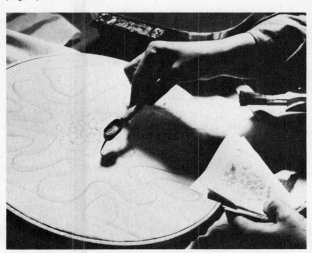

Pipe cleaners can also be formed into simple designs. An extra pipe cleaner can be tied into the form and twisted into a handle. Printing blocks made of pipe cleaners are effective because the covering holds the wax while the thin wire retains the heat.

The temperature of the wax for stamping can be a little lower than the temperature for brush and tjanting work. If the wax is too hot, it will spread too much as the block is stamped onto the fabric. One way of helping to avoid this is to place a piece of foam rubber on the bottom of the wax pan—wax should just cover the surface. The printing block can be pressed onto the foam pad to pick up the wax and then stamped onto the cloth. The hot wax will penetrate the cloth so that a better resist occurs when the fabric is immersed into the dye bath.

Stencils can be cut in simple, geometric designs from commercial stencil paper or from a waxy tagboard. One way to apply stencil decorations to fabric is by placing a stencil on the cloth and drawing around the shapes lightly with pencil. Move the stencil and repeat until the fabric is covered with the designs. Then carefully brush hot wax within the shapes to create repeat patterns. Several stencil designs can be drawn on one fabric piece.

Self-adhesive stencils can be made from plastic preparations such as contact paper. After the designs and their placement are planned, the paper backing can be peeled off and the stencils adhered to the cloth. Hot wax is brushed carefully over the stencils. After the waxing is completed, the stencils can be pulled away, one at a time, and attached to a plastic surface to be saved for later use. In fact, contact stencils can be used about fifty times before they deteriorate. After the stencils are put away, check the waxed areas on the cloth. If the wax has penetrated the cloth, apply hot wax to those areas of the fabric which need retouching. The fabric is then ready for dyeing.

The creative craftsman may wish to combine various waxing techniques: brush and tjanting; brush and stencil; stencil and tjanting; stencil and block; or block, brush, stencil, and tjanting. Other interesting effects can be created by drawing lines into the wax before final dyeing. This can be achieved by scratching into the wax with a sharpened dowel, a bamboo skewer, or an orange stick. The process is called *sqrafitto*.

Wax can be removed from the cloth by ironing the fabric between newspapers. Old newspapers should be layered on a large work surface, an old pattern-cutting board, or on the floor. Layer the paper approximately one-half inch in thickness. Place the fabric on the newspaper padding, put more sheets of newspaper on top of fabric, and then iron with dry heat. After ironing, pull out one newspaper sheet from under and over the fabric and repeat the process. When wax no longer stains the newspapers, the fabric is ironed suffi-

Figure 8. Stencils may be used to make repeated patterns on the fabric. After the design is cut from stencil paper, place the sheet on the material and brush hot wax within the open shapes. Continue waxing the stenciled areas until the desired effect is achieved.

*Figure 9. To prepare a dye bath using household dyes, begin by pouring the powder into a mixing cup (above). Then, add enough water (above right) and stir to make a paste (opposite.).*

ciently and will be stiff. There will always be a residue of wax in the fabric.

## DYES

There are many kinds of dyes available to the batik craftsman. For the beginner, there are enough household dyes, direct dyes, and fiber reactive dyes to choose from to achieve excellent and successful results. Basic colors for developing a wide color range are lemon yellow, scarlet, and ultramarine blue. Other colors that would add to color exploration are magenta red, deep yellow, turquoise, brown, and black.

### Household Dyes

Household dyes (Rit, Putnam, Cushing, Tintex) are available at grocery, drug, variety, and department stores. They are basically multipurpose dyes, usually a combination of dyestuffs that react with an assortment of fabrics. The dyes are effective on cotton, silk, linen, and wool as well as on viscose rayon, which is a man-made fiber. They are easy to use and fairly inexpensive.

These dyes can be used for direct brushing by preparing a more concentrated solution. Most household dyes come in powder form. Disregard directions for soaking. One teaspoon of the dye, made into paste with cold water and then mixed with two cups of boiling hot water and three tablespoons of salt, is of sufficient strength for direct painting on fabric. The dye bath should be a colored clear liquid to which one more pint of cool water should be added. Remember that areas to be dyed should be drawn in with wax to keep one dye area from running into another. When working with immersion of fabrics in dye baths,

*Figure 10. A dye bath is made by diluting a concentrated dye solution in a large dishpan of hot water (above). The transparent liquid can be intensified in color by dissolving table salt in the mixture (below). It is a good idea to wear rubber gloves when working with dyestuffs.*

always wear rubber gloves and a cover-up such as a rubber apron. Dyes can be removed from hands with household bleach solution.

Dyes usually work best when they are very hot because they will be faster and more fadeproof.

However, in batik work hot dyes are impractical because the wax designs on the cloth would be obliterated. Therefore, even though the dyes for wax batik should be prepared hot, when the fabric is finally immersed in the dye bath, the mixture should be cool.

The fabric should be immersed in the dye for 45 minutes to an hour. If more dye is needed, follow the same proportions for each additional quart required. Also, if darker or more intense colors are desired, add one-half cup of plain salt to the dye bath—be sure the salt is thoroughly dissolved.

After the fabric has been in the dye bath about an hour, take the cloth out of the dye, rinse in cold water, and let it dry. The fabric can be laid on layers of newspapers or on a drying rack. Do not hang it in direct sunlight or put it in a dryer because the wax will melt. After the fabric is dry, rinse it in cold water until all excess dye has been removed and the water runs clear. The fabric can then be dried again.

For additional dyeing, wax can be applied to the cloth again by repeating the dyeing process. Start with light colors for the first dyeing and go to darker colors. Household dyes are not light-fast or washable and should be dry cleaned, a process which preserves the dye color.

## Direct Dyes

Direct dyes (Aljo, Dick Blick, Craftool, Fezan) are available in art stores, craft supply shops, and batik supply resources. These dyes work best at high temperatures: the dye can be mixed with water as hot as it can be from the faucet. Because direct dyes should be cool to the touch when used for batik, twice the amount of dye powder should be mixed to a paste. Usually two to three heaping teaspoons will be sufficient for about one pound or three yards of fabric. After the dye has been made into a paste, hot water is added to yield one-half gallon of dye bath, to which three heaping tablespoons of plain salt should be added before the fabric is immersed. Fabric should be left in dye bath for 40 minutes to an hour. For brush painting on fabric, a concentrated solution can be used. Make a paste of one teaspoon of dye and a little water. Add one pint of hot water from the faucet and three tablespoons of salt. Brush on the fabric and let dry.

After the fabric is taken from the dye bath, it should be rinsed in cold water until the water runs clear. Because direct dyes are not light-fast or washable, dry cleaning is again recommended.

Fabric dyed with direct dyes and with household dyes should be steamed for a little more color fastness.

## Fiber Reactive Dyes

Fiber reactive dyes (Dylon, Hi-Dye, Fibrec, ICI Organics, Pylam), which react with and affect fibers, work very well in cool dye baths. The colors are bright to brilliant, light-fast and can be washed—fabrics do not have to be dry cleaned. Moreover, because they mix well, only a few basic colors are needed to create an adequate range. These dyes are effective on cotton, linen, silk, and viscose rayon; they are not effective on polyesters, dacrons, acetates, or other man-made fabrics.

Fiber reactive dyes can be purchased with packages of fixitive and with paste activators. The user needs only to follow directions on the packages. For the beginning batik artist, buying just what is needed is a logical way to proceed. If the craft is continued, then it is wise to buy larger quantities of dyes.

A dye bath with fiber reactive or Procion dyes can be prepared by making a paste of one teaspoon of dye powder with a little cold water. Two pints of very hot water (from the faucet) should be added and six tablespoons of salt also dissolved in the solution. Finally, two tablespoons of washing soda (e.g., Sal Soda) should be dissolved in a little warm water and added to the dye bath.

After the cloth is put into the dye bath it should be moved about constantly for a half-hour. If the fabric is not covered by the dye, increase the amount of dye powder, water, salt, and soda according to formula.

There is also a long-method fiber-reactive dyeing procedure, explained here for one pound of cloth (about three yards), which is done as follows:

**1.** Dissolve 1 or 2 teaspoons of dye in 1 cup of hot water (140° F).

**2.** Add the dye solution to 2 gallons of warm water (100° F).

**3.** Place the clean cloth in the dye bath for 10 to 15 minutes. (All cloth should have been washed before dyeing except for mercerized cotton, which need not be washed.)

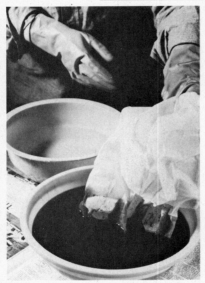

**4.** Add 2 tablespoons of plain salt every 5 minutes for 15 minutes. Then leave fabric in bath for 20 minutes more. (Stir fabric in bath occasionally.)

**5.** Dissolve 3 tablespoons of washing soda in 2 ounces of water and add to dye bath. Stir occasionally for 1 hour.

**6.** Rinse the dyed cloth in warm water and soap (Lux or Ivory).

**7.** Rinse well until water runs clear. Let the fabric dry.

Always wear rubber gloves. Pans for dyes should be plastic, enamel, or stainless steel—do not use copper, aluminum, or galvanized metal.

In order to brush dye directly on cloth, mix two teaspoons of dye powder (pasted in water), one pint of hot tap water, six tablespoons of plain salt, and two tablespoons of washing soda (dissolved in warm water). This solution will be active for about five or six hours. The fabric should be allowed to dry in a warm humid place for a day or two, or ironed for five minutes between paper towels with a steam iron.

## COLOR

The one-color process is an excellent way for the beginner to start batik. In using one color at a time, there can be dramatic contrasts of dye color to the white or light background color—trying a dark or intense color will bring the designs out even more. An experiment for the beginner follows.

Begin by waxing out all areas that are to remain the original color of the fabric. Then, wet the fabric and immerse in a red dye bath. Rinse the fabric and let dry.

Once this process is mastered, plan a design using the following four-color dye bath process. Wax areas that are to remain the original color of the fabric, wet the fabric, and immerse it in a yellow dye bath, following dye directions previously given. Rinse and dry. Next, wax out areas to remain yellow and rewax white if necessary. Wet

*Figure 11. Waxed cloth is immersed in cold water (top) before it is placed in a dye bath (center]. The fabric should be removed from the dye bath in about an hour (bottom).*

*Figure 12. When the batik cloth is dry, place it on a thick padding of newspapers and iron the fabric until all the wax has been removed from the finished piece.*

the fabric in plain water and then put into a red dye (unwaxed yellow areas will become orange). Follow the dyeing procedure then rinse and dry. Now wax areas that are to remain orange, wet the fabric, and immerse it in a brown dye. Rinse and dry. Wax out any area to be left brown and rewax other areas if necessary. Wet the fabric and finally put it into a dark-blue or black dye. Follow dyeing procedures, then rinse and dry. Iron out wax between newspapers until the fabric is as free of wax as possible (there will still be dark wax outlines left). Dry clean to remove all remaining wax.

Because dyes are transparent, one needs to think about color and experiment with it. Remember that red over yellow produces orange; blue over yellow produces green; and blue over red produces violet. It is always a good idea to have some small pieces of fabric available as test pieces and to keep a record of successful combinations. In this way one accumulates information and acquires an expertise in working with dye colors.

## Projects You Can Do

As mentioned above, the beginner in batik work should start work simply with one- and two-color designs. Concentration can then be on design and craftsmanship. Learning to work with the application of hot wax, the dyeing of fabrics, and the removal of wax are basic to all batik work. Planning a good design and careful procedure will result in success and satisfaction.

### BRUSH BATIK PANEL (ONE DYE BATH)

**1.** Wash piece of white cotton cloth, rinse, dry, and iron.

**2.** Place several layers of newspapers on working surface.

**3.** Heat paraffin or batik wax in an old electric skillet or double boiler to 240° F.

**4.** While wax is heating, draw design on cloth with pencil or artist's charcoal.

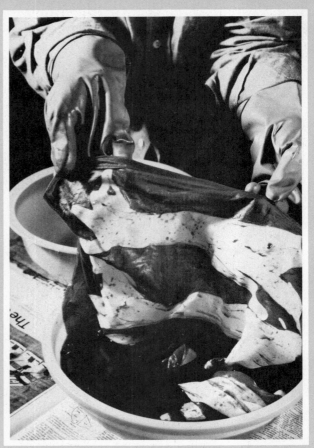

Figure 13. Hot wax is brushed on the design (left), and the waxed cloth is immersed into a dye bath (above). The waxed areas on the finished batik (below) remain white.

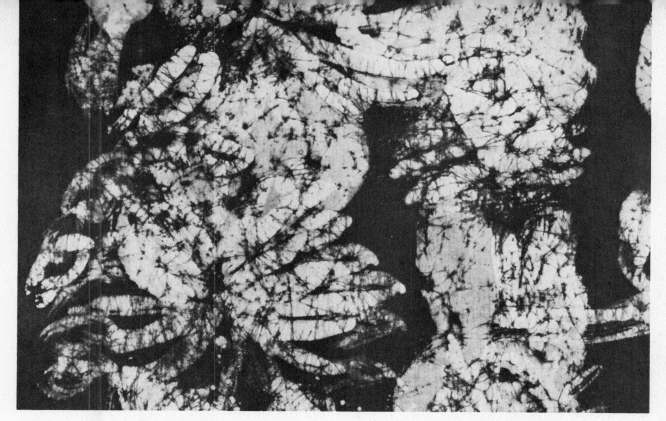

5. When wax is hot enough to penetrate cloth, apply it with a brush to areas which are to remain white.

6. After wax is applied let it cool on cloth.

7. Make a paste of one color of dye and pour mixture into a plastic or enameled pan. Add water and three tablespoons of salt to make dye bath and stir well.

8. Wet the waxed cloth with cold water.

9. Immerse wet waxed cloth in dye bath. Remember to use rubber gloves. Leave in dye for 30 minutes to an hour.

10. Remove cloth from dye and rinse in cold water until it runs clear.

11. Let cloth air dry (place on newspapers on floor or hang on line).

12. Place several layers of old newspapers, newsprint, or paper toweling under batik cloth and also over cloth.

13. Iron out wax. Keep removing wax-laden papers and adding fresh papers until all wax is out of cloth.

14. Finish cloth by dry cleaning.

15. Finished batik can be tacked over stretchers and framed as an art work.

*Figure 14. Dramatic effects can be achieved with one color dye baths. The brush batik above has bold designs which dominate the background color. The brushed patterns on the batik below make the solid background an important aspect of the design.*

## WAX PRINTED BATIK FABRIC (ONE DYE BATH)

**1.** Wash two or three yard lengths of white cotton cloth, rinse, dry, and iron.

**2.** Prepare working surface with newspapers.

*Figure 15. After preparing the fabric and organizing a work area, dip printing object in hot wax and stamp material (below). The finished batik cloth (opposite) has many decorative uses.*

**3.** Heat paraffin or batik wax in electric skillet or double boiler to 240° F.

**4.** When wax is hot enough to penetrate cloth, use block, stamp, or other object to pick up wax and apply to fabric in overall design. Wax should be maintained at even heat so that the block or stamp prints the wax design evenly on cloth.

**5.** After design is applied to whole length of cloth, let it cool.

**6.** Follow steps 6 through 14 as described for previous project.

**7.** Fabric can be used for skirts, dresses, pillows, or wall hangings.

## TJANTING BATIK (ONE DYE BATH)

**1.** Wash piece of white cotton cloth, rinse, dry, and iron.

**2.** Place several layers of newspapers on working surface.

*Figure 16. The cup of a tjanting tool picks up wax which has been heated in an old electric skillet.*

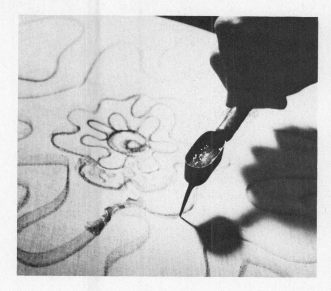

*Figure 17. Wax flows through a spout in the receptacle of the tjanting (above). By following the drawn patterns, this batik technique produces unusual linear designs (below and opposite).*

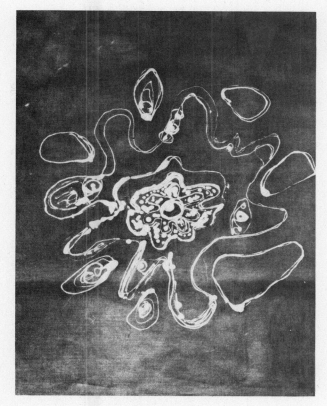

**3.** Heat paraffin or batik wax in an old electric skillet or double boiler to 240° F.

**4.** While wax is heating, draw design on cloth with pencil or artist's charcoal.

**5.** When wax is hot enough to penetrate the cloth,

pick up wax with tjanting. Carry over to cloth and follow drawn lines with flow of hot wax. Put dots of hot wax in some of the wax outlined shapes or areas.

**6.** Follow steps 6 through 14 for first project.

**7.** Tjanting batik can be matted and framed under glass.

## BATIK WALLHANGING (TWO OR THREE DYE BATHS)

**1.** Wash piece of white cotton cloth, rinse, dry, and iron.

**2.** Place several layers of newspapers on working surface.

**3.** Heat paraffin or batik wax in an old electric skillet or double boiler to 240° F.

**4.** While wax is heating, draw design on cloth with pencil or artist's charcoal.

**5.** When wax is hot enough to penetrate cloth, apply it with a brush to areas which are to remain white.

**6.** After wax is applied let it cool on cloth.

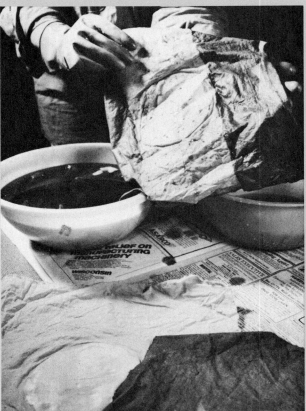

Figure 18. *Multicolored wallhangings require several dye baths. Brush wax on the portion which is to remain white and immerse the fabric in the lightest dye bath first (top left). Dry the fabric and repeat the waxing process, covering only those areas that are to remain the initial color. Then, place the cloth in a second, darker dye bath (bottom left). Three dye baths were used to produce the color variations in this piece (below).*

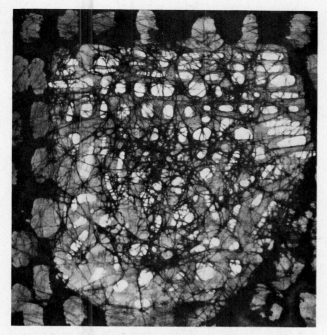

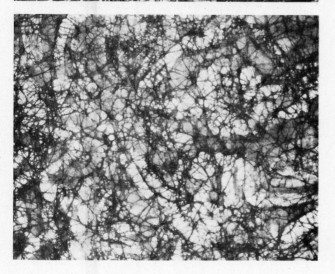

**7.** Make a paste of a light-colored dye, pour mixture into plastic or enameled pan, and add water to make dye bath. Stir well.

**8.** Follow steps 8 through 11 for first project.

**9.** Wax areas of design to remain first light color. Repeat steps 7 and 8 for each additional color. The second dye should be darker than the first and the final color should be the darkest. Example: first color, yellow; second color, red; third color, blue.

**10.** Put cloth between newspapers and iron out wax. Use as many clean newspapers as needed until all wax is removed.

**11.** Finish cloth by dry cleaning.

**12.** Batik can be hemmed on all raw edges. Casings can be sewed at top and bottom. Curtain or dowel rods can be put through casings for hanging batik as a decorative wall hanging.

## *For Additional Reading*

Belfer, Nancy, **Designing in Batik and Tie Dye,** Davis, 1972.

Johnston, Meda, and Kaufman, Glen, **Design on Fabric,** Reinhold, 1967.

Keller, Ila, **Batik: The Art and Craft,** Tuttle, 1966.

Krevitsky, Nik, **Batik: Art and Craft,** Reinhold, 1964.

Meilach, Dona Z., **Contemporary Batik and Tie-Dye,** Crown, 1973.

Nea, Sara, **Batik,** Reinhold, 1970.

*Figure 19. Once the batik method is learned, cloth design becomes a uniquely personal form of artistic expression (opposite page).*

# Color in Crafts

*Every craftsman needs a guide to the confident and stimulating use of color.*

From prehistoric times to the present, color has been an integral part of people's lives. The museums of the world are filled with portrayals of the dreams and realities of mankind. Throughout history, these images have been expressed in thousands of different and colorful ways. The craftsman has always been guided by nature, climate, the relative advancement of his civilization, and the materials available to him. His inspiration was drawn from the time and place in which he lived.

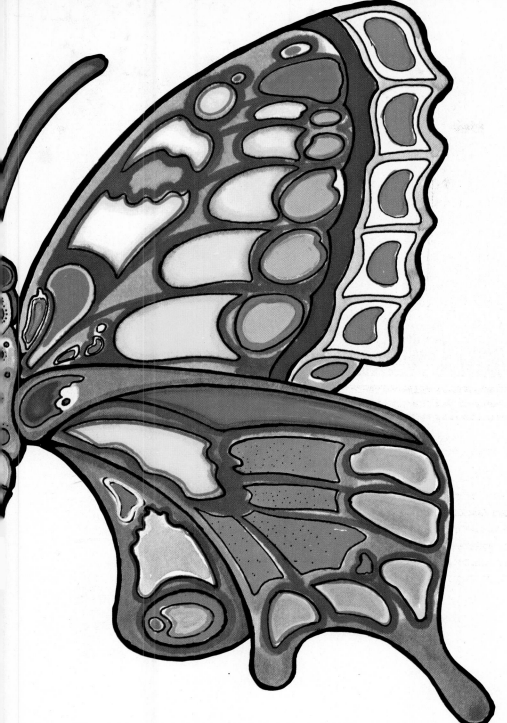

Prehistoric man could use only materials which were readily at hand. Since earth pigments were at his disposal, he painted in earth colors. These colors were derived from the juices of plants and insects, soot from fires, and natural materials in the earth. As a result, his colors were restricted to black, brown, red, yellow, and gray. The cave artists' drawings of animals were done with surprising realism: outlines were usually black, with the remainder of the picture consisting of a skillful mixture of yellow, red, and black.

Early craftsmen often employed a mosaic technique to express their attitudes and ideas. The large mosaic found on the floor of a Palestinian synagogue, circa 520 A. D., shows that colors were few and, although arranged artistically, were imposed according to colored substances that could be derived from the surrounding environment.

Early Egyptians were, and still are, renowned for their knowledge of dyes and skilled use of color.

Figure 1. This prehistoric cave painting (above) was done in earth-tone colors. (Ralph Morse/Time-Life Books.) Only a few colors were used for this mosaic floor (right) in a synagogue. (The Photographic Archives of the Jewish Theological Seminary of N.Y., Frank J. Darmstaedter.)

The museums of Cairo contain many fine examples of objects depicting the relationship between early Egyptian civilization and nature. It is not surprising that the vast, sterile deserts and the continuously warm and sunny climate of Egypt produced arts and crafts with warm, bright colors. Because the craftsman depended upon color and texture for beauty, rarely were ornaments of any kind found on the many jars and bowls used by the common folk. Egyptian jewelers also displayed great technical skill in their lavish use of such materials as gold, blue-green feldspar, lapis lazuli, and carnelian — each of which was bountiful throughout the country.

The ancient Greeks, free from extremes of temperature and surrounded by brilliant colors of the sea and sky, reacted with great sensitivity to their surroundings. Undoubtedly, the science of color had its beginnings in the vast growth in human wisdom which occurred in Greece hundreds of years ago: the poet Sophocles employed an artist to paint what seems to have been the first scenery for plays. This artist may have been one of the first to recognize the relationship between light, shade, and distance.

To the Greeks, man was the measure of all things. Their black pottery served as a background on which to display this human involvement in decorative beauty. Their knowledge of color mixture

became highly developed. Roman pottery, on the other hand, was made of fine, reddish clay to which a redder glaze was added. Then, when the blowpipe was invented, glassmakers were able to produce beautiful, colored glassware. The craftsman was able to use his inspiration in arranging nature's colors to form a very private expression of himself.

A natural consequence of the fusion of East and West was evident in the bright, Byzantine crafts. Gold mosaics, fine marbles, and rich color in gold and jewels were lavishly used. Sometimes, color became practically synonymous with a craft. For instance, the "Delft Blue" of Dutch tiles was an imitation of early Chinese porcelain which, when first made, was painted blue because it was the only color that would withstand the heat of the kiln. The Delft potters succeeded in imitating this color, and the blue tiles and pottery became a popular part of their industry. Great influence on modern-day color came from the French Impressionists. They developed a technique called pointillism: rather than mixing colors on palettes, they obtained a one-color effect by placing many colors in tiny dots on the canvas. (For example, to make violet, dots of red and blue were placed next to each other.) A visual mixing of light and dark, and warm and cool spots of complementary colors resulted in a vibrancy of color never before

*Figure 2. Delft pottery work is a prime example of a craft associated with one color, blue. This Delft kettle and brazier date back to 1744. (Reproduktieverkoop Rijksmuseum Amsterdam.)*

obtained. The Impressionists' use of color was imaginative, gay, and involved.

As civilization spread across the Atlantic to the North American continent, the American Pilgrim women did their best to apply color to the materials available to them. Using only natural dyes to put color into their woven cloth, they discovered how to produce a soft, very serviceable gray by combining one-third each of black sheep's wool, white lamb's wool, and wool dyed in indigo. This gray, which eventually became known as Pilgrim gray, was more practical than pure white and more adaptable than pure black. However, historians note that the capes brought to America by Pilgrim gentlemen were lined with scarlet. It would appear, therefore, that hard times rather than choice dictated the predominance of gray in early America.

Dyeing in the early colonial days utilized such natural dyes as indigo for blue, madder and cochineal for red, and fustic and quercitron for yellow. Logwood was the most commonly used black dyeing ingredient. The dry outer skins of onions have also long been used for coloring yarns and fabrics.

But natural dyes fade unless the yarn or fabric is first treated with a mordant, a setting agent such as alum or tannic acid. The discovery in the mid-1850s of a lavender dye made from aniline, a coal-tar product, marked the end of the natural dye era. As colors became more easily obtainable, the American woman began to express herself in woven coverlets, quilts, and hooked rugs with the brightest colors available. Many craftsmen today, however, prefer the "imperfect" look of natural dyeing for hooked rugs, weaving, and knitting yarns. These craftsmen are seeking a "one of a kind" look, or colors that are unique.

Early American settlers brought to the New World their cultural inheritance. This and regional differences are readily discernible in their early crafts. Although clay, for example, was an important substance used by these settlers, potters in the other colonies could not match the decorative ceramics of the Pennsylvania Germans. These craftsmen, newly arrived from Germany, had an innate ability to use color as emphasis for ornamentation. One favorite technique of these potters was sgraffito. This method of scratching a line through a coat of white clay laid over a red clay base will rpoduce a dark pattern on a light, golden background when glazed and fired. In the horseman plate shown here, the use of bright red color emphasizes the design of the bold, daring horseman.

Just as the early craftsman and homemaker wished to express their creativity, people today find that many of their happiest hours are spent in a chosen craft. Because of the technological revolution which took place at the close of the nineteenth century, the reliance on handmade crafts dwindled, but did not completely disappear. Today there is an intense revival of crafts, a searching for the same self-expression, personal independence, and self-reliance which our ancestors possessed.

Indeed, the craftsman who made a quilt in Pennsylvania in 1890, and the craftsman of today who uses strips of colored ribbon to fashion a desk set have touched hands across the years. They both have seen the world in bold, bright colors and will leave heirlooms that will inspire future generations to retain these arts.

## An Introduction To The Use Of Color

Many people avoid creative craft work because they lack formal training in science or art. Some people do have difficulty using color effectively, but this usually stems from a lack of confidence and experience rather than a lack of ability. The ability to use color is not necessarily an inherited gift or the result of scientific training. It is usually more a matter of good taste and sensitivity to one's surroundings. Even those people who appear to have a natural ability to use appropriate colors can benefit from some basic knowledge about color.

There is a definite pattern and order in the use of color. Understanding this is important in expressing ideas in an easy, confident way. Sometimes, just the simple knowledge of a particular color harmony makes starting a project easier. Personal taste and style will develop, and satisfaction will increase as one becomes more involved in a craft.

Being surrounded by color every day and reacting to it strengthens likes and dislikes. Perhaps the best advice that can be given a beginner is to choose colors that one likes. Should a color choice in a project prove disappointing, it is advisable to change it. If, for example, a rug has a disturbing color value in a flower, remove it.

Because color is so personal, there cannot be any hard and fast rules concerning its use. Nevertheless, one should not always rely too heavily on natural insights and guesswork, for sometimes the cost of making a mistake is too great. Understanding the makeup of color adds to skill in its use.

Imagination, perception, and execution all play essential roles in craft work, but the ability to "see" perhaps takes precedence over all. Is grass just green, or many colors of blue, green, and yellow? Is a color just blue, or a variation of the hue? Is a rose just red, or five or six different values of that color? It is seeing the color values in a rose, for example, that enables the craftsman to better understand the way to use color. Constant observation and learning to look is a large part of a craftsman's education.

*Figure 3. Photographs can provide color inspiration for the craftsman. This intriguing photo shows the wavelengths generated by a laser. (Fritz Goro.)*

A collection of pictures and illustrations of all kinds is an invaluable aid to every craftsman, working in any craft. Almost every magazine uses a variety of color — as do greeting cards, advertisements, wallpaper, fabrics, ribbon, wrapping papers, and so forth. It may be a good idea to keep a file of such items to use as a source of color inspriation whenever needed.

Study nature. A walk in the woods is inspiring. Be aware of the colorful plumage of birds; of the soft and subtle brown, black, gray, and white mixture of furry animals. Notice the many warm, soft colors in stones. Find the bright hues in fish and insects. Observe very closely the woods, sea, and sky.

Visit museums. Look at the colors used in paintings. Note those color combinations that are personally appealing. Study the blending of colors. Make note of how one color is played against another. Study proportion of dark and light. Find a favorite color and note how it was used with other colors. All this thoughtful give and take, *before* starting a project, is excellent preparation and helps to build confidence.

Because everyone sees things differently, any two people can work the same design and have it look completely different when finished. A standard design can take on a different personality when worked in a different color. A visit to any craft show is most rewarding: seeing several interpretations of one design provides realization that color is what makes the biggest difference between one piece of work and another.

## The Color Wheel

Anyone working in arts and crafts should make and use a color wheel. This is the single, most important aid and in learning about color, and the easiest method for showing basic color relationships. The first color circle was arranged by Sir Isaac Newton in the latter part of the seventeenth century. He chose red, orange, yellow, green, blue, violet and indigo as major hues, and allied them to the seven known planets and seven notes of the diatonic music scale. The color wheel is a constant, useful source of reference. And, a sound understanding of its makeup is an important first step in attaining a working knowledge of color.

## ARRANGEMENT OF THE COLOR WHEEL

The arrangement of a color wheel is made in an orderly fashion. Using the accompanying illustrations one at a time, try to create a wheel on paper as well as memorizing it.

### Primary Colors

The primary colors, from which all other colors are obtained, are red, yellow, and blue. These are pure colors — they do not have a trace of any other color in them. For example, primary red is a red with no trace of either yellow or blue — it is not an orange-red or a blue-red.

### Secondary Colors

The secondary colors are orange, green, and violet. They lie between the primary colors and are obtained by mixing two primary colors in equal proportions. Hence, red and yellow make orange, yellow and blue make green, and blue and red make violet.

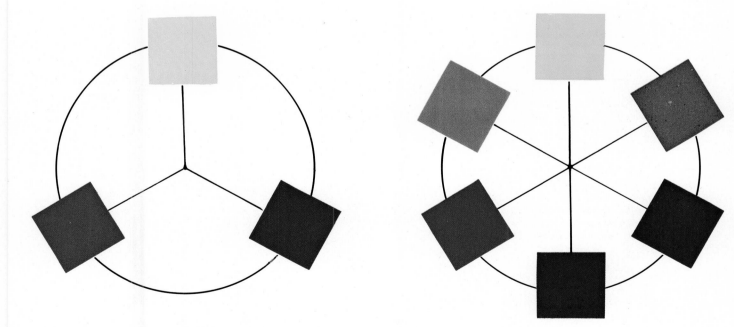

*Figure 4. The three primary colors (left) are red, yellow, and blue. All other colors are obtained from these three. The secondary colors (right) are organge, green, and violet. They are obtained by mixing adjacent primary colors in equal amounts. For example, yellow plus blue equals green.*

## Intermediate Colors

Intermediate colors are those formed by combining a primary color and its secondary color. For example, yellow (primary) combined with orange (secondary) produces a yellow-orange (intermediate). Yellow combined with its other secondary, green, produces a yellow-green.

It should now be evident that between any two colors there are any number of possible gradations. For practical purposes, however, it is enough to divide the color wheel into 12 sections. Hence, a color description may be refined to blue-green or yellow-green — or finer yet, to a green blue-green or a green yellow-green.

## Tertiary Colors

Tertiary colors are formed from a mixture of all three primary colors. These subtle colors are excellent foils for the bright primary colors. Mixing the primaries in different proportions yields a wide range of soft, subdued colors. For example, a predominance of yellow will yield khaki drab, a predominance of red yields browns, and a predominance of blue creates a blue-green. An equal mixture of the three primary colors produces a neutral gray. Gray, of course, can also be mixed from black and white.

## Opaque and Transparent Colors

Opaque colors are those that cannot be seen through, and which cover black and white. Transparent colors will look brilliant when painted over white, but are invisible on a black surface.

## DIMENSIONS OF COLOR

Color may be described as having three dimensions: hue, value, and intensity. *Hue* is another name for color. Red is a hue. In order to change a hue, it must be mixed with another hue. If yellow is mixed with red, the result is orange, a new hue.

*Value* designates the lightness or darkness of a color. The value of a hue can be changed without changing the original hue. Light values of a color are called *tints;* dark values of a color are called

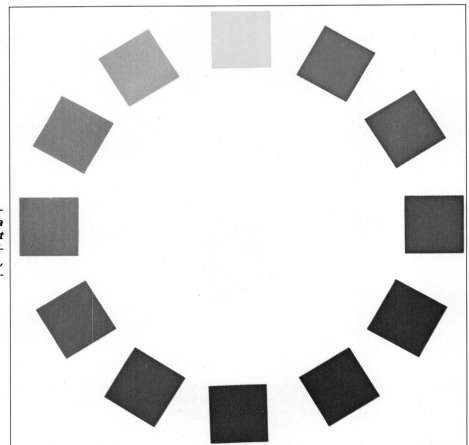

*Figure 5. To obtain an intermediate color, combine a primary with its adjacent second color. Note that yellow is combined with green, for example, to make yellow-green.*

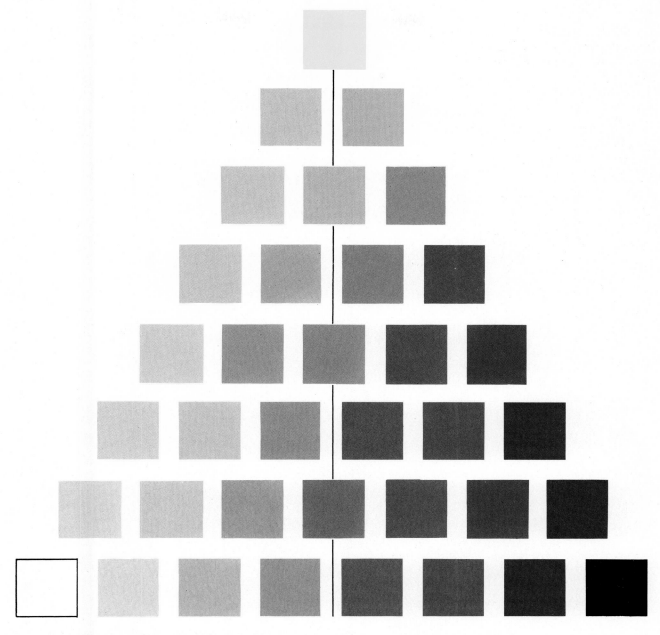

**Figure 6. This intensity scale demonstrates how colors dull as gray is added. The yellow is a pure color and thus has the highest intensity of the color blocks shown.**

*shades*. Pink is a light value, or tint, of red; dark red is a dark value, or shade of red.

*Intensity* (or chroma) refers to the brightness or dullness of a color, or the amount of pure color it contains. Color in its purest form has high intensity. As a color becomes grayer (grayed), it loses its intensity; therefore, a grayed color is said to be low in intensity. Scarlet red has high intensity, as opposed to the low intensity of a rosy hue.

## Color Organization

The Munsell color system, worked out by A. H. Munsell, provides an easy explanation of the organization of color, as well as classifying color relations. Imagine a sphere with all the hues of color around the equator. Now, imagine a vertical pole through the center of the sphere. This is called the neutral pole because there is no trace of color in it. The neutral pole changes from black at the base, gradually going through several values of gray, to white at the top. Just as the neutrals in the neutral pole make up a scale of values, so too, do all hues. Black must be eliminated because no hue can be as dark as black, and white must be eliminated because no hue can be as light as white.

Next, imagine a horizontal line extending from the gray center to the equator. This line represents the intensity or chroma. Notice how the hue becomes more intense as it extends horizontally from the neutral pole to the outer edge of the sphere. This very important dimension of color gives us an understanding of a grayed color (low intensity) or of a bright color (high intensity). When color harmonies fail, the fault is usually in the intensity dimension, even though there is a proper balance of hue and value.

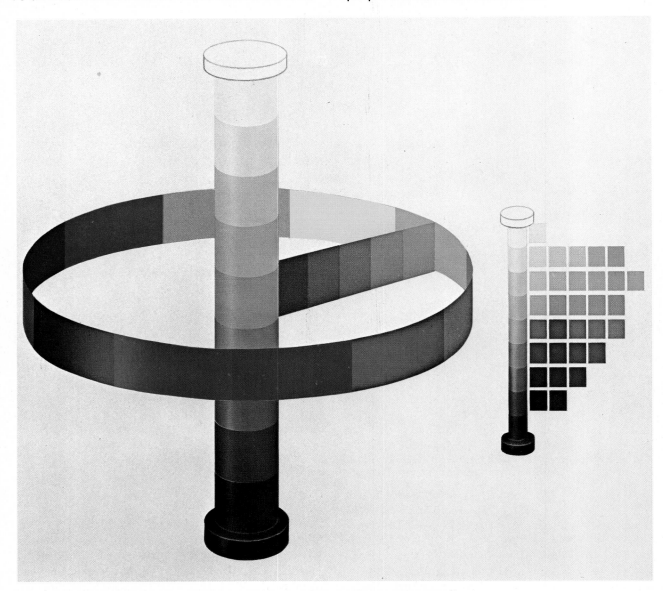

Figure 7. The Munsell color system is used to classify colors in three ways: (1) light and dark values, represented by the pole; (2) hue, the circle; and (3) chroma, the connecting band. (Courtesy, The World Book Encyclopedia © 1974, Field Enterprises Educational Corporation.)

# Color Harmonies

Webster's dictionary defines the word harmony as a "fitting together, a combination of parts into a proportionate and orderly whole, an arrangement of color, size and shape that is pleasing to the eye." This is the goal to achieve in color harmony.

## MONOCHROMATIC COLOR HARMONY

In this harmony only one color is used. For example: only red, only blue, only yellow. (Mono means one, so it will be easy to remember.) The usual monochromatic color scheme is made of carefully graded values of one color placed imaginatively to relieve the monotony.

In order to hold a monochromatic color scheme together, the one hue must be used in several values and intensities. However, if a dramatic effect is desired, jump, the values and use brighter intensities of the one color. If a smooth, calm effect is desired, use the colors in the middle range of values and intensities. In a monochromatic scheme, a safe rule of thumb is that the middle values and intensities are the most pleasing, with smaller areas of extremes used for accent or emphasis.

The next hue on the wheel can also be used while still retaining a monochromatic scheme if the hue has weak values and intensities. This will only work, however, if the largest areas or motifs in the pattern strongly state the basic hue.

## COMPLEMENTARY COLOR HARMONY

There are several arrangements of color which make up complementary color harmonies.

### Direct Complement

A direct complement is just what its name implies — one color used with one other color, which is directly across the color wheel. Thus, red is the direct complement of green, blue is the direct complement of orange, violet is the direct complement of yellow.

*Figure 8. The needlepoint pillow makes striking use of a monochromatic color harmony in blue. (Courtesy, Elsa S. Williams.)*

When direct complementary colors are placed next to each other, each color appears to increase in strength and intensity. However, in the mixing of paints and dyes, mixing complements in equal proportions produces gray at the neutral pole. This seems like a contradiction, but the phenomenon can be observed by actually mixing paints of complementary colors and, by putting one color of yarn or paper next to its complement.

In mixing complementary colors, the amount of the complementary color added to another color will determine the extent to which the color has been grayed. To create a dramatic effect, the direct complementary scheme is used to great advantage.

## Split Complement

A split complementary color scheme uses the colors found on either side of a direct complementary color. For example, the use of red-violet and blue-violet opposite yellow. Most often this type of color harmony is more pleasing than a direct complementary scheme.

Because split complementary colors are not in a direct line with each other, there is no gray area in the middle as occurs with the direct complements; thus, split complementary colors remain brighter. Also, when these colors are laid side by side (try it with beads, yarn, or paper), the combination is more pleasing to the eye because the colors do not have the strength and intensity of direct complementary colors. This knowledge is important to the individual working in any craft where dyeing is involved.

*Figure 9. A direct complement (above left) uses one color with the color opposite it on the color wheel. Also shown are a split complementary scheme (above center) and an adjacent complementary scheme (above right). Complementary colors were used in the macrame hanging (below). (Transworld Feature Syndicate, Inc.)*

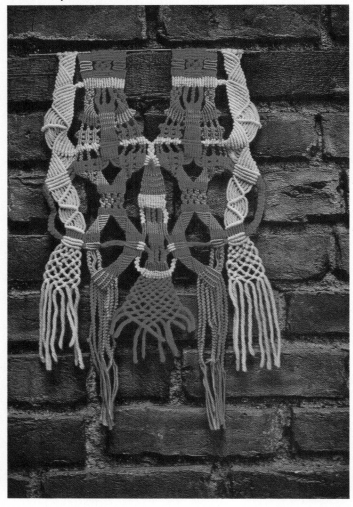

Figure 10. This butterfly potato print by Barbara Cohn makes use of an adjacent complementary scheme. The yellow and the green are complementary to the red.

## Adjacent Complement

Another variation of the complementary color scheme is the adjacent complementary. In this harmony only one color adjacent to the direct complement is used — for example, blue-violet opposite yellow. This is a more subtle use of the complementary color scheme (choosing a complement and merely moving over one hue on the color wheel).

## ANALOGOUS COLOR HARMONY

Analogous colors are those hues that are next to each other on the color wheel. They are related colors because each hue contains some of the adjacent color. For example, green goes comfortably with blue-green because both have some blue (remember, blue and yellow make green). Similarly, blue-violet will blend comfortably with violet because both have some blue (remember, blue and red made violet).

Using hues that go from one primary color to its nearest secondary color creates a close analogous harmony. In a regular analogous harmony, it is possible to move to three or more adjacent hues as long as these are between two primary colors and include only one primary color. For example, using red as the primary, the hues can range all the way to yellow-orange, but not include yellow; or all the way to blue-violet, but not include blue.

Analogous color schemes are often used to balance the cool or warm aspect of color. A color scheme that includes blue, blue-green, and green can be warmed by yellow-green. Or a warm combination of yellow, yellow-green, and green can be cooled by blue-green. Analogous color harmonies are most pleasing when similar values and intensities are used. However, dramatic effects can be obtained by jumps in values and intensities.

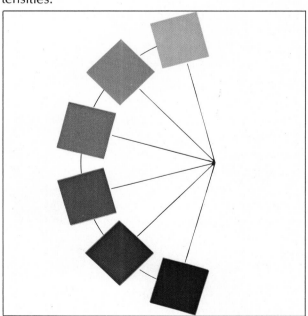

Figure 11. Analogous colors are those adjacent to each other on the color wheel. Each color has something of the next in it.

## ALL-COLOR HARMONY

In an all-color harmony, any number of all hues may be used. With such a wide range of color, beginners often feel this harmony can be the answer to a color planning problem. This may be true, but it requires caution. It has been said of the old masters that they restricted their palettes as they advanced in age and experience.

An interesting and beautiful effect in all-color harmony can be produced in such crafts as dried flowers, hooked rugs, mosaics, stained glass, and crewel embroidery. However, it is wise to remember that the more hues used, the greater the need for moderation in value and intensity. The effect of too many colors at full strength can be overpowering. Use less pure color of the primaries, and more of the secondary and intermediate hues. Softer, more subdued values of these hues will avoid discord. Here, use of a color wheel becomes necessary.

It is best to use a color more than once: repetition adds unity and contributes to good balance. In order to keep an all-color harmony from running wild, one hue should dominate. Use it in grayer shades for large areas and in stronger intensities for smaller areas. Let other hues be decreasingly pronounced. This will assure a rounded-out richness to the color arrangement. The larger the motif, the more careful the craftsman must be with color and color contrast. Often the use of neutrals gives the eye a needed rest. Color contrast, simple dark against light and light against dark, can be used quite successfully in an all-color color scheme.

Black and white are frequently used in an all-color harmony, but great caution should be taken in introducing them. In some instances, if properly used along with other colors, they can sharpen or point up all the other colors to produce a dramatic effect. In most cases, however, black and white should be used merely to enhance the other hues.

## TRIADIC COLOR HARMONY

As its name implies, triadic color harmony is made from three colors equidistant on the color wheel. For example, red, yellow, blue (the primaries; violet, orange, green (the secondaries); yellow-green, red-orange, and blue-violet (the intermediates); or any other combination forming an equidistant triangle.

It is suggested in using triads that the three hues not be of equal value and intensity. This would result in a disturbing scheme. It is much wiser to have one color set the theme and the other two colors be in unequal proportions as well as unequal values and intensities.

## BLACK AND WHITE

While black and white are not hues but extremes of value, they do have to be taken into consideration in color harmony. Black and white are two of the most misused colors. When using these absolutes, it is important to remember that large areas of both black and white are seldom pleasing. In most cases, one should dominate decidedly and the other merely enhance.

In every medium, there are a number of different shades of black and white. White in paint can be brighter than white in yarn. When trying to match black and white in fabric or yarn, this becomes quite apparent.

# Description Of Color

In working with color, descriptive terms other than color names are often applied.

## COLOR TEMPERATURES

Colors fall into two families: warm colors and cool colors. Warm colors are those covering the color wheel from yellow to red-violet; cool colors are those from yellow-green to violet. Strictly speaking, red-violet and yellow-green are neutral because they contain equal parts of both families. Knowing this, it becomes apparent that these two colors can be compatible for either a warm or a cool color scheme. In fact, they can be used to tie the two schemes together.

An intermediate color will fall into the warm or cool group according to the proportions of the warm or cool color used in producing that hue. For example, those colors on the color wheel which contain red appear warm; those which contain blue appear cool. However, the reds on the blue side appear comparatively cool, while the reds on the yellow side appear comparatively warm. Hence we have warm reds and cool reds.

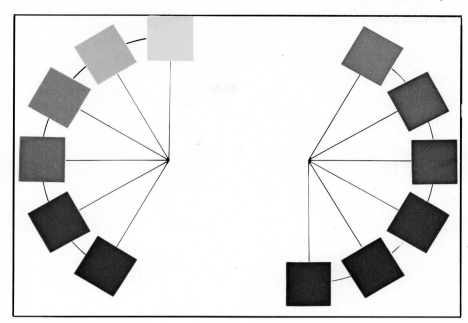

Figure 12. Warm colors (left) include yellow and orange. Cool colors (right) includ blue and yellow-green.

Reds can be cooled by incorporating blues and greens in a color scheme, or by using a cool background. Of course, the opposite is true if the colors are reversed.

In working with complementary colors, the neutral gray (resulting from mixing equal amounts of two complementary colors) can be made warm or cool by slightly varying the amounts of the warm or cool color. With red and green as complements, for example, more red than green would produce a warm gray, and more green than red would produce a cool or steel gray. Therefore, the balance between complements at the neutral pole determines color temperature.

## VISUAL ILLUSION

The study of visual illusion and its effect on how color is seen, is fascinating. Mask making and scrap art are particularly enhanced by illusion. Craftsman working in collage, papier-mâché, and cardboard also can develop new means of expression. Quilt makers can and have used this technique to great advantage. With an understanding of visual illusion, attractive creative effects can be produced.

### Border Contrast

In the illustration depicting the visual illusion known as border contrast, each vertical band appears to be lighter in color on its left side than on its right side. Each band, however, is of an even shade from one edge to the other. The illusion of gradation of value at the edge is the result of contrast with the adjacent value. Craftsmen working in crewel embroidery and rug making constantly use this illusion.

Figure 13. The border contrast is one type of visual illusion. Each band of color looks lighter on its left side, but in fact each band is the same color from side to side. The effect of gradation is achieved by contrasting color values.

*Figure 14. Heightened contrast is another kind of visual illusion. White looks whiter when placed next to a color at the opposite end of the value scale. Note that white surrounded by black looks whiter than the paper, even though it is not.*

## Heightened Contrast

White can be made to appear whiter by using it at the opposite end of a value scale. Thus, white next to black appears whiter than the white paper on which a figure is printed.

Many of today's so-called "mod" colors are the result of heightened contrast. Looking at the color wheel, notice that yellow is the lightest tone and violet is the darkest. If the colors are used undiluted from yellow to violet on either side of the wheel, there is a gradual darkening. The eye is comfortable with this flow of color. If the colors are used out of context, disturbing the flow, there is discord. For example, red is darker than orange, but if red is lightened to pink and put on top of orange, the effect is a "shocking" or unusual color scheme. It is these color discords which produce a great many of today's modern color schemes. Degrees of light and dark affect people when they are seen "out of phase."

## Weight Illusion

Color has a visual property of weight. Light colors appear to have less weight than dark colors.

## Temperature Contrast

Warm and cool colors have visual temperature relationships. Warm colors appear to advance, while cool colors appear to recede. On warm backgrounds the warmer colors seem to appear warmer. On cool backgrounds the warmer colors seem to appear cooler.

*Figure 15. On a cool background (above), warm colors seem cooler. On warm backgrounds (below), cool colors look warmer.*

## Simultaneous Contrast

The way a hue is seen is influenced by the color of the background. The accompanying illustration contains several examples of this phenomenon. The red dot on the white circle appears to be much brighter and more intense than on the black circle. In fact, it is exactly the same color. Yellow appears brighter on orange than on green, and brown appears to be smaller in area on violet than on yellow-green.

## Outline Effect

Outlining colors defines them and makes them appear more intense.

*Figure 16. The outline effect is another kind of color illustration. Outlining colors makes them look more intense. In the example shown the black outline (bottom) brings out the yellow and lavender shades. Note the contrast between the figures that are not outlined.*

*Figure 17. This photo of a needlepoint piece demonstrates the outline effect. The fruits are outlined in white and the main design in red. (Courtesy, Elle; photo Transworld.)*

## Color Vibration

The eye cannot focus on red and blue at the same time to form one image. Alternating lines of red and blue will result in visual vibration, causing a stimulating effect or an uncomfortable feeling.

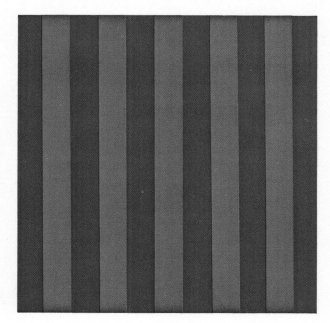

## Area Effect

Color used for the largest area appears to have more influence than the color used in an area or lesser size.

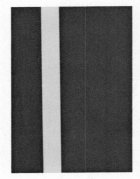

## Depth Effect

Effects of depth can be created with color. If the three primary colors are placed on a black background, the yellow will appear to float in the foreground; the red will come forward, though not as much as the yellow; and the blue will appear to cling to the background. This is due to relative brilliance, or tone value, of the three colors. If the three primaries are placed on a white background, the reverse will happen. The blue will come forward and the yellow will appear farthest from the eye.

Craftsmen who are involved with background know only too well than tonal relationships are relative. In other words, the same hue which looks dark against a white background will appear light against a dark background.

## Visual Mixing

The eye will mix hues. If several different hues of yarn are twisted together, they can be "mixed" into a new hue.

*Figure 18. Hues of yarn blend together to create a visual mixing of colors. (Courtesy, Ladies Home Journal Needle and Craft; photo, Transworld.)*

## Background

The qualities of any color are only valid in relation to other colors near it. Background color can visually influence the way colors are seen. For example, if identical chips of green and blue-green color are put on a green and on a blue background, the chips appear green on the blue background and blue on the green background.

In rug making and similar crafts, the background color must be chosen *first*. Then all other colors are laid on the background color to be sure that there is a proper balance in values and intensities. Consideration of light colors on dark and vice versa will prevent a motif from being lost in the background.

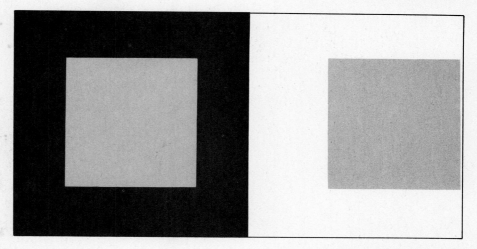

*Figure 19. Background color makes a difference in perception of the main color. The two gray squares are the same hue, yet they look different against black and white backgrounds.*

Background may be used for emphasis or subordination. Where a startling effect is desired, a background color could be quite dramatic. A subdued background can make a motif prominent. In most cases, however, as its name implies, background color should remain "behind" and function as a foil for the other colors. The lessons of nature teach bright in front of dull; warm in front of cold; smaller, bright areas in front of larger, more subdued ones.

Color need not be the only consideration for proper background use. Consider the craftsman who uses shells in all their natural colors against a pale-green chiffon background. The texture of chiffon, as well as its color, suggests that this craftsman is sensitive to nature. A smooth surface for the shells would not be as outstanding.

Often background becomes a part of the design. Thus, the interplay between motif colors and background colors can be the most important part of the design.

There is one very subtle consideration of background: Where will the crafted piece be displayed? For instance, a bold quilt with bright colors must be allowed to shine on its own. The room in which it will be used must harmonize as background. Certainly, the importance of harmony between a craft and its surroundings cannot be overemphasized.

Because color has the power to set a mood, it can become a distraction rather than an attraction. The objective is simplicity and strength; but, of course, this does not mean emptiness or lack of refinement. Creating with color, as stated earlier, is indeed a matter of taste.

## For Additional Reading

Committee on Colorimetry, Optical Society of America, **The Science of Color,** Crowell, 1953.

Halse, Albert O., **The Use of Color in Interiors,** McGraw-Hill, 1968.

McGown, Pearl K., **Color in Hooked Rugs,** Boston: Buck Printing Co., 1954.

Munsell, Albert H., **A Color Notation,** Munsell Color Co., 1946.

Sargent, Walter, **The Enjoyment and Use of Color,** Dover, 1964.

# Crafting With Gourds

**Of all the ecological materials that have been used by craftsmen, the gourd is one of the most versatile and beautiful.**

Throughout recorded history artists have selected simple natural materials from their environment to create beautiful pieces of art. Depending on geographical location, craftsmen have utilized stones, sand, mud, animal skins, feathers, bones, and many other earth-related items.

Indians in the northwestern part of North America, where trees were lush and abundant, turned out massive pieces of wood sculpture. Indians in the southwestern United States became expert potters, utilizing the natural clay of their environment to make pots of incredible beauty. These were fired in open pits and then colored with pastes made from other kinds of earth. Eskimos in Canada made objects for both utility and beauty from soapstone native to their area. The skin boxes, shields, and shelters of the Plains Indians would have been just as useful without decoration, yet they were elaborately embellished with paints, feathers, beads, and porcupine quills. It is interesting to note that when people had no need for shields, boxes, or shelters, they used their decorative talents on their bodies. The Nubian tribes of Africa, for instance, developed an elaborate system of body decoration.

One of the most durable environmental materials which has been used for craft purposes is the gourd. Gourds in perfect condition have been found in Egyptian tombs dating as far back as 3500 B.C. and, symbols representing gourd cultivation have been found in almost every primitive society.

The variety inherent in the gourd is amazing. The fruits of this plant vary in size from that of an orange to some twice the size of a pumpkin. Because of the hard outer shell and hollow interior,

**Figure 1. The techniques of incising and relief are beautifully illustrated on this contemporary gourd by Peter Nzuki, Nairobi, Kenya. (Courtesy, The Field Museum of Natural History, Chicago.)**

gourds have been utilized for containers of all kinds. In the islands of the South Sea, 36 different uses have been documented for the gourd, including ladles, dippers, bowls, strainers, funnels, carrying-baskets, and musical instruments. They were decorated with feathers or paint, and some were encased in baskets woven from the vines of the "ieie" plant.

The Japanese grew a bottle-shaped variety of gourd in which they stored wine. These were highly polished and many of them were decorated with floral patterns. Chinese craftsmen used a tiny variety of gourd to make cages for pet crickets. The gourds were decorated as they grew.

A two-part carved mold was placed over the gourd about midway in its growth. As it grew, the pattern became incised on the skin of the gourd. Examples of these cages can be seen at the Peabody Museum in Salem, Massachusetts.

All over Africa gourds were turned into useful objects decorated with a variety of materials. The simplest was a gourd stained with millet leaves or dyes made from earth pigments. More elaborately decorated gourds were created by cutting, scraping, or engraving techniques. Hats were even made from gourds by cutting them in half and decorating them with cowrie shells.

Both colonial and frontier Americans found many uses for the gourd. Today, interest in their growth and use is once again growing rapidly. Craftsmen turn gourds into containers for display materials. They are used to show off arrangements of wild flowers and for table centerpieces. They are also used for holiday decorations such as Easter eggs and Christmas ornaments. And, as a result of a resurgence of interest in old time music, people are shaping gourds into copies of the once-popular gourd fiddle and banjo.

Figure 2. The Japanese stored wine in bottle-shaped gourds which were specially grown for this purpose (left). (Courtesy, The Peabody Museum, Salem.) Africans made useful hats by cutting gourds in half (right). (Courtesy, Smithsonian Institution Photo No. 72-3652A.)

## Common Terms Used In Crafting With Gourds

Gourds once grew wild. But, even after years of cultivation, their promiscuous breeding habits still result in new, curious shapes with each growing season. Gourds not only mate indiscriminately with most other gourds, they are also happy to join families with cucumbers, squash and pumpkins. Hence, there are several dozen basic shapes plus all the different variations as a result of cross breeding. This gives the artist an almost unlimited choice of shapes from which to choose his craft material.

Within this mixture of shapes and sizes, two basic types emerge which relate to craft work. One type consists of the small colorful green, yellow, warted, and striped varieties that are seen in many supermarkets in the fall. These are called "ornamentals" and, with few exceptions, are not suited for craft work. Their deep colors and waxy natural sheen will look beautiful for several months. But, with age, they have a tendency to develop a terrible kind of acne on the skin. This discourages any kind of craft work.

The other main type of gourd is called a "hardshell." These are much larger and will age with a smooth, wood-like hard shell that lasts for many years. Hardshells grow in such a wide variety of shapes and sizes that it is not practical to describe each. But, a few of the most popular ones are listed below by their common or "country names" as a reference for purchasing gourds or seeds by mail.

**Apple and Pear Gourds:** shaped like the fruits for which they are named, these gourds are quite small — no more than 3" to 4" in diameter. They are most often used as decorations. Those with stable bottoms can be cleaned out, lacquered, and made into unusual wine cups.

**Baseball Bat Gourd:** a spectacular gourd which grows to lengths of 3 feet or more and measures 15" to 30" in circumference at its widest part. The smallest ones are sometimes made into percussion instruments by scoring a section across the middle of the body. Larger ones are left uncut and become decorative objects.

**Bird House Gourd:** the term applied to almost any gourd which looks like it could be turned into a home for a bird. It is actually used for that purpose and hung out in early spring.

**Bottle or Vase Gourd:** a gourd with a rounded bowl-shaped bottom and an extended neck that is sometimes narrow and sometimes thick. These

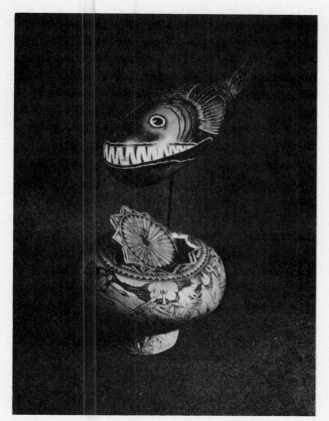

Figure 3. *The breeding habits of gourds have produced an almost unlimited variety of shapes and sizes. Selection for craft purposes depends partly on the proposed function of the gourd.*

gourds are often manipulated during their growth by tying parts of the neck with strips of soft cloth. Generally, their bowl is 6″ to 20″ in diameter and the neck ranges from 8″ to 20″ in length.

**Club Gourd:** a gourd with an extremely long neck that gradually widens into an elongated bowl. These are often covered with welts and warts about the size of a thumb tip. The combination of long neck and bowl-bottom makes them useful for fashioning gourd fiddles or banjos.

**Dipper Gourd:** a gourd with a long and slender neck which, if allowed to hang free as it grows, will have a perfectly straight neck. Sometimes the gourd reaches a length of 2 to 4 feet. If it grows on the ground, the neck twists and curves into interesting shapes. One type of dipper gourd has a short handle only 5″ to 6″ long.

**Powder Horn Gourd:** this is a medium-sized gourd with a short neck which curves gently into the bowl. Once, this gourd was actually used as a powder horn by hunters on the frontier. Powder horns make interesting animal shapes.

# Basic Equipment And Supplies

Because gourds are so inherently handsome and adaptable, they are fun to work with. The exterior of the gourd is smooth and wood-like, making it easy to paint, stain, dye, cut, drill, or glue. In some instances, it can even be sewn with threads made of grasses or wire. Gourds, quite inexpensive to buy, can be grown by the home gardener. They require nothing more than sun and a little space to climb. Their unpredictable shape is an asset because one is tempted to elaborate on the ideas the body of the gourd suggests: some look like birds, others like fish, and still others like natural baskets. Primitive craftsmen painted gourds with coloring materials from the earth or from plants. They also used cutting tools that were no doubt made from stone or bone. Today, the commercial colors and craft tools that are available should be used. But, these should not overpower the simplicity of the gourd itself.

Following is a list of equipment and supplies needed for making the simple projects which are described later in this article.

## COPING SAW

This saw should have a 1/8″ removable blade. These blades come in 4″ to 6″ lengths and are easily removed from the frame. The blade is then fitted with a handle by winding all but 3″ with tape. Because of their flexibility, they are particularly helpful when a gourd is to be cut in half and then fitted back together. A wood saw would remove too much of the gourd.

## HALF-ROUND WOOD FILE

After a gourd is sawed, the cut surface needs to be smoothed. One side of this file is flat and the other has a gentle curve. This makes it adaptable for both curved and straight surfaces. The file cuts quickly and takes off jagged or splintered edges.

## CRAFT KNIVES

There are many different kinds of craft knives suitable for cutting. Because gourds are easy to carve, only two different blades are needed: one to give sharp edges to figures; the other for piercing and

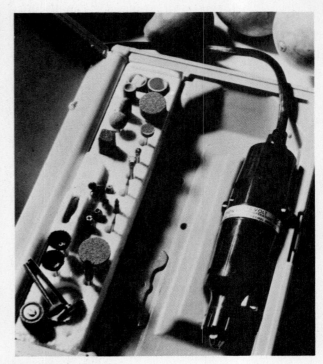

*Figure 4. Equipment needed for crafting with gourds (left) includes a saw, file, knives, sandpaper, detergent, and a scrubber. Other materials required are wax, stain, lacquer, and felt tip markers. An electric craft tool (right) may be purchased as part of a "set" with all of the necessary attachments.*

making holes or for outlining and then removing small sections of skin. A 5" aluminum handle with a tapered razor-sharp blade is a good choice for the former operation. This blade can also be used to score and cut away unwanted portions of gourds. The blade for the latter operation should be tapered and about 1/8" wide. A kitchen paring knife can be substituted for either knife if it is very sharp and has a thin blade.

### FELT-TIP MARKING PENS

Sets of felt-tip markers (permanent colors) can be found in most craft and stationery stores. They are also available from those mail-order firms that sell to craftsmen in Indian Arts. Non-toxic, instant dry pens are best for these projects. They come with fine tips and write on any surface. A few broad-tip felt markers will also come in handy and can be used to cover broad areas. Though the colors are brilliant, they are translucent and the shadings of the gourd skin can still be seen through the color of the marker.

### FOAM WOOD STAIN

This is used to add depth and color to designs. It is rubbed into cuts and marks in the skin, then rubbed away. The stain stays in the cracks but rubs away from the skin. Wood stain also is used to deepen the overall color of the gourd.

### METALLIC WAXES

Waxes with a metallic base are fairly new. They are creamy, semihard, and available in tubes or small glass containers. Originally designed to use as an aid to antiquing wood and metal, they are especially suited to the task of applying color to a gourd. There are a large number of colors available which can be used as highlights or to cover the whole gourd.

### LIGHTWEIGHT ELECTRIC CRAFT TOOL

This is a compact motorized tool weighing less than a pound. It comes as part of a "set" which contains all the attachments necessary for making the projects in this article. Other attachments are available for the craftsman who wishes to work with other kinds of raw materials or to perform a wide variety of other skills.

These motorized tools are available from hardware stores and from general household mail-order catalogues. At this writing, their cost is in the $25.00 to $35.00 price range. More powerful models are also made, but their price is double

*Figure 5. Gourds are available in a great variety of shapes, sizes, and colors. There is a plentiful market stock of gourds during the fall season, and they may be purchased through suppliers year-round.*

that of the lightweight model. The more expensive motor is mounted on a stand instead of being held in the hand and the attachments fit a flexible shaft. Because the mounted model is less tiring to use, it might be worth the investment for anyone planning to do an extensive amount of this kind of craft work.

## GOURDS

Gourds grow abundantly and can be found in many markets beginning in September. Supermarkets, farmers' markets, and county fairs all display them through the early part of winter. After that time, gourds can be purchased from people who grow them as a hobby and from commercial growers. A list of hobbyists who have gourds for sale is available from the American Gourd Society, Box 274, Mt. Gilead, Ohio 43338. A large number can be purchased at one time because gourds do not deteriorate with age. Only usage will wear them out.

## OTHER SUPPLIES

In addition to the items described above, other materials also needed for gourd projects are: (1) several sheets of medium-coarse sandpaper to smooth edges or rough spots on the skin; (2) de-

---

To determine when gourds are dry, tap them with a fingernail as one would tap a table top. When dry, they will give off a sharp crack instead of a thump. Depending on the size and the drying conditions, it takes from one to three months for gourds to dry. Small, apple-sized ones will be ready long before Christmas. Larger bowls may not be dry until January or February.

When dry, gourds need to be washed and scrubbed to remove the thin outer layer of skin. As they bob around in the water, the rough moldy material begins to disappear and smooth golden skin appears. To make the job easier, soak the gourds overnight. Because they are hollow and will float, they need to be weighted down to keep them submerged. Put a bit of detergent in the water to help loosen the skin. A metal pot-scrubber, such as the ones used to scour pots and pans, is useful for cleaning the skin. Heavy collections of debris or scar tissue can be removed with the side of a knife, but care should be taken not to damage the skin. After the gourds are clean, they are set aside to dry.

Some projects described here call for the gourd to be cut open. The hollow, ivory-colored interior contains clumps of seeds attached to glossy layers of membrane. These should be removed and may be put aside in a dry place for planting them in the spring. The interior can then be smoothed with the back of a spoon.

## PLANNING THE DESIGN

Every project described later in this article includes a photograph which can be used as a design guide for the project. However, one may want to create an original design. If so, suggestions may be in order. Gourds do not come in perfect shapes. Some may have flattened areas, warts, or knobs. There may even be, in some of the larger models, areas where the skin has split and holes have opened up. These "flaws" are to be taken advantage of — not scorned — as they can be incorporated into the design. African craftsmen repair gourds that have cracked by stitching them together with copper or brass wire. The stitching then becomes a decoration rather than a patch.

Anything done to gourds should be in harmony with their shape. Do not impose a rigid design.

Colors should only enhance, not obliterate or overpower the natural shadings. One should work out a design on paper first; the, apply it to the gourd with a pencil. Go over the whole gourd in pencil before beginning to work. Do not depend on luck to match up lines which disappear around a curve. Pencil lines can easily be erased and adjusted — corrections are not possible if a knife or a marker is used.

## USING THE WAXES

A double layer of soft cloth covering the end of the finger makes a good applicator for soft waxes. A small amount is rubbed directly onto the skin of the gourd. Several thin coats can be applied to get the desired effect. Allow each coat to dry for a few minutes. When wax is dry it can be buffed to a soft glow with another soft cloth. When markers are being used over the wax, these are applied after the surface has been buffed. If wax becomes hard in the container, it can be thinned with a drop of turpentine. It also can be thinned considerably and then applied with a brush if this seems desirable.

## MARKERS

The purpose of these almost transparent colors is to give a stained-glass effect to the gourd. Two kinds of markers are used: the fine-tipped ones can fill in a small areas and outline the designs; the broad ones are used to cover large areas. The skin should be completely dry before color is applied. Fine lines should be filled in first and allowed to dry before another color is applied. One color can be added over another if the first color proves unsatisfactory, or if a deeper color is wanted. Keep a spare gourd on the side for testing colors and combinations of colors.

The broad areas are covered more smoothly if broad-tipped pens are used. The colors flow freely at about the consistency of watercolors. They can be wiped off if a mistake is made, but this must be done very quickly.

## DRILLING

Though gourds are sturdy, they are also hollow and care needs to be taken not to put too much pressure on one spot. To drill a hole with an electric drill, choose the smallest cutting attachment

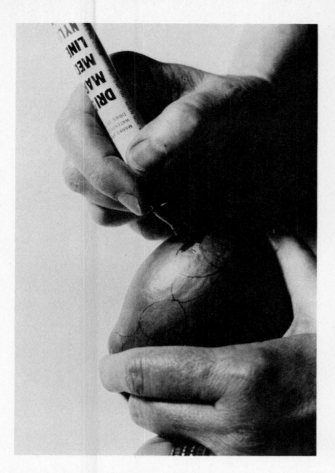

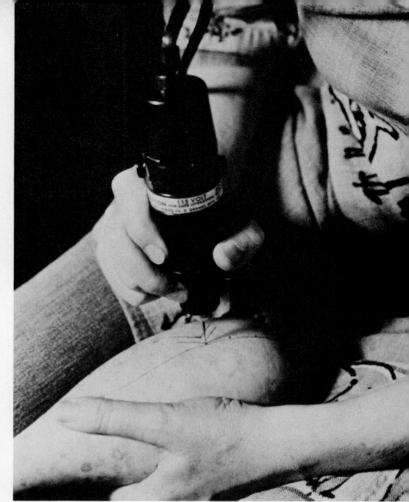

Figure 6. Once a design has been penciled on a dried gourd, use a fine-tipped marker (above) to outline the pattern and to fill in small areas. For larger shapes, a broad-tipped marker should be used. A hole may be made by using the electric drill (top right) or the sharp tip of a knife (bottom right). Increase the size of the cutting attachment or twist the blade until the hole is sufficiently enlarged.

first. After drilling with that, enlarge the hole with the next largest attachment. First, mark the spot to be drilled with a pencil; then, lay the gourd across the legs while drilling. Because a gourd is round, it is difficult to control if placed on a work bench or table.

It is possible to make a hole without an electric tool by using the sharp tip of a knife. Hold the gourd steady, insert just the tip of the knife, and twist it until it pierces the skin. Continue to twist the blade until the hole is enlarged to the proper size.

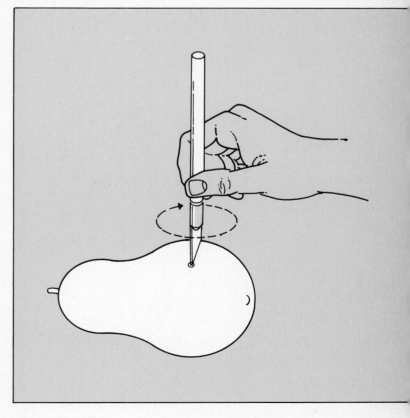

## SAWING

To begin sawing, a hole large enough to admit the blade is first made by the above method. The saw blade is then inserted into the hole. The blade should be held as if it were a feather and the sawing should be done with long, slow, even strokes. It is not necessary to apply pressure. If the body of the gourd is accidentally cracked during this process, it can be glued back together with ordinary white glue.

## USE OF THE KNIFE

To begin a long cut, such as one needed to separate the neck of the gourd from the bowl, use the craft knife with the wider blade. Insert the tip of the knife and then go around the pencil line once, just scoring the line. Repeat this process several times until the inside is reached. Care should be taken not to use too much pressure. It is better to go over the line many times rather than risk cracking the gourd.

To make purely decorative cuts, such as those needed to remove triangular-shaped pieces, use the narrow-bladed knife. Holding the gourd in one hand, insert the tip of the knife and score along the triangular-shaped pencil line. Go over the line several times, being careful not to cut all the way through. Only the top layer of skin is to be

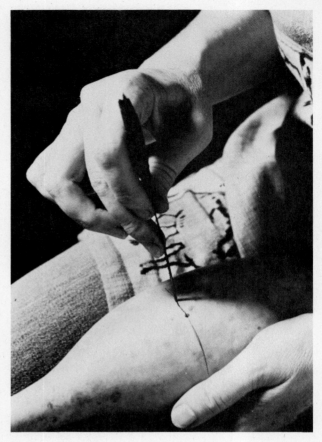

*Figure 7. A hole must be made in a gourd before a saw blade can be inserted. All sawing should be done with long, slow, even strokes to avoid damaging the gourd. If breakage does occur, the gourd may be repaired with glue.*

*Figure 8. Before beginning the cut to remove the neck of the gourd, draw a line where the cut will be made. Insert the knife and follow the line several times until the inside is reached.*

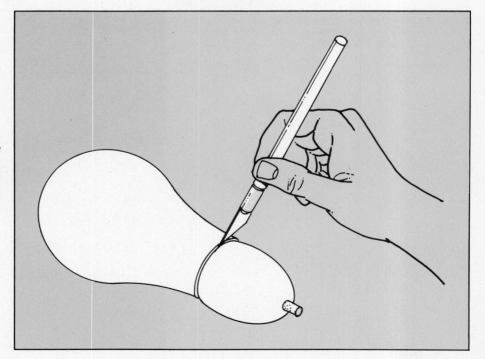

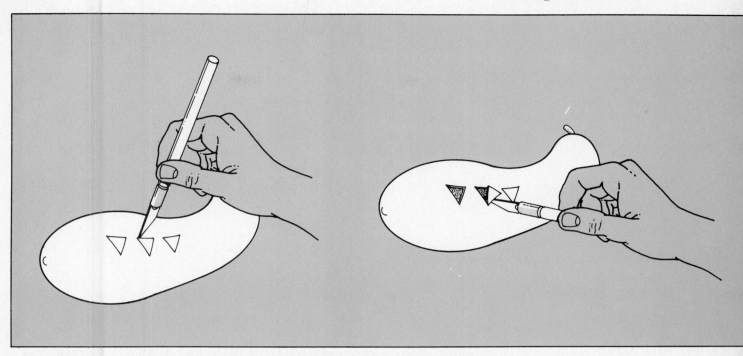

*Figure 9. The narrow blade craft knife is used to cut decorative shapes. Score the design on the top layer so that all lines are joined (top left) and insert the blade under the skin to remove unwanted sections (top right). To smooth the cut surfaces, use a half-round wood file (below). When filing two pieces that are to be joined together, do not remove too much of the surface.*

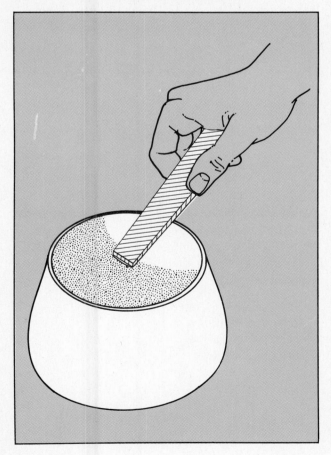

removed. When all the lines are cut and joined, insert the tip of the blade just under the skin and pry out the unwanted portion.

A variety of decorative lines can be made with just the tip end of the knives. Kitchen paring knives often have blades that are wider on the noncutting side of the blade. These produce an interesting elongated triangle. A running stitch design can be formed by just pricking the skin with the sharp end of any small knife.

## USE OF THE FILE

The file is used in one direction only, just as would be the case with wood. Heavy pressure is not necessary. When smoothing the edges of two pieces to be fitted together, care should be taken not to remove too much surface.

## FINAL FINISH WITH LACQUER

After gourds have been decorated with color, it is important not to apply too much lacquer at one time. This will cause colors to run. Hold the spray can about 12″ away and let the spray float down on the gourd rather than reach it directly. Moving

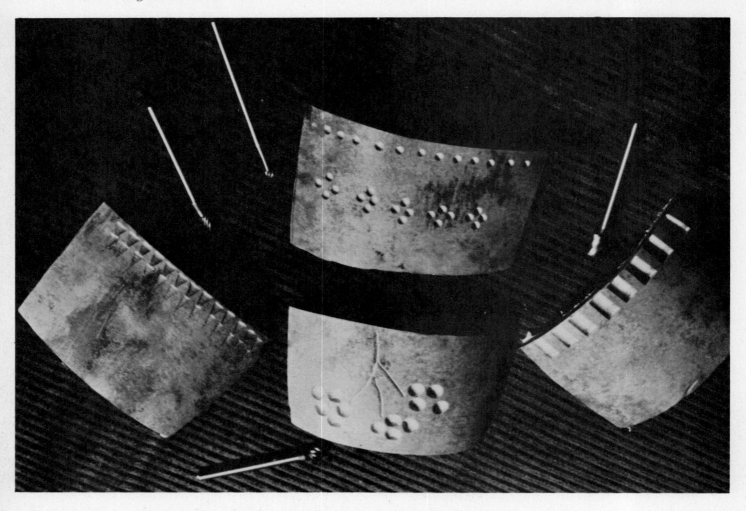

*Figure 10. The electric craft tool is used to create a wide variety of decorative effects on the surface of the gourd. The tool comes with bits in a number of sizes; the smallest bit is used to make simple lines. A large bit is used for making broad strokes and carving massive designs.*

around the gourd, let each thin coat dry before applying the next. Five or six coats may be necessary to completely cover the surface. It is better to take time with this step rather than risk having the colors run together. Spraying is best done in an open area. As with all materials from pressurized cans, it is wise to work where there is plenty of air to minimize the danger of inhaling too much of the material.

## USE OF THE ELECTRIC CRAFT TOOL

The craft tool will come equipped with its own set of instructions for general usage. The directions which follow here are those which relate specifically to its use with gourds. Remember that this is a high speed tool which will cut very quickly. Before using it, practice on one or two gourds. Try each of the attachments to see what kind of mark it will make. Also check to see if variations can be made by holding it to the side or from above. Experiment to see what kinds of patterns can result by combining two different lines or dots. Because the gourd has no straight edges, it is better to hold it on the lap rather than trying to secure it to a work table or bench.

Gourds have an imperceptible grain which will help to determine the direction of the cut. Test to see in which direction the tool moves easiest. There will be more resistance in one direction (against the grain) than the other; and, if not heeded, the tool will not hold steady. Once the grain line is established, continue to make all the cuts in that direction. There are also small areas on the skin of the gourd which seem to resist the tool altogether. Simply move the tool away a fraction of an inch and set it down in a new area.

To make a simple fine line, the smallest of the cutting tools is used. Holding the gourd on the lap, steady it with one hand. The tool is held to the side with the tip just touching the cutting line. A broader line is made in the same fashion, but with the next largest tool.

To drill a hole, use the smallest of the cutting tools. The tool is held like a pencil and approaches the place marked for the hole from above. If a larger hole is needed, the same hole can be enlarged by the next largest cutting tool.

To scrape away areas, leaving a raised design behind, use short clean strokes with the small cutting tool. The tool is held to the side so there is good control. It is better to cut right up to the pencilled design in short strokes rather than try to outline it with the tool first. If a razor-clean outline of a design is desired, it can be outlined first with the craft knife.

## Projects You Can Do

Gourds can be altered to such a degree that their former identity as a living plant can be lost completely. The projects in this article, however, have been designed primarily in the hope that the gourd's identity will still be apparent — that its natural form, color, and spirit dominate the finished product.

The projects which follow are meant to be copied or to be used simply as a take-off point for original ideas. The simplest ones to execute are described first. None of them, however, is complicated or requires great skill.

### SMALL DECORATED SPHERES

**1.** Select six small apple- or pear-shaped gourds that have been cleaned and dried. Have ready a

*Figure 11. Short clean strokes are used to carve a raised design with a small cutting tool (left). Small gourds, colored with metallic wax, are displayed in a basket (below).*

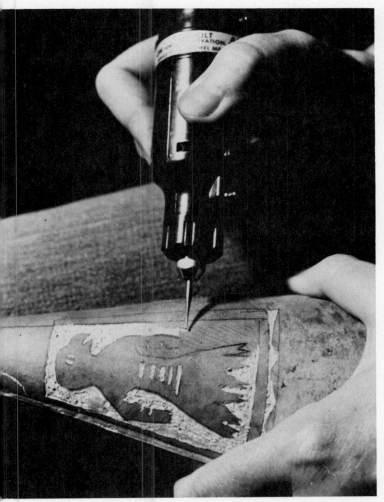

selection of metallic waxes of assorted colors, a selection of felt-tipped marking pens, a can of spray lacquer, and one soft dry cloth.

**2.** Using the soft cloth, apply a small amount of wax at a time until the gourd is covered with a base color.

**3.** Allow the base color to dry for five minutes; buff so the color takes on a soft sheen.

**4.** Following the illustration as a guide, use a pencil to apply the design to the sphere. Taking advantage of the wax's color and sheen, try for a design with much open space.

**5.** Fill in or outline the design with markers, letting each color dry before applying the next.

**6.** When the sphere is completely dry, spray it with four thin coats of lacquer.

These spheres can be displayed in a nest as though they were eggs, or they can be hung as Christmas tree decorations if a small hole is drilled in each end and a thread run through for hanging. These last for many years and make excellent gifts.

## HANGING PLANTER

**1.** Select one bird house gourd with a bowl measuring approximately 6″ in diameter. Supplies needed are a coping saw blade, a knife or electric craft tool, felt-tip markers, file, sandpaper, lacquer, and a 20-inch cord for hanging the planter.

**2.** Cut the top, unwanted portion off the gourd. Mark the cutting line with a pencil 5″ from the bottom of the gourd. There should be an "ear" on each side of the gourd to allow for the hole which will hold the hanging cord.

**3.** Following the sawing procedure as described previously, saw away the top portion. (The discarded top can be used for practicing designs or to try out color combinations.)

**4.** Pry off the top of the gourd, clean out the seeds and membrane, and file the rim free of rough spots. Sandpaper to further smooth the edge.

**5.** Drill one hole in each "ear."

**6.** Decorate the gourd with markers and with the tip of a small knife.

**7.** Apply four thin coats of spray lacquer. Allow to dry. Tie cord through holes for hanging.

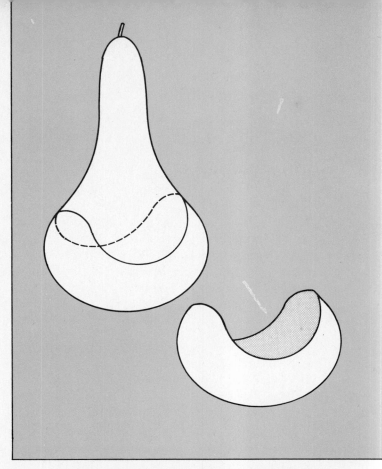

*Figure 12. Gourds make unusual containers for hanging plants. Measure from the bottom of the bowl to mark cutting line, saw away the top section, and clean out the inside (above). The plant should be put in a clay pot and surrounded with moss before it is placed in the gourd (below).*

The plant which goes into the planter should be planted in a clay pot before being put into the gourd. Surround the clay pot with moss to absorb excess moisture and to enhance the beauty of the planter.

## BOWL WITH FITTED LID

**1.** Select a bird house gourd with a bowl 6″ in diameter. Also needed are a set of markers, two craft knives, and spray lacquer.

**2.** Mark the cutting line for the lid. The line should be drawn at the point where the bowl just begins its inward curve toward the neck. After a straight line is drawn around the bowl, mark another line 1/2″ directly below it and join the two lines with a zigzag mark.

**3.** Cut off the lid with the saw. Before trying to lift it off, go along the cutting line with a knife to be sure all the edges are free and clear. Pry off the top and remove the seeds.

**4.** Decorate the gourd with the markers. The one shown here is red with brown, green, and orange accent lines. The overall color of red is applied first to the bottom of the bowl, after which a green line is drawn 1-1/2″ up from the bottom. This is followed by a 1/4″ strip of brown. Draw one final thin line of green above the brown. Cover the lid of the gourd with red and brown. Draw a thin accent line of green at the base of the neck and a thick line of green to accent the zigzag edge of the lid.

**5.** Using a craft knife, cut a triangular design into the top green stripe at the bottom of the bowl. Then, with the same knife, cut ascending decorative lines on four sides of the bowl.

**6.** Put the lid on the bowl and make an indention with the knife on the lid just above each ascending line. This acts as an aid for repositioning the lid after it has been removed.

*Figure 13. A zigzag pattern (below) is easily made by drawing two equidistant lines around the bowl and connecting them with smaller lines. The pattern is then cut and the seeds removed. The finished bowl (left) is not only an attractive object, but also serves a utilitarian purpose.*

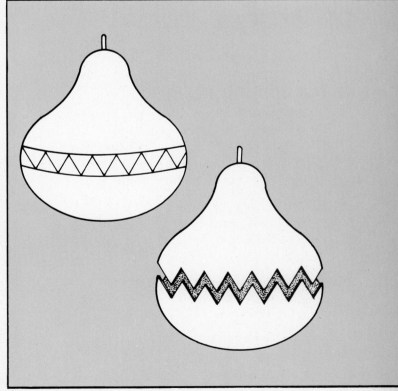

*Figure 14. Decreasing sizes of gourds strung with beads (above) add a natural and decorative touch to a room. The painted dolls (below) accentuate the interesting shapes of gourds.*

*Figure 15. The wall hanging (left), the painted nut dish (bottom left), and the sun-faced gourd decorated with feathers (below) are imaginative designs that have been created from a variety of gourds.*

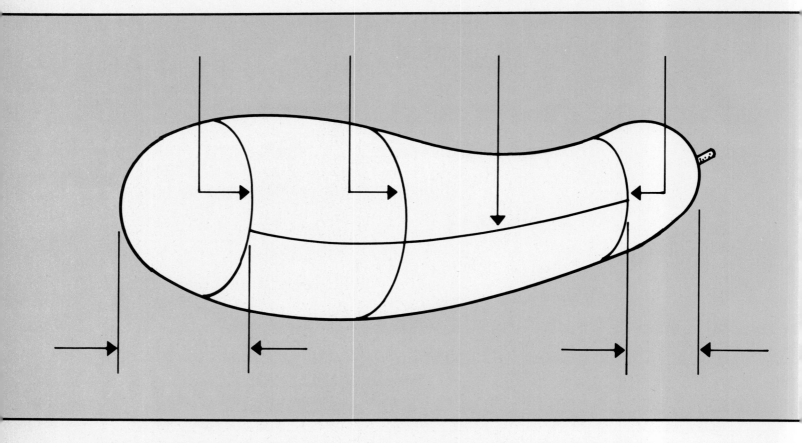

*Figure 16. Before applying a design to the baseball bat gourd divide the gourd into sections (above). The sections will serve as a guide for filling in the intricate details of the planned design (below).*

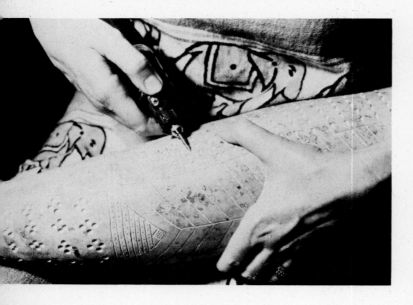

## LARGE DECORATED GOURD

**1.** Select a clean, dry baseball gourd. Also needed are the electric craft tool, a can of foam-wood stain (fruitwood stain is used here), and a spray can of lacquer.

**2.** Decide on a design. It is not necessary to duplicate the design illustrated here, although it might be helpful to use the larger blocks as a starting point and then fill in as desired. Block out the general areas of the design by starting at the bottom of the gourd. Draw one line, 2″ up from the bottom, all the way around the gourd. Draw a similar line 2″ down from the top. From this point draw one line straight down from the top to the bottom of the gourd. Though the line is straight, it will have a slight curve to it to match the curve of the gourd. One more line can be drawn around the circumference about one-third of the way down. These four lines can serve as base lines for filling in the rest of the design.

**3.** Using the electric tool, cut all the major lines first. Then fill in with the holes, flowers, and other decorative cuts.

**4.** Covering a small area at a time, apply foam to the gourd. Allow it to soak into the cuts. Rub the surface color away immediately — color should remain only in the cuts.

**5.** When the gourd is thoroughly dry, spray it with four thin coats of lacquer.

## GROWING GOURDS

Although it is possible to purchase gourds for craft projects, they are quite easily grown. The vines are prolific climbers and can be used as a natural decorative screen for porches, patios, and fences. Not only will home-grown gourds provide abundant raw material for craft work, but it is fun to watch the bright-yellow, white, or orange blossoms turn into bowls, dippers, bottles, or other handy containers.

### Shaping the Gourds

People have found some very dramatic ways to shape gourds while they are growing. Any shaping has to be done while the gourds are still young enough to feel soft. It is possible, for in-

*Figure 18. The smaller type of gourds, called ornamentals, are colorful and have beautiful natural designs. They are available in a wide range of shapes and sizes.*

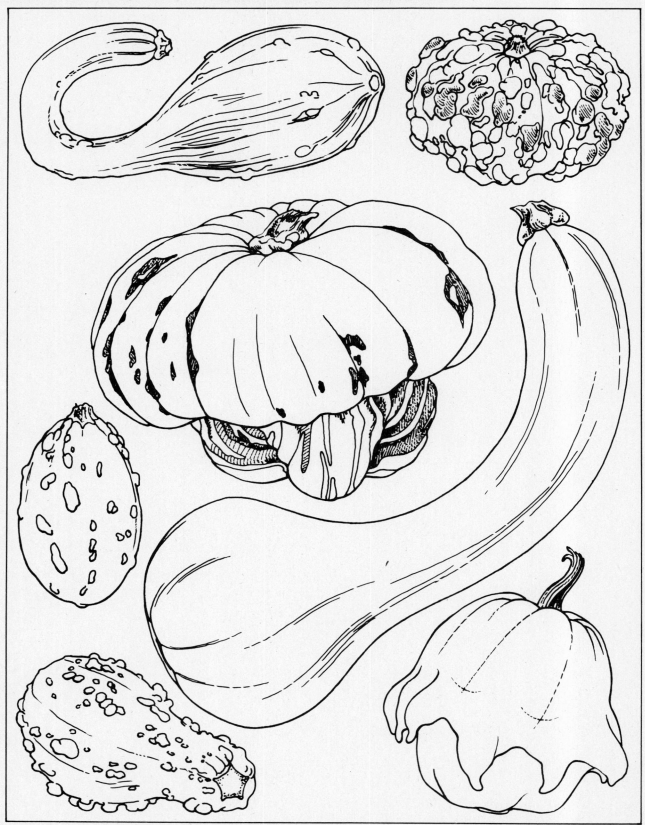

stance, to tie a knot in the long neck of a dipper gourd. This must be done on a hot day, when the gourd is limp, and it must be done very gently. The gourd will then continue to grow to its normal size with the knot in its neck. Or the neck can be lengthened by tying a bag of sand around the bowl and gradually adding more sand to the bag each day. However, there is a risk involved when doing this to the gourds. But because there is usually a good supply available, it's fun to try. Elongated or cylindrical gourds can be given a wasp waist by wrapping them in the middle with strips of cloth. The cloth should not bind too tightly or it will cut into the gourd.

## Types of Gourds to Grow

When making a decision about the kinds of gourds to grow, don't just buy a package marked "Mixed Ornamentals" or "Mixed, Large Variety, Hardshells." The difference between these two is very pronounced. Ornamentals are those gourds which look beautiful for one season, and then decay. Melons and pumpkins are in this group, as are most of the small and beautifully shaped green, yellow, orange, striped, warted, and twisted gourds usually seen in the autumn. Hardshells, on the other hand, are the ones described in this article. They grow in large, rounded, and sometimes grotesque shapes. They are pale green when ripe, then age to a golden yellow. Their blossoms are white, while those of the ornamental are golden.

When buying gourd seeds, be more specific than just buying the mixed packages. Choose from those listed earlier in this article or widen the choice by considering one of the following.

**Mammoth.** This gourd can reach a weight of 100 pounds and have a circumference of 50". Because the body is more pear-shaped than round and the bottom is flat, it can be utilized very nicely as a basket.

**African Giant.** This is similar to the Mammoth, but larger around. It has the appearance of a large ball that has been flattened at the top and bottom.

**Hard Basket (or Kettle).** This grows with a nice flat bottom and a bowl that measures about 20" in diameter. The neck is short, giving a pyramidal shape to the gourd. It makes an excellent basket because it grows with an extremely hard shell.

**Knob.** This is a bowl-shaped gourd with a slender neck topped by a knob.

**Baby Dipper.** This is a miniature dipper, as its name suggests, and is great fun for children to grow. It is possible to buy seeds for miniature bottles, too.

**Penguin.** The body and neck of this gourd flow into each other, and the stem at the end suggests a penguin's bill. This is a variation of the Powder Horn gourd.

**Eel.** This is a very long, slender gourd that looks like a snake as it hangs from a vine. It is only 2 to 3 inches in diameter, but can attain a length of 3 feet.

## For Additional Reading

Bailey, L. H., **The Garden of Gourds,** The Gourd Society of America, 1958.

Gardi, Rene, **African Crafts and Craftsmen,** Van Nostrand, 1970.

Organ, John, **Gourds,** Faber and Faber, London, 1963.

Plummer, Beverly, "Gourds Become Ornaments and Entertainments for the Eye and Hand," **Earth Presents,** Atheneum, 1973.

Publications and Bulletin of the American Gourd Society, Box 274, Mt. Gilead, Ohio 43338.

Trowell, Margaret, **African Design,** Praeger, 1960.

# Silk - Screen Printing

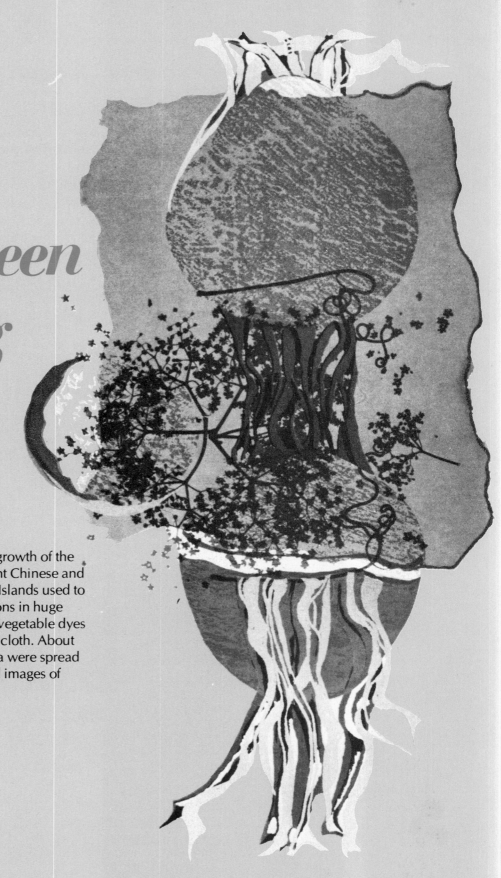

*A contemporary printing process done on silk represents an ancient Oriental technique of graphic expression.*

Silk-screen printing is a direct outgrowth of the common stencil as used by ancient Chinese and Japanese artists. People of the Fiji Islands used to make stencils by cutting perforations in huge banana leaves and then applying vegetable dyes through these openings onto bark cloth. About 500 A.D., the teachings of Buddha were spread by decorating walls with stenciled images of religious dogmas.

The Japanese adapted stenciling to their own uses for decorating the backgrounds of ceremonial robes and kimonos. They cut their stencils with skill, patience, and fine detail from specially treated mulberry tree paper that was water-proofed by oil, making it impervious to dyes. The sheet was coated with glue and stuck on a cardboard frame, then a brush was used to press color through the stencil and onto fabric. The Oriental artists used as many as five colors in combination to print their designs. This Japanese process is undoubtedly the origin of silk-screen printing.

During the Middle Ages stencils were used for decorating playing cards, murals, and wall hangings. In the sixteenth and seventeenth centuries, the art of stenciling spread through Europe, reaching its height of appeal in Germany and France where it became an established art. It was used in conjunction with woodblock and brush painting for religious pictures and illuminated manuscripts. During the seventeenth century in England, the stencil was used to apply an adhesive to wallpaper, after which a flock dust was sprinkled over the sticky paper to produce flocked wallpaper. A Frenchman, Jean Papillon, used a stencil roller to print the first wallpapers in the eighteenth century. Early stencils, made from oil paper, were being used in America by 1787 to decorate on wallpaper, furniture, and directly onto walls with designs of the federal eagle, vines, flowers, and fruit.

*Figure 1. A paper stencil, glue, and maskoid were used in the printing of this original serigraph, "Ribbonscape," by Dorothea Bilder (opposite). It is a fine example of the varied possibilities of modern silk-screening.*

In 1907, Samuel Simon of Manchester, England, received a patent to manufacture a screen using a silk fabric. Then, in 1923 John Pilsworth of San Francisco developed a multicolor method of printing called Selectasine. This method, which consisted of using the screen to print multicolor work, was used to produce the great variety of commercial signs that sprung up all over America and Europe. The silk-screen technique continued to develop not only for printing posters and for general advertising, but for decorating such items as furniture, lamp shades, tablecloths, rugs, book jackets, and scarves.

The process was considered only of commerical value until 1938, when a group of artists convened to study the artistic possibilities of the techniques. Inspired by Anthony Velonis, the group received permission from the Works Progress Administration of New York City for a silk-screen art project. This experiment ultimately produced original prints of such high caliber that they were shown in exhibitions and museums. The artists' works received much praise and proved that the ancient process of stenciling had tremendous possibilities for contemporary fine art prints.

Carl Zigrosser, an art critic and writer on the subject of graphic arts, coined the word "serigraph" for this new fine art printing technique. The serigraph (derived from the Greek word *serikos* meaning silk) came to be recognized in the United States on a level with engraving and lithography. Largely responsible for promoting this new print form as a fine art was the National Serigraph Society in New York. Certainly, as a result of this recognition, more and more artists have become and continue to be aware of the silk-screen process as a means of creative expression.

Figure 2. Silk-screen printing is believed to have originated with the Japanese process of stenciling. Ceremonial garments were designed by utilizing detailed stenciling techniques. The Japanese No Robe (below), dated 1800, was worn for theatrical performances. Oriental motifs found graphic expression in the early hand-cut Japanese stencil (below right). Contemporary artists have adapted this technique to produce modern designs such as the wrapping paper (opposite) created by Roy Lichtenstein. (Courtesy, The Art Institute of Chicago for two bottom pictures.)

## Common Terms Used In Silk-Screen Printing

**Base:** that part of the printing table on which a sheet of paper to be printed is placed and to which a screen frame is hinged; can be made of masonite, plywood, or baseboard.

**Block-Out:** the process for covering or coating the meshes around the design to be printed; to control the open and closed areas of the design, glue or paper are most often used for this purpose.

**Draw-Direct Method:** the drawing of the design directly onto the silk, usually by using Vaseline, grease, or litho crayons.

**Frame:** a wooden structure stretched with fabric that constitutes the screen. For a screen larger than 16 inches by 20 inches, 2-inch by 2-inch lengths of wood are used; 1-inch by 2-inch lengths can be used for smaller screens. A cardboard box, shoe box, or shirt box can be used by children for a simple frame. Frames with silk already stretched over them may be purchased commercially.

**Hinges:** hardware that allows the screen to be lowered or raised.

**Lock-In:** a method for setting the screen in place for printing by placing a corner of the screen in the right-hand corner made with two C-clamps and wood attached to the edge of a table; used when baseboard and hinges are not used.

**Padding:** a base made by stacking newspaper and placing a clean sheet of any unprinted paper on top of the stack, which is then attached to a table top with masking tape.

**Pin Holes:** tiny holes not covered by block-out and through which ink leaks. Check for these by holding the screen up to the light after the glue is dry. Then, using a small brush, dab glue on any pin holes and wait for them to dry before printing. These holes also can be covered with masking tape.

**Prop:** a piece of wood, old brush handle, or paint stick attached to the side of a screen frame to hold it off the baseboard.

**Puddle:** ink poured from a jar into the well or border of the screen at the uppermost section of the frame.

**Pull:** the action of printing or squeegeeing the puddled ink down from the top and across the silk.

**Registration:** the accurate positioning of each sheet of paper so that each color will occupy the same position or place in relation to every other color on every sheet of paper.

**Registration Tabs:** brown paper tape squares folded and taped in three places on the baseboard as a guide to insuring that the various colors fall properly onto each sheet of paper.

**Resist:** a substance, such as an oil-based ink, applied to keep an area free from dyes; does not affect a glue block-out.

**Screen Clogs:** any buildup of glue or dried ink that clogs pores of the silk.

**Silk:** the fabric that is stretched over the frame, usually with a mesh count of 10, 12, or 14, and costing anywhere from $4 to $8 a yard.

**Solvents:** substances used for cleaning oil-based inks from the silk; if tempera paints are used, the screen is cleaned with water.

**Squeegee Angle:** the 55- or 65-degree angle at which the squeegee is held as it is being pulled or pushed across the screen: enables a tight close contact between the ink and silk, forcing color through the fine mesh.

**Stencil:** a paper design that determines through which parts of the screen there will be a passage of ink.

**Wash-Out:** the process of cleaning the screen after each printing.

## Basic Equipment And Supplies

Silk-screen printing, as a graphic art process, has unlimited possibilities. The work can be done at home and there is no need for the assistance of other individuals. All supplies and equipment—such as inks, silk, squeegees, transparent base, bamboo pens, litho crayons—may be purchased or ordered at art supply stores. Any form of wood may be obtained at a nearby lumber yard. Following is information about the various supplies needed.

*Figure 3. Materials used for silk-screen printing are readily available and may be purchased at any art supply store.*

## BAMBOO PEN

This Japanese pen, or reed pen as it is also called, is used for drawing with maskoid (see below) directly on the silk. Pens with metal points tear fibers and should be avoided.

## BRUSHES

Inexpensive, small brushes should be used for the application of glue. A scrub brush three inches by one inch, which is made of natural fiber and has a wooden handle, should be used to wash out ink from the silk.

## CRAYONS

Because crayons are used to fill in fibers of the silk, the softest, greasiest type to draw with is suggested. Oil crayons or grease-litho crayons are best.

## DRYING RACK

By simply spreading the print or paper directly on the floor (covering the floor first with an old sheet, newspaper, or large sheets of cardboard), one has an adequate drying rack. A clothes line and clothes pins are preferable.

## ERASER

Use a natural rubber square for removing maskoid (see below).

## FABRIC

Silk, preferably with a mesh count of 10, 12, or 14, can be purchased at any art supply store carrying silk-screen supplies. Organdy or nylon may also be used. When considering how much fabric to buy, be sure to add, for stapling purposes, two inches to the measurement of all four sides.

## GLASS JARS

These are necessary for the storage of inks and should preferably be four to eight ounces in size, with large mouths and metal lids.

## GLUE

Used for the block-out procedure, two-thirds parts glue should be mixed with one-third part water in a glass jar. It is both wise and economical to purchase glue in large quantities.

## INK

Oil-based ink sold expressly for stencil or silk-screen printing is available in pint or quart cans. To begin, buy white, black, raw umber, red, yellow, and cobalt blue. The raw umber can be used for dulling the intense colors. (Tempera or poster paints can be used for simpler screening methods.)

## MASKOID

Used as a block-out and insoluble in water, this glue-like substance may be removed with a natural rubber eraser or with mineral spirits.

## MAT BOARD

Stiff cardboard, cut in 2-inch squares, used to spread glue or to remove excess ink from screen after printing.

## PAPER

### Contact Paper

This is adhesive-backed paper that can be cut to the required shape and applied to the back of the screen as a block-out.

### Newspaper

This is used for padding and also for the wash-out of ink from silk.

### Newsprint

This may be used as a block-out or for experimenting with colors and shapes.

### Paper Towels

These are used for the wash-out process and are handy for general clean-up processes.

### Printing

Any relatively smooth surfaced paper may be used for printing, such as drawing paper, heavy rice paper, index paper, manila paper, cover stock, card stock, or oak tag. Watercolor and charcoal paper have a definite grain or tooth that is not very desirable.

## Q-TIPS

When saturated with water or a solvent, a Q-Tip will dislodge glue or ink from a clogged area.

## SANDPAPERS

After constructing the frame, use sandpaper to smooth any rough edges.

## SHELLACS

The brown water tape (see below) for covering the silk where staples or tacks are used is given two coats of shellac to protect them from water, inks, and solvents.

## SOLVENTS

Mineral spirits or any paint thinner are acceptable solvents. The fumes of the former are less toxic and both are less expensive than turpentine. Alcohol should never be used.

## SQUEEGEE

A rubber blade with a wooden handle that is used to force ink through the silk. A squeegee should be long enough to cover the width of the silk on the frame. Squeegees are easy to clean and should be kept clean because caked inks will eventually rot the rubber and cause poor contact with the silk. The blade can be sharpened, if it gets dull, by rubbing it over a long sandpaper board. A wooden ruler or a tongue depressor can also be used as a squeegee.

*Figure 4. There should be ample work space on top of a large, sturdy table in order to accomodate all the silk-screening supplies and equipment.*

## SPOON (METAL)

Used for mixing ink and for applying and removing it from the frame. Ink also may be removed from the frame with a rubber spatula.

## STAPLES

These are used to attach the silk to the wooden frame. Carpet tacks and a hammer may be used instead.

## TABLE

Preferably, this should be an old workbench-type table. If new, be sure to cover it with plastic cloth or newspaper to protect the surface.

## TAPES

### Brown Water Tape

This is used to make registration tabs and to cover the silk in areas where staples or tacks are to be used.

### Masking Tape

This can be used as a quick block-out.

## TRANSPARENT BASES

Commercially manufactured, this substance is used to thin down colors for transparencies or glazing. It is sold where inks are purchased. Note: It is always useful to have at least a tablespoon of transparent base in every color used. This keeps the color opaque and allows the ink to be washed out of the silk more easily and quickly.

## WOOD

Used for baseboards; the wood—preferably pine or fir—may be purchased at any lumber yard.

## VASELINE

Sometimes used as a block-out, Vaseline creates an interesting effect.

# Basic Procedures

The technical considerations in silk-screen printing are limitless—the process is particularly adaptable to flat-patterned or painting-like effects through a build-up of various successive colors. By tightly stretching a piece of finely woven fabric such as silk, organdy, or nylon over a wooden frame, the basic piece of equipment is ready for use. Printing and the making of stencils can be done in a number of ways until the desired image is completed.

Prepare the mesh of the silk by sealing with glue or covering with a crayon those areas not to be printed. Cover the entire surface of the screen with glue, let the glue dry, and then, using mineral spirits, wash out the meshes where any previous design was applied.

## MAKING THE FRAME

Using two-inch by two-inch strips of pine or fir, nail or glue together two lengths and two widths to form a rectangle. The corners can be butted together or mitered. It is most important that the frame be rigid and that corners join at right angles. Any poor construction will make for poor registration and distortion of the stencil. Remember, the function of the frame is as a support for the silk and as a basin for the ink. After the frame is nailed and glued together, use joiners or angles for reinforcement of the corners. Using sandpaper, remove any rough or splintered edges. The frame is now ready for the silk to be stretched over it.

## STRETCHING THE FABRIC

It is advisable to use silk, as opposed to organdy or nylon, because silk produces sharper and clearer printed images. The higher the mesh count, the finer the mesh and the clearer the the print. The number 12 mesh is of a medium fine quality and recommended for all work.

Measure the size of the frame and cut the silk two inches larger than the frame to allow for stapling or tacking. Place the frame on a flat surface and then place the silk directly and evenly onto the frame. Using a staple gun or carpet tacks and a hammer, stretch the silk as follows. Place a tack or staple in the middle of each length, keeping the fabric taut by gripping it firmly. Then place staples alternately on the opposite sides of each center staple, doing this on all four sides of the frame and continuing to pull the fabric tightly. Tack or staple until within one inch of the corners of the frame, then fold under the remaining silk to form a folded

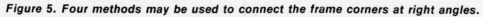

*Figure 5. Four methods may be used to connect the frame corners at right angles.*

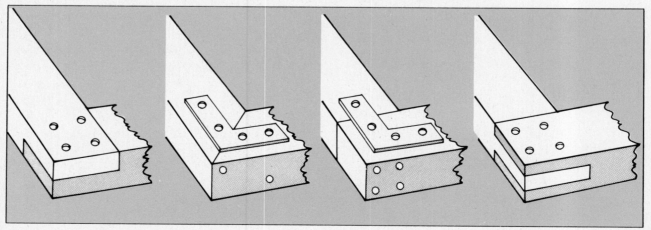

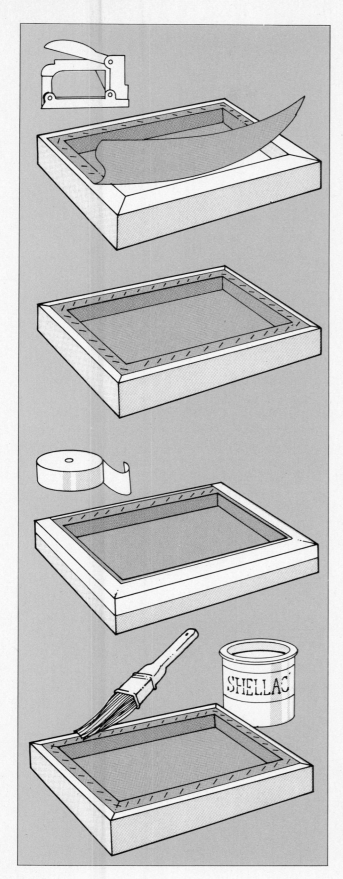

corner, pull it tightly, and staple or tack the fabric in place. The stretched fabric should be "tight as a drum." Trim off any excess silk that extends beyond the frame.

Now cut four strips of brown water tape. Each strip should correspond to the lengths of the sides of the frame. Use these strips to cover the tacks or staples and to hold the silk in place. Turn the frame over, with the basin side up, and cut four more brown paper strips. Fold the paper tape in half lengthwise and seal the four inside edges of the frame by pasting the paper strips so that half of the tape goes on the silk and the other half goes on the wood frame. This will prevent the ink from seeping through the frame during printing and will also reinforce the silk.

The brown taped areas of both sides of the frame should be shellacked to make them waterproof; the shellacked areas will also make it easier to remove the paint from the tape and wood. Be sure to extend the shellac one-half inch or so into the screen (fabric) on all four sides. This will assure an area for holding the paint during printing.

Finally, wash the silk with detergent and a rag or sponge to remove the fabric sizing. If the silk ever develops a hole or is torn, take a piece of masking tape and attach it to the silk, covering the area on the back of the screen. This tape must be removed and replaced for each color. If the tear covers a large area, the silk has to be restretched.

## PREPARING THE BASEBOARD

This flat board, upon which the screen rests, should be two or more inches larger (on all four sides) than the frame and about one-half inch thick. The baseboard allows for a flat, level area on which to print and on which the entire frame and wood can be easily stored. (An alternative to making a baseboard and hinging it to the frame, is to lock the screen in place with C-clamps, making a permanent set-up on a table. Tape newspaper padding to the table as a support for printing.)

*Figure 6. To stretch the fabric, cut the material two inches wider than the frame and staple the material with a staple gun (a). After the fabric has been stapled (b), cover the staples with brown water tape (c). Then, shellac the taped portions and about half of the adjoining screen on all four sides (d). The finished screen should be washed before the first print is made.*

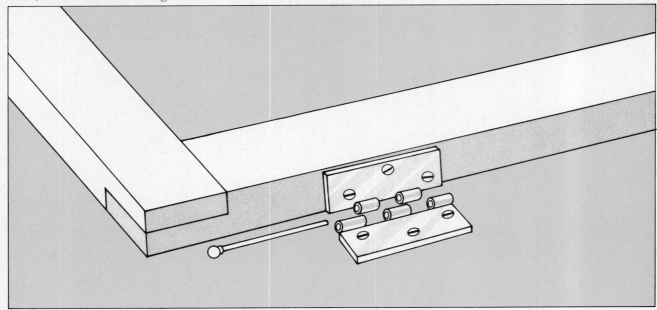

*Figure 7. The frame is attached to the baseboard with two sets of slippin hinges.*

## HINGING

The purpose of hinging the frame to the baseboard is to allow for a more portable arrangement for painting. Two sets of 2½-inch or 3-inch slip pin hinges should be attached to a long side of the frame. Center the frame on the baseboard with the silk side down. Use ¾-inch flat-head screws and fasten the hinges—one side to the baseboard and the other side to the frame. The frame can now be lowered or raised easily. Be sure the slip pins are oiled for easy removal.

## PREPARING A PROP

This is nothing more than a leg stand used to support the screen at approximately a 40- or 45-degree angle from the baseboard, making it easier to remove the printed sheet and to insert and register a clean sheet of paper. A wood, metal, plastic, or formica wedge—four to seven inches in length—can be nailed or screwed into the side of the screen frame about eight inches from the hinged end to serve as a prop.

## DRYING PRINTS

The time for drying a color or print varies, based on the mixture of ink used as well as its build-up. Inks mixed with transparent base will dry faster, but a humid climate as well as a rainy day often will slow down the drying process. Drying time may vary anywhere from ten minutes to two hours—most prints dry in 20 to 30 minutes.

The simplest drying method is to clip each individual print to a strong wire line, clothesline, or rope with paper clips, clothespins, or metal clips. It is also possible to place cardboard or large sheets of paper on the workshop floor and simply set the printed sheets there until dry. Usually, the next color can be printed immediately after the screen has been washed and the next stencil prepared. This is because the first color usually has dried during the time that it takes to prepare the next stencil.

*Figure 8. A prop is used to support the screen at a 40- or 45-degree angle from the baseboard.*

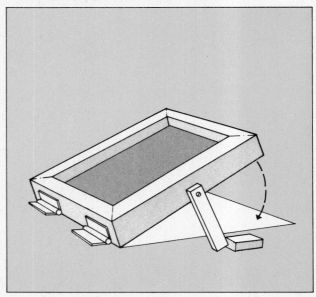

*Figure 9. After the prepared screen is hinged to the baseboard and raised on the prop, it is ready for printing. Note the various sized squeegees used for prints of different widths.*

## REGISTERING THE DESIGN

The registration of each sheet is to insure that the design is lined up properly—especially when one is working with various stencils and colors. There are a few methods for registering prints, but the following one is extremely accurate as well as convenient.

First of all, make sure the paper is cut with straight edges and that each sheet is equal in width and length. Registration tabs can be made from brown water tape. Cut the tape into three small strips, two inches by two inches, and fold them in half. Then, on each folded strip, fold each half back to the center fold, creating an accordian-type fold. Wet or lick the center of the fold and glue the top half of the strip together. When attaching the tabs to the baseboard, have handy the sketch, design, or sheet of paper on which you will be printing. Align the sketch or paper under the screen and lightly tape it down. One half of the registration tab is placed under the paper and then the center portion (the part that has been taped together) is

*Figure 10. Prints are dried most easily by attaching a clothspin to each corner and hanging them on a strong wire.*

**Figure 11. Registration tabs are cut and folded, then glued together in the center.**

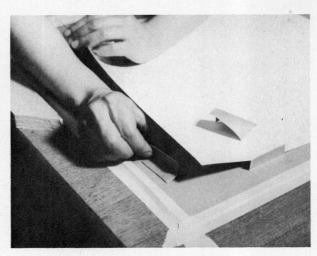

**Figure 12. Position tabs so that paper edges fit tightly against the register folds.**

**Figure 13. When the tabs are secured and the printing paper is aligned, uniform prints can be made. Place the paper on the baseboard so that the edge of the paper rests against the edge of the inside tab fold. Tape the paper to the baseboard and attach the tabs in place.**

**Figure 14. Fold the center portion of the tab over the paper to firmly hold it in place.**

folded over the paper. Now tape down the other half of the tab to the baseboard, lift the corner of the paper, and tape the over end of the tab down. It is a good idea to wet the tape just before setting it under the paper because then it glues itself to the baseboard.

Place two of the tabs at either the top or botton of the sketch and the remaining tab on one of the sides. These hold the paper in place during printing and insure that each sheet of paper aligns properly to a design of several colors. When working with a free or spontaneous design or print, it is also helpful to mark with an "X" the top of the paper to avoid confusion with the bottom.

**Figure 15. The print appears on the paper in the desired position. Keep register marks in place for multiple printings.**

*Figure 16. After mixing the inks (left), a transparent base is added (right).*

## PREPARING THE INK

The amount of ink used depends on the number of prints being made. The ink should be the consistency of heavy cream. Ink that is left over may be easily stored in glass jars for at least a year. When using ink straight from a can or when mixing colors, always use at least a tablespoon of transparent base; this will thin the ink as well as facilitate the wash-out. Ink also can be thinned with mineral spirits. An ink supply usually needs replennishing after printing ten prints.

## PREPARING THE PAPER

The kind of paper used is based on personal preference as well as what works best with a particular design. Remember that the paper should be cut to allow for a two- or three-inch margin extending beyond the design. This margin can later be cut away, but it allows for fingerprints, matting, and easier handling in general. The paper should always be prepared before printing: determine and cut the necessary number of sheets.

## PULLING A PRINT

After positioning the printing paper, make sure the registration tabs are secure and accurate. Assuming the screen to be used has a stencil or glue block-out on it, place the screen down and puddle some ink in the well at the top of the frame. Spread the ink across the top of the frame from one side to the other along the tape, so that it is evenly distributed. Take the squeegee and, holding it at about a 55- or 65-degree angle, pull it very firmly across the silk towards you. Then, at the same angle, push the squeegee firmly back to the top of the frame. Leave the squeegee resting against the top of the frame or set it next to the frame on a cookie sheet, board, or waxed paper. It is better to use more ink than not enough. Also, try to keep all of the ink on one side of the squeegee; this helps to produce a cleaner, more even color.

Now lift the screen, prop it up, remove the printed paper, and set it somewhere to dry. Take another sheet of paper and continue the process. When all of the prints of the first color (or only color) have

Figure 17. After the paper is securely aligned and the screen is placed down, puddle the ink from jar into the well at the top of the frame.

Figure 18. Spread the ink with a metal spoon along the tape from side to side across the uppermost section of the frame.

Figure 19. Position the squeegee in the ink-filled well and take a firm grip on the handle to insure even coating of the screen's surface.

Figure 20. Pull the squeegee at about a 55-to 65-degree angle toward you, forcing the ink through the silk onto the printing paper.

been made, remove the remaining or excess ink with a spoon or rubber spatula and place the ink in a clean glass jar for further use. This procedure, after a wash-out, is repeated for the remaining colors. Finished prints should be stored in flat, dry areas.

## WASH-OUT

It is necessary to do a wash-out before each new color is applied. This means cleaning the screen, squeegee, spoon, and anything else that is covered with ink. The screen need not be removed from the hinges. Sheets of newspaper can be spead between the underneath side of the screen and the baseboard and mineral spirits (or another such solvent) sprinkled over the silk and tapes. Use paper towels to wipe the ink from the silk as well as from the tapes, and to wipe off the squeegee, spoon, and other materials. It will be necessary to wash out the silk two, three, or even four

times in order to cleanse it thoroughly. Change the newspapers each time. The amount of ink left on the towels shows whether the silk is clean. (Note: After two wash-outs, prop up the screen and rub it with mineral spirits and paper towels on both sides. This will knock out the ink from the pores of the silk and prevent the ink from clogging.)

If, after four wash-outs, ink still seems to be clogged in an area, use a small-bristle scrub brush with a wooden handle and, sprinkling mineral spirits on the silk, lightly scrub the silk on both sides. Some people will always do this to assure a thorough cleaning. To tell if an area is clogged, remove the hinge pins and hold the screen up to the light. The clogged ink is easily seen. If the silk is clogged, continue to use the brush and mineral spirits. Do not be concerned if ink appears to be lodged in the fibers even though the paper towels

Figure 21. *Before applying additional colors, all the equipment should be cleaned. Begin by placing the excess puddled ink in a glass jar.*

Figure 22. *Place newspapers beneath the screen and, using a paper towel, wash out any inked portions with a solvent such as mineral spirits.*

Figure 23. *For ink-clogged areas, it may be necessary to use a small brush to lightly scrub the surface (*above*). Unhinge the frame and thoroughly clean both sides with mineral spirits (*right*).*

are without ink. Many colors stain or dye the fibers and a faint trace of color is almost always evident. Repeat these procedures after each color printing.

## Projects You Can Do

Successful silk-screen printing depends on the ink being forced through the silk and onto the paper underneath to be printed, producing the desired image. The stencil and block-out must be soluble in water, since oil-based ink is most often used.

There are several methods and materials which can be used for both the stencil and block-out methods. Three of these stencil processes—glue block-out, paper stencil, and direct drawing with oil crayons and Vaseline—will be described here, step-by-step. These processes are all direct, spontaneous, easy, and inexpensive. They use very

basic skills which can produce exciting and versatile items, resulting in finished prints, posters, cards, or announcements.

Cut-film stencils or photo silk-screen processes are not described here because both of these necessitate more expensive materials, a greater variety of solvents, and complicated techniques. Each of the processes discussed here, on the other

A  B  C  D

*Figure 24. A glass jar is used to mix two-thirds parts glue to one-third part water (a) for the glue block-out. This mixture is applied to the raised screen with a brush (b) or with Q-Tips (c), depending upon the effect desired in the finished print. A portable hair dryer may be used to speed the drying process (d). The dried screen is then positioned on the baseboard for printing.*

hand, is simple and direct and can be used separately or combined in any number of ways. Always remember to precut the paper before printing and to determine at the beginning how many sheets will be printed.

## GLUE BLOCK-OUT STENCIL

In a jar, mix two-thirds parts glue and one-third part water. This will be used for the block-out to create a textural drawn spontaneous image for the first color.

**1.** Remove the hinge pins and either hold the screen up with one hand or, as mentioned earlier, prop it up with two strips of wood or jar lids. This will allow the frame to dry from both sides. Have newspaper underneath to catch any dripping of glue.

**2.** Spatter on glue with a brush, letting it drip or flow and dotting it on the silk with Q-Tips or fingertips to create a free flowing image. Make no attempt at this point to control the image—it will become more organized later.

**3.** Allow the glue to dry. To speed up the drying time, a portable hair dryer or the nozzle of a vacuum cleaner can be used.

**4.** Before the glue has set or dried completely, added textures may be created by pressing into wet areas of glue with crumpled waxed paper, aluminum foil, or crushed paper towels. Use paper towels to wipe off any excess glue that accumulates on the tapes.

**5.** When the glue is completely dry, place the screen in position on the baseboard. Now take a sheet of inexpensive paper, such as newsprint, and place it under the silk.

**6.** Mix ink, puddle it, and print two or three experimental proofs in a desired first color.

**7.** After noting the image, place the proofs to dry, register the actual paper to be used, and begin printing, following the instructions described above. The glue is the block-out—the untouched silk will be left open, letting the color pass through.

**8.** After printing all sheets of paper, follow instructions for the wash-out. However, the same glue block-out can be used again, before removing it from the silk, by using either of the following two methods:

**a.** Place the printed sheet with the first color on it back under the screen frame, but shift the paper slightly out of the registration tabs. Use a new color and print each sheet a second time, making sure each is lined up properly in its new position. Use new registration tabs if desired. This process creates an interesting double image.

**b.** Reversing the printed sheet from top to bottom, overprint the first two colors with a third color. The same glue block-out acts as a resist, and can create interesting effects by being used with three different colors.

**9.** When the glue block-out possibilities have been exhausted and all the ink has been thoroughly washed out of the silk, take the screen and remove the glue by using plenty of warm to hot water. This can be done in a sink, bathtub, shower stall, utility tub, or with a garden hose out of doors, depending upon the size of the screen.

**10.** Wipe the excess water from the silk, using paper towels and rubbing from both sides.

**11.** Hold the screen up to the light to check for any clogged areas. If necessary, repeat the water wash-out and use a scrub brush on the silk to dislodge any remaining glue. Ink will sometimes collect around glued edges and the silk may also be washed out with mineral spirits after it has dried following the water wash-out.

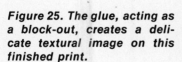

*Figure 25. The glue, acting as a block-out, creates a delicate textural image on this finished print.*

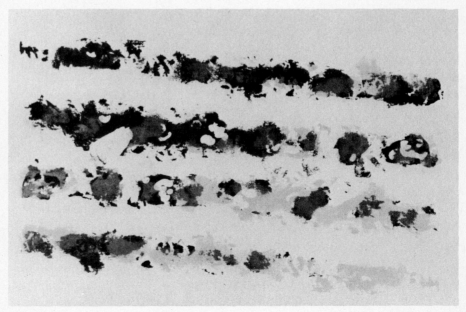

**1.** Create a paper stencil by cutting or tearing newsprint paper. The torn edge gives a soft effect compared to a crisp, cut edge. Newsprint—not newspaper—should be used because it is not absorbent, it is less expensive, and it may be used as a block-out for printing approximately 30 prints. This particular project utilizes abstract geometric forms. Of course, the design is up to the individual.

**2.** After the design is complete, cut out the shapes with scissors or with an X-acto knife. Save the cut-out pieces for the second color.

**3.** With masking tape, tape the cut newsprint stencil to the frame on the underneath side of the silk. The newsprint stencil must cover or extend onto the taped areas of the frame.

**4.** Put the frame back in the hinges, prop up the screen, place the paper in the registration tabs, lower the screen, puddle the ink, and print all the sheets of paper. Remember to pull a few experimental newsprint proofs first to check both the image and the color.

**5.** After printing, remove the excess ink, remove the paper stencil (carefully if it is to be saved), and wash out the silk with mineral spirits.

**6.** Return the screen to the baseboard and place one of the already printed sheets under the silk in the registration tabs.

**7.** Take the pieces of newsprint that were cut out from the previous stencil and arrange them in any random position or directly upon the colored areas which were created by the first stencil. Mix the second color of ink.

**8.** Lower the screen, puddle the ink, and squeegee across the silk. The cut-out sections will adhere to the underneath side of the silk as the squeegee is drawn across.

**9.** Continue printing all of the paper. Then remove the cut-out stencil shapes, remove the excess paint, and wash out the silk with mineral spirits.

**10.** Take the first printed sheet, which now has two colors on it, from the drying area. Place this back in the registration tabs on the baseboard,

*Figure 26. Newsprint may be used for paper stencils. A design is drawn on the newsprint, then cut out with an X-acto knife (above). Masking tape is used to hold the cut newsprint to the frame (below).*

and place one of the newsprint proofs on top of the printed sheet.

**11.** Take a clean sheet of newsprint and tear some random or drawn shapes out of it. The ragged, soft edge will give a new dimension to the print. Mix the ink, making it transparent this time by using three-fourths transparent base to one-fourth ink.

*Figure 28. The printing process has "glued" the cut shapes to the silk (above), resulting in a second paper stencil. An additional printing with torn shapes placed on the printed newsprint produced a three-colored print (below).*

*Figure 27. When the newsprint sheets have been pulled, the screen is cleaned. The cut-out pieces of stencil are re-positioned on the registered print (above). The printing process is repeated, using a second color (below).*

**13.** If the results are desirable, lower the screen, puddle the ink, squeegee across the silk two or three times, lift the screen, remove the proof sheet, and set it aside to dry.

**14.** Register the print paper in the tabs, lower the screen, continue printing all sheets of paper, and set them aside to dry.

**15.** Remove the excess ink, remove the paper stencil block-out, and wash out the screen with mineral spirits.

It is possible to continue overlaying and building a print of numerous colors and shapes. A stencil also may be created by cutting shapes out of contact paper. The sticky side of the contact paper will dissolve with the mineral spirits during the wash-out.

**12.** Place the torn shapes on the printed newsprint sheet, arranged as desired. Lower the screen, puddle the ink, and pull the squeegee across the silk, to which the torn shapes will again adhere. By taking a proof on the newsprint, the arrangement of shapes and the transparent color can be tested.

## DIRECT DRAWING

Oil crayons, grease crayons or pencils, and Vaseline can be dissolved by mineral spirits. These materials yield soft paint-like qualities.

**1.** Take a clean screen and prop it up. Using oil or grease crayons, draw on the silk, pressing firmly so as to fill in the mesh that *will* print.

**2.** Coat the silk evenly with glue, using a small piece of matt board to spread the glue over the entire screen.

**3.** After the glue has dried, check the silk for pin holes by holding the screen up to the light. If there are pin holes in many areas, coat the entire screen with glue a second time. If the pin holes are in only a few places, dab the screen with glue. Wait for this second coat to dry and wipe the excess glue from the tape wells.

**4.** Now wash out the oil crayon drawing with mineral spirits and paper towels. The glue will work as a block-out and the crayon drawing will print as the image.

**5.** Put the screen back in the hinges, place a sheet of newsprint for proofing under the screen, mix the ink, puddle the ink, and squeegee it across the screen. Remove the print.

**6.** If ink is coming through some pin holes that were not part of the original drawing, do one of two things. Either take masking tape and block-out the pin holes with small strips of tape, or leave the pin holes alone—they will plug up with ink or add to the image.

**7.** Register the print paper, lower the screen, and print. After printing all the sheets of paper, set them aside to dry, remove the excess ink, and wash out the silk with mineral spirits.

**8.** Wash out the glue, using hot water and possibly a scrub brush, rubbing on both sides to unclog stubborn glue. It may be necessary to do a wash-out with mineral spirits after the glue wash-out, as ink has a tendency to collect on the edges of glued areas.

**9.** Prop up the clean screen and, using the fingertips, smear Vaseline on the silk in any desired manner.

**10.** Spread glue over the entire silk and wait for it

Figure 29. To create the third project (a), the soft edges of the first color (b) are drawn with crayons. A Vaseline smear (c) adds a transparent look to the second color. The third color is a combination of a glue resist and presssed aluminum foil (d).

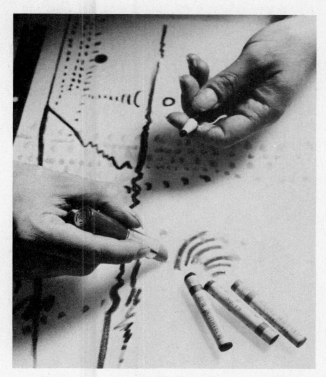

***Figure 30. Paint-like qualities are achieved by drawing directly on the screen with lipstick as well as with oil and grease crayons.***

to dry. The Vaseline will create a very soft, cloudy area. Wipe excess glue from the tape wells.

**11.** When the glue is dry, wash out the Vaseline with mineral spirits, replace the screen, and place the newsprint proof sheet under the screen.

**12.** Mix and puddle the ink, then print the image on the newsprint proof. After checking the proof sheet, place the sheet with the first color printed on it in the proper position. Make sure to check the registration tabs and remember which is the top of your printed sheet.

**13.** Print the Vaseline-smeared image on all the sheets. This will create an interesting effect over the previously drawn image. After printing each sheet, set it aside to dry. Remove the excess ink and wash out the screen with mineral spirits. Again, the glue block-out must be washed out with hot water and possibly a scrub brush.

**14.** For the third color, prop up the screen again and spread mineral spirits all over the silk. Make sure there is newspaper under the screen frame. (This is an example of a mineral spirit and glue resist.)

**15.** Before the mineral spirits dry on the silk, spread glue over the entire screen, using a piece of matt board. Wipe off excess glue along the taped wells with paper towels and let dry.

**16.** There is nothing to wash out at this point. Merely position the screen frame, position the newsprint proof sheet under the silk, mix the ink, puddle the ink, and squeegee the third color across the screen. If the third color is transparent, the underneath colors will show.

**17.** After printing the proof, register the printed sheet (now with two colors on it) in the tabs, lower the screen, and continue printing until all sheets have the new images upon them. Set the prints aside to dry.

**18.** Remove excess ink from the screen frame and do a wash-out. Wash out the glue resist with hot water and a brush if necessary. Again, rub both sides of the silk.

This direct drawing process can be continued any number of times, repeating with oil crayon to build areas, as well as with Vaseline or the glue-resist method. Another idea is to draw directly with lipstick. Because it is oil-based, lipstick can be used the same way grease pencil, oil crayon, or Vaseline is used.

## *For Additional Reading*

Auvil, Kenneth W., **Serigraphy: Silk Screen Techniques for the Artist,** Prentice-Hall, 1965.

Biezeleisen, J. I., and Cohn, Max A., **Silk Screen Techniques,** Dover, 1958.

Caza, Michael, **Silk Screen Printing,** Van Nostrand, 1974.

Chieffo, Clifford I., **Silk Screen as a Fine Art,** Van Nostrand, 1967.

Schwalbach, Mathilda V. and James A., **Screen Process Printing,** Van Nostrand, 1970.

Shoklu, Harry, **Artist's Manual for Silk Screen Print Making,** Tudor, 1960.

*Hand-crafted items have been made not only for decorative purposes, but for ceremonial and functional reasons as well. The sampler (top) is an example of early American needlework. It was customary to work the name of the designer and the date into the embroidered piece. (Courtesy, The Henry Francis du Pont Winterthur Museum.) Masks have been used for ceremonial purposes throughout history. The Japanese No mask (above left) was used for theatrical performances. (Courtesy, The Tokyo National Museum.) Both the Egyptian and Greek masks (above center and right) date back to at least the third century A.D. and were used in burial rituals. (Courtesy, The Field Museum of Natural History.) The fireplace broom (left) has long been a part of many households. This broom was decorated with felt to give it a contemporary flair.*

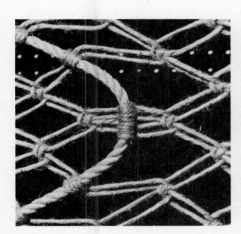
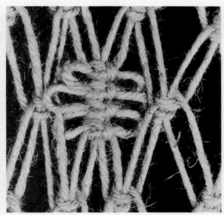

*Many age-old crafts are experiencing a new revival. Modern silk-screening processes grew out of the ancient Oriental techniques used for graphic expression. The detail of the contemporary silk screen (top left) illustrates the effect that can be achieved by using the direct draw method of printing fabric. Although needlepoint was originally confined to aristocratic circles, its popularity grew and today this form of stitchery has widespread appeal. The detail of the eighteenth-century Italian embroidery (top right) is an example of bargello work. (Courtesy, The Cooper-Hewitt Museum of Decorative Arts and Design, Smithsonian Institution.) The art of macrame has been practiced for centuries. Early civilizations used this technique as a means of making articles of clothing. In addition to its practical purposes, macrame is also used to make decorative items such as wall hangings. The three bottom pictures show some of the ways in which string can be knotted and intertwined to make interesting patterns.*

# Felt Craft

Felt was surely one of the earliest types of fabricated cloth known to man. It was used in ancient times for blankets, tent coverings, and garments. Fleeces and loose matted fibers collected from sheep were washed and laid out on the ground, with much of the natural oil left in as a lubricant. The mass was then beaten with rods until the desired thickness and cohesiveness were obtained. This method was called "felting."

Felt manufacturing has greatly progressed since these early crude methods, going through several developmental stages before reaching today's expertise. However, ancient felting methods and modern methods accomplish the same results.

After fibers are washed and carded, heat, moisture, and pressure are applied. This process is called "hardening." In the next step, "fulling," the matted fibers are pounded by a series of wooden hammers which forces the fibers into closer contact with firmer entanglement. Felt may be made in any thickness, from a fraction of an inch up to several inches. After fulling, the felt is washed, dyed, and finally dried on frames with a pulling tension in each direction.

To achieve density in felt, wool is necessary. Under the right conditions of temperature, moisture, and pressure, wool scales will curl up into perfect coils. When combined with agitation, these will cause other fibers to interlock and mat together in such a manner that they cannot separate. Because wool is the only fiber that will produce this effect, all felt fabric contains some percentage of wool.

*Figure 1. Felt craft is accessible to all age groups. This cheerful hanging created by an elementary school boy utilizes a burlap background for the felt cutouts. (Courtesy, Noah Weiner.)*

Felt has many advantages over other fabrics. Because it is a nonwoven fabric it will not ravel and, therefore, does not require hemming. It can be cut in any direction because there is no bias. Nor is there a right or wrong side to felt. It can be molded, shaped, and cut into intricate designs; it is extremely flexible and forms soft rounded shapes when stuffed.

Probably one of the earliest uses of felt for other than practical purposes was in the early 1920s. Items requiring trimmings, such as hats and slippers, were most often decorated with flower shapes cut from felt pieces of contrasting colors. Soon these decorative methods spread to such fields as the toy industry.

Many new shades were added to the felt color line and, because of growing interest, felt was made available to the public by the yard or in small cut pieces. Many craftsmen saw the unlimited possibilities with this fabric and today there are hundreds of craft items made of felt. There are precut shapes and designs which attach to embroidered backgrounds and are used for pictures and pillows. There are kits which contain sequins, beads, and other trimmings which can be glued in place on various items. In fact, new ideas are constantly being developed to make felt craft a fun and exciting hobby.

Figure 2. These pixie dolls were made from a kit. The bodies are made of felt; other materials are used for trimming and padding.

## Common Terms Used In Felt Craft

**Felt Sheets:** because of the availability and low cost, most items in this article are made from 9" x 12" sheets of felt which may be purchased packaged or loose in most craft stores or departments; felt may also be purchased by the yard in fabric stores or departments, or through art needlework mail-order houses.

**Stuffing:** kapok, shredded foam rubber, or cut up scraps such as nylon stockings may be used as stuffing.

**Tacking:** to sew lightly with hidden stitches.

## Basic Equipment And Supplies

The felt craft items mentioned in this article are for suggested projects. After accumulating several colors of felt, it is a good idea to start a scrap box. Do not discard any pieces, for even the smallest piece may be valuable in making pictures or trimming toys.

### FOR STUFFED TOYS

If sewing by hand, use a large-eyed, sharp-pointed needle. For both machine or hand sew-

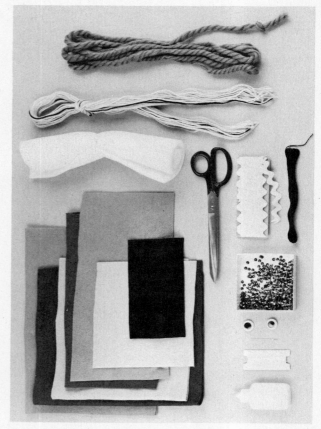

Figure 3. Materials needed for felt craft are easily available and generally inexpensive. They include pieces of felt, yarn, trim, sequins, white craft glue, a needle, and scissors.

*Figure 4. These Christmas tree ornaments are made from a kit. The animals range in size from 3¼" to 7¼" tall.*

ing, matching thread, scissors, felt, and stuffing are needed.

## FOR PICTURES

Needed are scissors, white craft glue, and felt in several colors. A frame should be purchased after deciding upon the size of the picture. If the frame does not include a backing, obtain a piece of cardboard cut to size. To hang the picture, two small eyelet screws and picture wire are necessary.

## FOR BEADED ITEMS

A beading needle, a very fine needle about 2 inches long with a large eye, is necessary. This is usually available wherever beads are sold. Also needed are scissors, matching thread, beads, a regular sewing needle, and, of course, felt.

# Basic Procedures

## JOINING

Felt can be joined by hand or machine sewing. Items can be inverted to appear seamless or trimmed close to the seam with seam side out. Felt adheres very quickly and can be glued to felt or other surfaces. Be careful to use glue sparingly to prevent staining. If staining occurs, blot with a cloth dipped in cold water.

## CUTTING

Use sharp scissors when cutting felt. A simple method for cutting shapes such as small circles is to draw a pattern on paper, then pin or staple the pattern to felt. Cut pattern through paper and felt. For intricate designs, draw the design on contact paper. Remove backing from paper and press over the felt. Cut out the design, using manicuring scissors for small spaces. Do not remove contact paper but glue paper to background.

## BEADING

When working on beaded projects, always use nylon thread. The invisible or colorless nylon thread is very helpful because it matches all backgrounds. Work beaded designs before assembling projects.

To sew bugle beads in a line, work in a back stitch as follows. Place bead on needle, insert needle on line to fit length of bead, bring needle out on line the same length ahead, place next bead on needle and insert needle at end of last bead, bring needle out on line at start of second bead and repeat the procedure. After working one row, run needle and thread through beads to straighten the line.

## ENLARGING PATTERNS

It is not always possible to give actual pattern size. To enlarge patterns, redraw them on 1" graph paper, using the background lines as a guide.

## BASTING

Use a contrasting colored thread and an ordinary sewing needle. Work a running stitch through felt 1/4" from edges to hold pieces in place. Remove thread when project is completed.

## CARE OF FELT

Felt does not wash well. Therefore, if cleaning is necessary, dry cleaning is suggested. To avoid fading, do not expose felt to direct sunlight or bright artificial lighting for long periods of time.

## Projects You Can Do

These projects are simple and suggest a variety of items which can be made, including a doll, a picture, a Christmas stocking, a pillow, and a circus elephant. Read through the projects before deciding which one to do first. Materials required for each are listed separately.

## DOLL

The materials necessary to make this doll, which is 17 inches tall, are: 1 sheet each of black and white felt, 2 sheets of hot pink, 3 sheets of flesh color, and scraps of red and blue; 14 yards of brown yarn; 1 yard of 1" lace; small buttons; 1 spool each of hot pink, brown, black, white, and flesh-colored sewing thread; 1 fine sewing needle; masking tape; and 1/4 yard of press-on

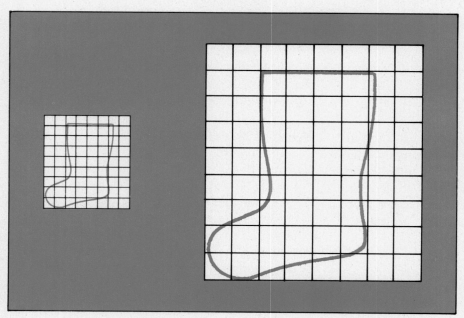

*Figure 5. Any pattern can be enlarged to suit the dimensions of a project. A grid is placed over the design, and the proportions are increased by a uniform number.*

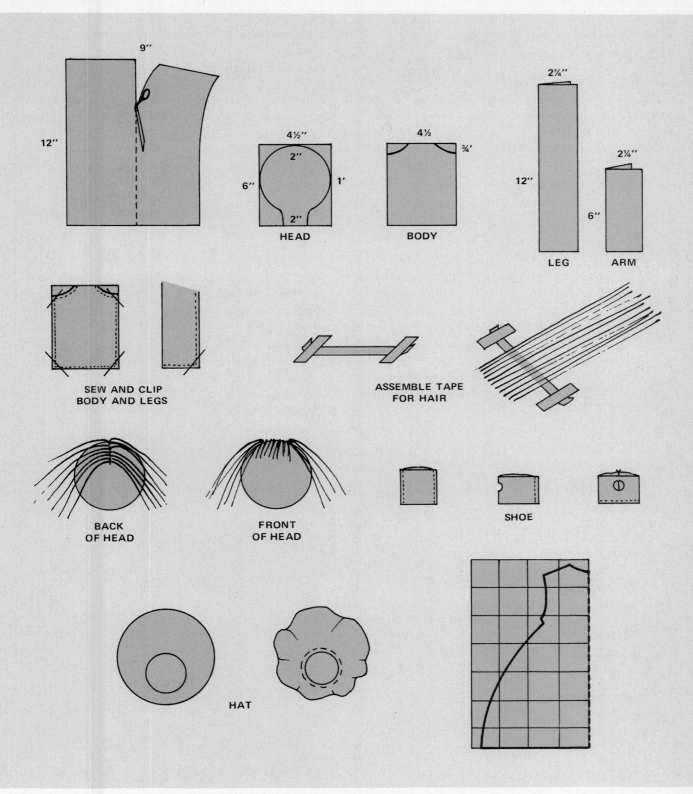

Figure 6. This diagram shows the pieces necessary to make a felt doll. Several colors of felt are used, and the pattern calls for matching thread. The finished doll will be 17'' tall.

Pellon, which has a glued surface on one side that adheres to fabric when ironed on.

### Cutting and Assembling the Doll

To cut the body of the doll, begin with the head. Cut one sheet of flesh-colored felt in half lengthwise. Fold one piece in half to make a double piece approximately 4½″ x 6″. Pin this together. Following the diagram, cut off and shape corners. Set aside.

For the torso, fold the second strip in half lengthwise also to make a double piece approximately 4½″ x 6″. Pin together. Cut around the upper edge as shown, leaving 2″ for the neck. Make shoulders about 3/4″ deep. Set aside.

For the legs, cut one flesh-colored sheet in half lengthwise. Fold and pin each strip together to form two double pieces, each approximately 2¼″ x 12″. Set aside. For the arms, cut the remaining flesh-colored sheet in half lengthwise and cut one strip through the center to make two pieces, each 4½″ x 6″. Fold each of these pieces in half lengthwise to make two double pieces, each approximately 2¼″ x 6″.

Now prepare to sew the body of the doll. With matching thread, sew pieces together as follows. Sew a 1/4″ seam around the head, leaving the neck open for stuffing. Sew a 1/4″ seam around three sides of the torso, again leaving the neck open. Clip corners at shoulders and lower edge, as illustrated. Sew a 1/4″ seam down the open edge of each leg and across one end. Clip corner of each leg. Sew a 1/4″ seam down the open edge of each arm and across the end. Cut off lower corner of arms.

To stuff the doll, turn pieces inside out and stuff each piece firmly.

Next, assemble the doll. Place head and neck over torso; pin these and sew in place with small stitches. Turn under 1/4″ at open end of arms. Pin together and sew to side seam of torso, starting at the shoulders. Turn under 1/4″ at opening of legs. Pin together and sew to lower seam of torso, starting at side seams. To make the face, use a penny as a pattern to cut out two blue circles for the eyes. Glue these to white felt and cut around the circles, leaving 1/8″ of white showing. Glue

*Figure 7. A red dress was chosen for this doll, but the basic dress pattern can be made up in any color and decorated in a variety of imaginative ways.*

and cut black felt around the eyes in the same way. Cut 1/8" square of black and glue this to the center of the eyes. Cut out a mouth about 1" long by 5/8" high from red felt.

### Making a Wig

Wind yarn around a 6" cardboard 13 times. Cut strands at one end. Cut a piece of masking tape about 6" long and tape each end to a table, with sticky side up. Place strands across 3" of the masking tape, leaving a 2" overhang on one side for bangs and 10" on the other side. With matching thread, sew across center of tape from beginning to end of yarn. Then, go back and forth over same stitches two or three more times.

Wind yarn around a 9" cardboard 18 times. Cut strands at one end. Cut another 6" piece of masking tape and attach to table as before. Crowd strands onto tape for about 1½", leaving a 9" overhang on each side of tape. Sew across tape as before. Tape may be removed if desired: it should not show through hair. Trim ends of tape close to first and last strands. Lay the 9" strands over the top of the head, with start of seam at top seam of head, and extend across back of head. Sew in place. Place bangs across top of head and sew in place, having 10" lengths to back of head. Bring some of the strands toward front of face and tack or glue in place. Tack remaining strands across back of neck. Trim strands.

### Making the Clothes

The next step is making the doll's clothes. To make the underpants, cut a piece of white felt 2¼" x 8" long. Bring the ends together and sew the seam. Turn right side out. Sew or glue lace around one edge. Place over body, then join lace between legs with a few small stitches.

Next, make a dress by enlarging dress pattern to actual size. Fold one sheet of hot pink felt in half lengthwise. Place pattern on fold and cut out front of dress. Cut out back from second sheet of hot pink the same way. Sew seam on each side of skirt only. Turn inside out. Glue or sew lace around inside of hemline of skirt. Glue or sew lace at inside of armholes, leaving shoulders open. Set aside. Make ruffle for neck by drawing white thread through edge of 10" piece of lace. Do not cut end on thread, but leave about 10" hanging from each end.

Sew three small buttons to front of dress, with the first at neck edge and each 1/2" apart. Place dress over body and sew together at shoulders. Draw ruffle around neck and tie ends in front. Clip threads.

To make socks, cut two pieces of white felt, each 2½" x 5". Fold each piece in half and sew seam at each side. Turn inside out and place over feet of doll. To make shoes, cut two pieces of black felt, each 5" x 2". Cut out a hole, using a dime as a pattern, in center 3/8" down from top. Fold in half and sew ends together. With seam at center back of shoe and hole in front, sew seam across bottom of shoe. Turn inside out and place over socks.

Next, make a hat by cutting two 5" circles and one 3¾" circle out of the remaining hot pink felt. Pin the two larger circles together. Place a straight pin at lower edge of each piece for center back. Cut out a 2" circle from both large circles, 1" from lower edge. Gather the edge of the 3¾" circle. Pin to inside of cut-out circle of one piece and sew in place by hand. The gathered circle should now puff out on right side of work.

Place second large circle on ironing board. Place glued side piece of Pellon onto felt. With moderately hot iron, press Pellon onto felt. Take a second piece of Pellon and press over first. Trim to same size as felt. Baste a piece of lace to wrong side, with 1/2" of lace extending over edge. Place circles with wrong sides together. Pin, then baste circles together. Machine stitch around 1/4" from outside edge. Trim around to within 1/8" of seam, trimming each side separately. Next, cut a 1/4" x 12" strip of black felt or use a 1/4" black satin ribbon. Glue or tack this around the hat, crossing ribbon in back. Tie a loose knot. Tack hat to head across top of bangs and at back of head.

## COVERED BRIDGE PICTURE

The materials required for this project, which measures 11" x 14", are: tracing paper and pencil; two sheets of light-blue felt and one sheet each of dark green, dark turquoise, apple green, loden green, black, light yellow, red, white, tan, gray, and dark brown; 12" x 12" piece of white contact paper; glue; a ruler; and an 11" x 14" frame without glass. If cardboard is not included, get cardboard and cut it to size. An extra piece of cardboard cut to the same size will be helpful in filling in the backing of the picture.

## Making the Pattern

To make the pattern, enlarge the illustrated bridge to actual size. Go over lines on wrong side of pattern with a pencil so pattern can be transferred. Use one of the sheets of 11" x 14" cardboard to draw the pattern. Write "top" at top of one long side. With ruler, measure down 5½" from top and draw a line across. Measure in 7" from each end and draw a line down, dividing cardboard into four sections. Measure down 1¾" from center horizontal line and draw a dotted line across. These lines will be guidelines for drawing the picture. Center the covered bridge pattern onto the cardboard with lower edge of bridge about 1/8" below dotted line and the left-hand corner of bridge on dotted line. Make a mark on lower edge of cardboard 3" in from the left-hand corner for the road and another mark 10" from left-hand corner for start of the water. Using the established guidelines, draw a curved line from left-hand corner of bridge to lower corner of cardboard. Draw other side of road, ending at the 3" mark. Draw water, ending left line at 10" mark and right

line at right-hand corner. Extend line for road on right side of bridge, 1/4" above dotted line. Draw a curved line for grass at left side of picture, ending 3¾" up from lower left corner. Draw two mountains behind this portion of grass, as shown in picture. Draw two clouds in the sky.

At upper right corner of the picture, draw a large tree about 5½" wide by 5½" high. Draw another tree behind the bridge, as shown, and one under both trees. Draw trunks of trees with branches as shown. Then, draw rocks in water.

## Cutting the Felt

Trace the pattern for the large 5½" x 5½" tree and the mountain behind the bridge onto paper and pin to apple-green felt. Cut out patterns through paper and felt, disregarding branches on tree. Next, trace pattern for three sections of grass, disregarding tree trunk. Pin pattern to dark-green felt and cut out patterns. Similarly, trace pattern for mountain at left side and lower tree onto paper. Pin pattern to loden-green felt and cut out pattern.

Continuing in the same manner, trace and cut out of tan felt the wide part of the road and the extension of the road at right-hand side. Trace and cut

*Figure 8. A pattern is provided for the covered bridge picture. Note that the lines — both solid and dotted — are used as guidelines for drawing and enlarging the picture.*

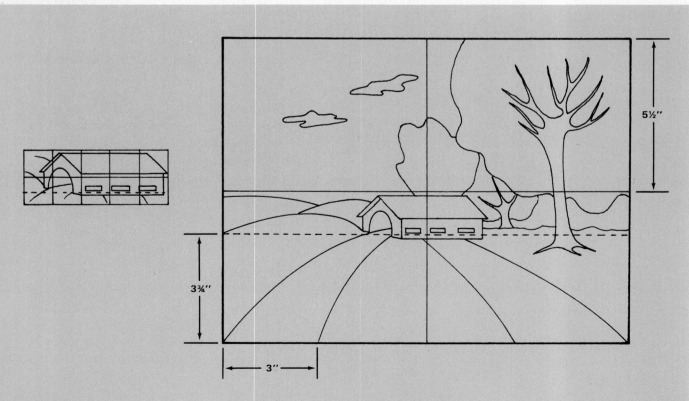

out two rocks of gray felt. Trace and cut the roof of the bridge out of red felt; the rest of the bridge and windows out of dark brown. (A pair of manicuring scissors will be helpful for windows.) Cut out a narrow strip of tan and glue it behind windows. Trace and cut out turquoise water and three light-blue pieces of sky, disregarding clouds. From white felt, cut out clouds.

Next, cut contact paper into two pieces, each 6″ x 12″. Then cut one piece into two pieces, each 6″ x 6″. Peel off backing on larger piece and place it over black felt. Cut out tree trunks through paper and felt (this will give added strength to the felt around branches). Cut out inside of bridge.

Peel off backing and press a smaller piece of contact paper onto apple-green felt. Cut out leaves and stems. Then peel off backing from last piece of contact paper and place over light-yellow felt. Cut out small ovals for flowers. With a red pen or marking pencil, make centers for flowers.

## Assembling and Framing the Picture

The picture is now ready to be assembled. Place glue around edges of wrong side of larger sky piece. Fit into upper left-hand corner of picture. Press in place with hands. Glue clouds over sky. Glue apple-green tree in place in upper right-hand corner. Glue blue sky and the remaining two trees in place; glue dark-green grass, turquoise water, tan roads, bridge, and roof in place. Glue trunks of trees and inside of bridge where indicated. Glue flowers and leaves where shown or as desired.

Place picture inside frame. If cardboard is not strong enough, cut additional pieces the same size until back of frame is filled in. Secure picture in place with small nails or with masking tape. Attach two small picture screws to back of frame about 6″ apart. Draw picture wire through and fasten by twisting several times.

**Figure 9. The assembled picture of a covered bridge is framed and ready for hanging.**

# CHRISTMAS STOCKING

To make a Christmas stocking that is 14½" long, the materials required are: 2 sheets of red felt and 1 sheet each of green, white, and chartreuse; 1 spool each of red, green, and white thread; glue; a large-eyed, sharp-pointed embroidery needle; 1 skein of green six-strand embroidery thread.

## Cutting and Naming

Enlarge the pattern illustrated to actual size. Cut one sock piece from green felt. Place green sock over 2 sheets of red felt with edges even at top and at least 1/2" of red showing around remainder of sock. Pin or staple pieces together. Carefully cut out red felt, leaving 1/2" around all sides except the top. If a cutting error is made, even up cutting to 1/4" around. For the cuff, cut a sheet of white felt in half. Then cut one piece in half again to make two pieces, each 3" x 9". Cut off a 3" piece at one end of each strip to make them each 3" x 6".

Next, write lightly with pencil the desired name on one cuff of the sock. Or, write the name in pencil on paper and pin the paper to the cuff, leaving at least a 3/4" margin of felt all around. Cut the six-strand embroidery thread into 1-yard lengths and embroider the name in a chain stitch (see Crewel article) onto cuff (through paper and felt if paper pattern is used). Keep stitches to 1/8" or smaller. If a name contains the letter "i," dot the letter with a French Knot (see Crewel).

## Sewing and Trimming

Now, remove staples or pins from top of sock only. Place white signature cuff across top of front, overlapping cuff 1/2" on right side of sock. With white thread sew across top of sock, starting and ending at red section. Attach other white cuff

*Figure 10. This pattern is easily enlarged to make a delightful Christmas stocking. Various shades of green felt are added to the red background for a holiday feeling.*

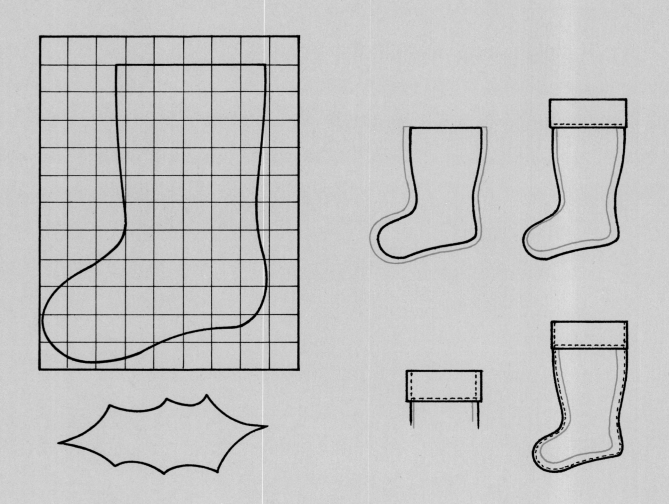

*Figure 11. Other Christmas decorations which can be made from felt include these ornaments. Railroad cars, a horse, and a reindeer should prove especially popular with children. The Santa figure has universal appeal to people of all ages. Note the liberal use of sequins and decorative braid. (Courtesy, Bucilla.)*

in the same way. Cut threads and bring to inside of work to end off. Pin sides of cuffs together, then repin top of sock together. With white thread sew a seam at each side of cuff in line with outside edge of red. Trim white felt to 1/4" from side seam. Cuff should extend 1/4" at each side of sock.

With green thread in the needle of the sewing machine and red in bobbin, sew a 1/8" seam around green sock on right side of work (or hand sew with two strands of green thread). Try to keep width from seam to edge of green as even as possible.

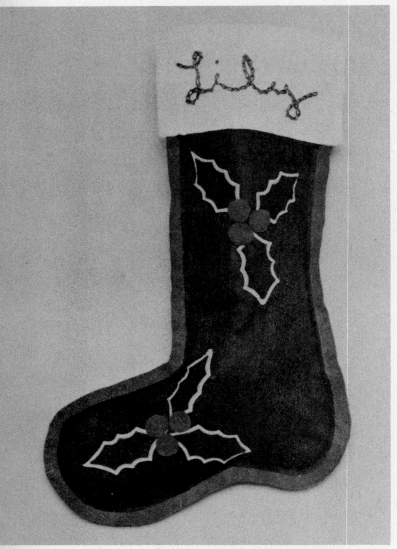

**Figure 12. A personalized Christmas stocking is a popular gift item for felt craftsmen. Use traditional or offbeat colors.**

Finally, for trimming, use a small button for a pattern and draw six small circles onto red felt. Cut these out; they will be used as holly berries. Using the pattern shown for a holly leaf, draw six leaves onto paper. Staple or pin paper to green felt and cut out the six leaves through paper and felt. Glue the leaves onto a piece of chartreuse felt and cut around leaves, leaving 1/8" of chartreuse showing. Glue leaves and berries to sock.

## FLOWER PILLOW

Materials necessary for this pillow, which is 16" in diameter, are: 2 sheets each of light-orange and medium light-orange felt and 4 sheets of dark orange; 1/2 yard of 72" width of medium dark-orange felt; 2 spools of orange thread to match darkest shade; regular sewing needle; 14" knife-edge pillow form or stuffing; 1 large white or clear plastic button to be covered; large thumb tack or T-pin; short pencil; large sheet of paper; small compass; ruler; and string.

### Making the Pattern

Place a large sheet of paper on a padded surface, such as an ironing board, drawing board, or corrugated cardboard. With ruler make markings at 16" width and at 8" for center. Push thumb tack part way into the center. Tie string around thumb tack, extending string at least 12" to side. Tie string to pencil at the 16" mark to form a compass. Holding thumb tack in center, draw a circle 16" in diameter. Be careful to hold pencil straight to make a perfect circle.

Using a small compass or the string and pencil, make a second circle on same paper 4½" in diameter (2¼" to the edge from the center marking).

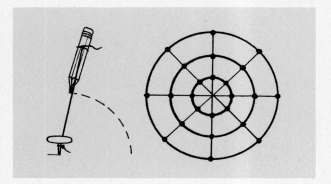

Make a third circle inside of the second 3" in diameter (1½" to the edge from the center marking). Make a final circle 1" in diameter (1/2" to the edge from the center marking). Remove paper from padded surface and cut out around the 16" *circle only*. Fold in half, then in half again, and in half again, making eight sections.

Mark positions for joining petals by marking off four quarters on the smallest circle and eight sections on each of the 3" and 4½" circles. Set aside.

For the large petals, make a pattern from paper or lightweight cardboard following the diagram. Draw lines 4½" in width and 4" in height. Mark center points at each side. From 1" on each side of center point at top, draw a curved line to the center point at each side. From 1¼" on each side of center point at bottom, draw a curved line up to

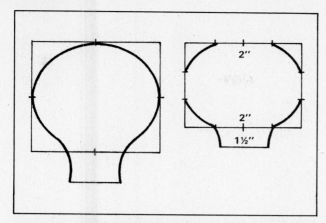

*Figure 13. Use these patterns for the large and small petals on the flower pillow. Lightweight cardboard is the best material for making the pattern.*

side markings. Extend lines at bottom down 1" to a 2" width, curving slightly. Cut out large petal pattern. For the small petals, draw lines on cardboard 4" wide by 3" high. Mark center of each side from 1" on each side of center point at top, draw a curved line to 1" above center point on each side. From 1" on each side of center point at bottom, draw a curved line up to 1" below center point on each side. Extend bottom lines down 3/4" curving slightly to 1½" width. Cut out small petal pattern.

## Cutting and Sewing

Now, pin or staple circle pattern to a double piece of felt from the 1/2-yard length. Cut out two 16" circles. On one of the circles, push pencil or pen through the marked points on each of the inner circles to mark positions for joining petals. Remove pattern.

Cut all sheets of felt in half lengthwise, then fold each sheet of felt in half across width and cut again, making four pieces, each 4½" x 6". Pin or staple two pieces together and cut out *double* petals. Make four small petals in light orange, four large petals in medium light orange, and eight large petals in dark orange. From the remainder of the medium dark-orange felt, cut out four large double petals. Using another scrap of the same color, cut out cover for large button. Draw button onto felt, then cut around felt 1/2" from circle.

Starting and ending at bottom, carefully stitch around all sides of petals, making a 1/4" seam. Trim seams to 1/8".

## Assembling the Pillow

To assemble the pillow, place the pillow form between the two 16" circles with marked side of

*Figure 14. Simple pattern instructions were followed to make this attractive pillow.*

felt facing out. Pin, then baste edges together. (If loose stuffing is used, cut out two 15" circles from white fabric. Sew 1/2" seam around, leaving 3" open. Turn inside out and stuff. Sew the 3" opening together.)

Bring needle threaded with six-strand embroidery thread between the two layers of felt. Join pieces by working a running stitch through the two thicknesses 1" in from edges; keep stitches to about 1/4" on each side. Tie and hide ends between the two layers of felt. Attach another six strands and stitch over the running stitch on one side of pillow, then end off. Attach another six strands of thread and stitch other side in the same way.

To attach the petals, draw the end of a large dark-orange petal together with a running stitch and sew to marking on the eight points of the 4½" circle. Alternating medium dark and medium light orange, sew petals to each marking on the 3" circle. Sew light-orange petals to the four markings on smallest circle or as close to center as possible. With needle and double strand of thread, make a running stitch inside edge of piece for button cover. Place over button, drawing as tightly as possible. Tie ends together. Sew button to top of pillow at center. Clip the 1" border around pillow 1/2" apart, clipping to within 1/4" of joining.

## CIRCUS ELEPHANT

The materials required to make an elephant 9" x 16" are: 6 sheets medium pink felt and 1 sheet each of purple, white, and red; 1 spool matching pink thread and 1 spool each of purple, white, and black; 1 tube each of gold and silver bugle beads; 1 yard of 1/2" silver braid; 24 3/4" red oblong beads; 24 turquoise beads which are 3 millimeters round; 12 small and 2 large pearls; 32 turquoise drop beads; 2 yards pink yarn for tail; 2 black 1/2" buttons for eyes; cardboard for stiffening legs; stuffing; beading needle; and glue.

### Cutting Patterns

Enlarge patterns to correct size. Pin or staple pattern for body to two sheets of pink felt; cut out both pieces. Fold one sheet of pink in half lengthwise. Pin or staple pattern for head to felt and cut out two pieces. Make a tracing of pattern for ear. Fold one sheet of felt in half widthwise and pin or

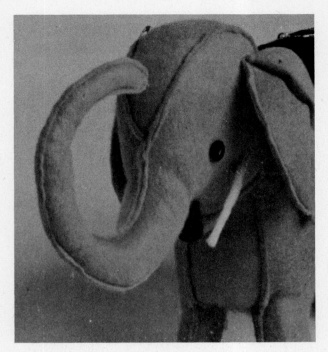

**Figure 15. Detail on the elephant's head is fairly simple, consisting of eyes and tusks. For some animal projects, the craftsman may want to include more elaborate detailing.**

staple two patterns for ears to felt. Cut out four pieces. Pin or staple pattern for underpart of body to one sheet of felt and cut out. Place a pin for marker where indicated on diagram. From remainder of same sheet, pin or staple breast strip to felt and cut out. Again place a pin for marker where indicated. From last sheet of pink felt, pin or staple pattern for back and hind insert to felt and cut out. Place a pin or marker where indicated.

### Sewing

Matching markers, pin breast strip to front of underpart of body. Pin strip for back and hind insert to back of underpart of body. Sew strips in place, making 1/4" seam (seam will be wrong side of work, to be placed inside of elephant). Pin a head piece to one body piece and sew a 1/4" seam. Attach other head and body pieces in the same way (seam side will again be wrong side of work). All other seams will be made on right side of work and trimmed.

Pin around legs of underpart of body to legs of elephant, matching pieces carefully. Baste around legs. Pin breast strip to front of elephant up to mouth opening and baste in place. Pin and

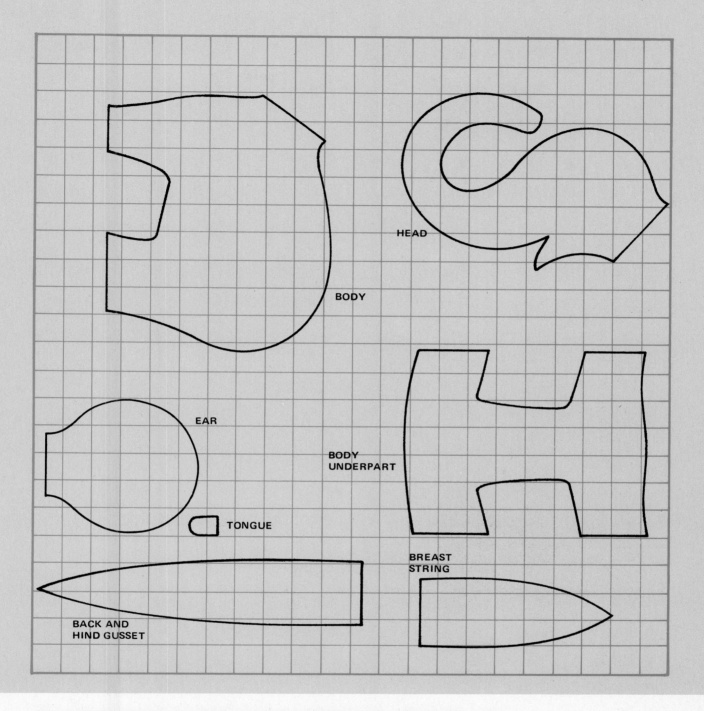

HEAD

BODY

EAR

BODY
UNDERPART

TONGUE

BREAST
STRING

BACK AND
HIND GUSSET

*Figure 16. The felt circus elephant is designed from simple patterns that can be enlarged to the correct size. The patterns should be pinned or stapled to the felt to insure accurate measurements.*

baste one side of back and hind insert strip around elephant, ending in a point at back of head. Pin and baste at other side around hind quarters, leaving one seam open across top back of elephant for stuffing. Pin and baste around head and trunk, ending at open mouth on other side. Mouth section will be sewn later.

Carefully sew 1/4″ seams around elephant, leaving unbasted section open across back. Tie threads at beginning and end of seams, drawing

*Figure 18. A pink elephant made of felt is a charming and whimsical gift. Note the elaborate ornamentation on the blanket; this gives an exotic flavor to the finished project.*

ends to inside of elephant. *Do not trim seams before stuffing.*

With needle and thread sew at each side of mouth by overcasting edges. Pin and baste two ear pieces together and sew a 1/4" seam around entire ear. Tie threads and draw to inside of ear. Trim to about 1/8" from seam and set aside.

To make tusks, fold and pin a piece of white felt in half. With pencil, lightly draw a line 2½" long. Leaving 1/2" at edge, lightly draw another line that joins the first line at a point, making a long triangle. Make a second long triangle about 1" apart from first. Sew triangles on lines, using white thread. Trim 1/8" from seam and set aside.

## Stuffing and Finishing

For stuffing, start with trunk and, using a pencil to push filling, stuff firmly. Stuff head, pushing the filling into mouth and chin area. Cut four pieces of stiff cardboard about 1¼" wide and 6" long. Put a piece inside of each leg. Stuff legs firmly, then stuff body.

Finally, make a fold in each ear at straight end and tack in place. Sew ear to each side of head, 3/4" down from top. Sew button for eye to each side of head, using black thread. With white thread sew tusks to each side of face as shown. Cut a tongue from red felt and glue over mouth section.

For tail, cut yarn into three strands. Fold strands in half and tack or pin to a board. Braid strands for about 2". Tie knot. Sew folded end to back of elephant. Trim seams carefully to 1/8".

*Figure 19. The blanket pattern is decorated with sequins or beads on the small floral areas. "Invisible" or nylon thread should be used for all sewing.*

To make the blanket, first enlarge pattern. Use purple thread or invisible nylon thread for all sewing. Cut a piece of purple felt 6″ x 8″. Sew silver braid around the four sides, cutting strips the length of each side or end, plus 1″. Turn under 1/2″ at each end. Sew silver bugle beads down center of braid. Sew 16 turquoise drop beads across each short end of blanket. Sew clusters of turquoise beads where indicated in diagram. Sew two large pearls where indicated, then form six petalled flowers around them, using large red oval beads. Sew remaining red oval beads where indicated. Sew small pearl beads to top of red beads. Sew gold bugle beads in a line where indicated. Place blanket on elephant and tack in place at back of head and at back of elephant.

## For Additional Reading

Janvier, Jacqueline, **Felt Crafting,** Sterling, 1970.

Moloney, Joan, **Making Toys for Children,** Drake, 1972.

Morton, Brenda, **Soft Toys Made Easy** Taplinger, 1972.

# Relief Printing

**Although one of the oldest forms of printing, relief printing offers the twentieth-century craftsman a simple, effective, hand-printing method.**

The development of the relief printing process can be traced back to the first century A. D., when the Chinese cut designs in stones or wood and pressed the images into wax tablets to create a signature. Eventually, they realized that these wax seals could be dipped in ink and would reproduce when pressed onto cloth. In the sixth century, the Egyptians are known to have used this printing process on fabric. Simultaneously, the Chinese were printing on blocks and transferring the work to paper.

Early relief printing was done with stamps, similar in size to present-day rubber stamps and therefore limiting the size of the created impression. It was not until the eighth century that the first full pages of type were printed. This was done by the Japanese, who discovered that a design could be transferred by rubbing the back of paper with a tool known as a baren, a stiff pad made by wrapping a large bamboo leaf around a coil of bamboo

rope. The first printed picture was done by the artist Wang Chieh in the ninth century and is presently in the British Museum in London.

In Europe, relief printing also began with the use of seals and extended to textile printing in the sixth century. These early examples were primarily decorative patterns; pictorial images did not begin to appear until the late fourteenth and early fifteenth centuries. These, however, were still printed on cloth. During the fifteenth century, paper became available to the Europeans. With Johann Gutenberg's invention of the printing press and movable type, the need for woodcuts as decoration and illustration in books became immense.

After the invention of the press, block printing expanded greatly. Early woodcuts were mostly concerned with religious subjects. They were used on holy cards and devotional pictures for private prayer. Woodcuts of patron saints were

*Figure 1. The woodcut "Riders on the Four Horses from the Apocalypse" was created by the German artist Albrecht Durer. The fine detailing on this print can be seen in a close-up of the angel (opposite).*

even sewn inside travelers' clothing or pasted inside lids of trunks. However, the majority of the early religious prints were made by monks who sold them to travelers as mementos.

As time went on, people began to purchase prints merely for enjoyment. Middle class merchants in Europe could not afford original paintings or sculptures by famous artists, so they bought the less expensive prints made by the same artists. It is because a print is a relatively inexpensive piece of art that woodcuts and relief printing have continued to flourish since the Middle Ages.

The first of the great woodcut artists was Albrecht Durer (1471-1528), a German who used woodcut printing to its full potential. His work, ranging from religious subjects to everyday themes to fantasy, was linear in character and always in black and white.

Color printing with wood blocks was developed in Japan and began with the Ekiyo-E school of art

in 1680 (Ekiyo-E means pictures of the floating world, or everyday life). The first Ekiyo-E prints were done in black and white and hand-colored with red watercolor paint after the print was dry. As more colors of ink were invented, blocks of wood were cut for particular colors. Thus the art of color printing began to be highly developed and prints were done in as many as 10 or 12 colors.

By 1880, this process was so common in Japan that dinnerware exported to Europe was wrapped in this kind of paper. In fact, these prints became collector's items and their style became very influential in Europe. Color came to be used even more in European artistry and certainly the brightly colored linoleum and woodblock prints of today are directly related to the first Japanese color prints. Indeed, some of the world's greatest artists, including Picasso, Matisse, Gauguin, and Winslow Homer, have employed relief printing methods, widely used by contemporary artists.

*Figure 2. The woodcut "Lovers in the Snow" (left) is the work of the Japanese artist Harunobu. (Courtesy, Honolulu Academy of Arts, Honolulu, Hawaii.)*

*Figure 3. "The Buxheim St. Christopher" (above) is a medieval woodcut portraying a religious scene. (Courtesy, The John Rylands University Library, Manchester, England.)*

## Common Terms Used In Relief Printing

**Bite:** slang term referring to etching (see below).

**Block:** general term referring to surface being printed.

**Caustic:** strong base used for etching linoleum.

**Collagraph:** block made by adding materials to a surface.

**Edition:** a group of identical prints.

**Etching:** the chemical removal of material from a surface.

**Fixed Sheet System:** a registration system in which the sheet remains in a fixed position until all colors are printed on it.

**Found Object:** any object not created by the craftsman.

**Kento:** Japanese registration system involving an L-shaped notch and a long notch at opposite corners of the block.

**Lost Block:** color printing method that involves the destruction of part of the image after each printing.

**Printmaking:** the process and practice of making multiple original works of art.

**Proof:** trial impression made of a block.

**Registration:** proper arrangement of colors and shapes printed from separate blocks onto the same page.

**Relief Printing:** surface printing, or the printing of images from a surface which has a design cut into it.

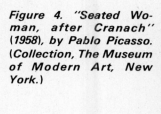

*Figure 4. "Seated Woman, after Cranach" (1958), by Pablo Picasso. (Collection, The Museum of Modern Art, New York.)*

**Resist:** any material which will prevent a caustic from etching a surface.

**Rice Paper:** a variety of thin, tough handmade papers produced in Japan from plant fibers.

**Rolling Up:** the application of ink with a roller to the block.

**Split Fountain:** a method of rolling up several colors on one roller in a rainbow effect.

**Woodcut:** print made from a wooden block.

## Basic Equipment And Supplies

Relief printing is, perhaps, one of the most popular current art forms. It is simple, inexpensive, and gives immediate results. Most of the equipment and materials listed below can be found at local hardware stores, lumber yards, or arts and crafts stores. For items not usually available locally, specific sources are given.

## TOOLS

1. Baren. A Japanese hand-printing tool made of a hemp coil covered with a banana leaf. The American variety is usually a smooth block of wood.

2. Bench hook. A board with a block attached to the top surface at the back and another at the bottom surface at the front. It is used to hold the block steady while cutting.

3. Brayers. Small rollers of varying hardness used to apply ink to the block.

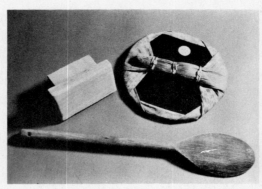

*Figure 5. Supplies for relief printing include brayers (left), barens (above), and an electric drill with attachments (right).*

**4.** Brushes. Various sizes used to apply wax, shellac, varnish, and other liquid materials.

**5.** C-clamp. A clamp used to hold the block to the table while cutting.

**6.** Drill bits. Small drilling and grinding tools which are attached to an electric drill to create various textures on the block.

**7.** Electric drill. Any one of the various makes of power drills.

**8.** Gouges. Cutting tools available in a variety of styles; used to cut images into the block.

**9.** Grinding bits. Small circular file-like bits used in an electric drill for texture and removal of surface area.

**10.** Knives. Any type with a straight edge and long handle; used to outline the forms on a block.

**11.** L-stop. An L-shaped piece of wood clamped to a table to hold the block in place while cutting.

**12.** Mat knife. A knife with a large handle and a small replaceable blade.

**13.** Propane torch. A simple torch used to burn a surface and melt wax.

**14.** Putty knife. A small spatula with a wide flat blade used to spread modeling paste.

**15.** Spatula.

**16.** Wire brush.

**17.** Wooden spoon.

**18.** X-acto knife. A small pen-like knife used for delicate cutting.

## SUPPLIES

**1.** Burnt plate oil. Used with ink to alter its consistency and transparency.

**2.** Clothes lines. The simplest method for drying wet prints.

**3.** Fabric.

**4.** Glass. A sheet of glass is used on which to roll up ink because it is very smooth and easy to clean.

**5.** Glue. White craft glue is used to glue objects to the collagraph. Lepage's glue is used to paste the design to the block.

**6.** Gouache. A water-soluble paint often used as ink.

**7.** Ink.

**8.** Linoleum. Only true linoleum which is usually gray or Indian red in color can be used. Most decorative floor coverings are not true linoleum.

**9.** Linseed oil. Used with an oil-based ink to change the consistency and degree of color.

**10.** Masonite. A compressed wood-like substance made from sawdust and used as a base for collagraphs.

**11.** Mat board. A decorative cardboard usually used in framing.

**12.** Mineral spirits. A solvent for wax and ink.

**13.** Modeling paste. A non-brittle, plaster-like substance useful for textures in collagraphs.

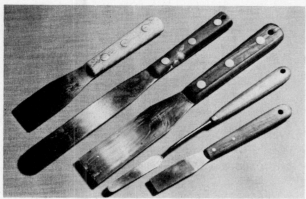

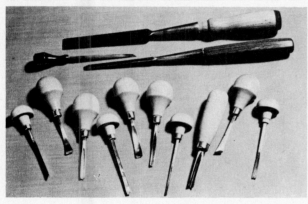

*Figure 6. Other important supplies include putty knives and spatulas (top), knives (center), and gouges (bottom). All are available in a variety of sizes.*

**14.** Oven cleaner. An easily available caustic used in etching linoleum.

**15.** Paint thinner. Used as a solvent for oil-based paints.

**16.** Plastic wood. A wood-like filler used to correct mistakes on a block.

**17.** Plywood. Layered wood useful as a block.

**18.** Poster board. Compressed cardboard that is useful in collagraphs.

**19.** Rag paper. Good paper for heavy and coarse printing.

**20.** Rice paper. Good paper for more delicate prints, although available in various thicknesses. Cost ranges from $0.10 to $1.00 per sheet.

**21.** Shellac. Used to seal and protect the block from ink and turpentine.

**22.** Sodium hydroxide. Used to etch linoleum.

**23.** Tempera. A water-based paint often used as ink.

**24.** Varnish. Used as a resist in etching linoleum.

**25.** Wax. Paraffin wax is used as a resist in etching linoleum.

**26.** Wood. A variety of woods are used for block printing. Cherry and poplar are best; pine is available in larger sizes, is inexpensive, and easy to use.

## Basic Procedures

There are several basic approaches to relief printing — woodcut printing, linoleum printing, collagraphs, and the use of found objects. With all these methods, however, there is one similarity: the print is taken from the raised surface of the blocks. The only difference in the various methods is the way the print is created — either by cutting into the block with a gouge or by adding onto the block with glue. All the procedures are simple and basic and can be used in various combinations to create literally hundreds of different effects.

*Figure 7. This drawing illustrates the "mountain and valley" effect in relief printing. As the brayer is rolled over the block, it inks only the mountains and not the valleys.*

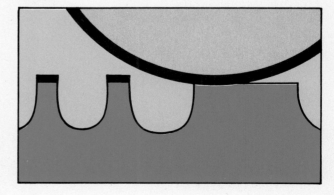

The following discussion deals first with the differences in creating blocks in various materials. It is followed by a general discussion of procedures for registration and printing used in all media of relief printing.

## THE LINOLEUM BLOCK

The simplest method of relief printing is linoleum printing because linoleum is soft and easy to cut, yet rigid enough to print from.

### Designing the Image

The first step in making any print is to decide upon its design. Do a drawing first on paper rather than on the block itself. Changes and variations in design can be made easily on paper — once the block is cut it is difficult, if not impossible, to change the design. After the design is finished, it can be transferred on to the block in one of several ways: (1) redraw the design on the block with a felt-tip pen; (2) place carbon paper on top of the block, place the design on top of the carbon, and trace over it; (3) glue the design to the block with a water-soluble glue. Any of these methods works well, and once the design is secured onto the block, the cutting may begin.

### Arranging Bench Supports

Before cutting the image, it is best to construct a simple bench hook or L-stop to prevent the block from moving while printing (see "Basic Equipment"). The block may also be clamped to the table with a C-clamp.

It is usually easiest to work on a block at the corner of a table because the cutting can be done from two directions without having to move the block. When working from the corner, however, use an L-stop or C-clamp and not a bench hook, for the latter only offers support while carving in one direction. The time spent arranging these supports is saved many times over while cutting. The height of the table should be roughly that of a kitchen counter, as cutting is always done from a standing position.

### Cutting the Block

The cutting of linoleum has several advantages over wood. The first, as stated before, is the relative softness of the material; second, linoleum does not split. Remember while cutting that the amount of resistance or pressure varies with the depth of the cut. Often while pushing hard, the gouge will slip when it reaches another cut-out area. To avoid this, ease the pressure. The gouge will also slip if the angle of the gouge is not consistent and allowed to decrease towards the surface. Because of this tendency to slip (even among experienced cutters), the cutting should *always* be done away from the cutter and the opposite hand should never be in front of the gouge at any distance.

Keep in mind that what is removed will remain white on the print. The choice of gouges to be used depends on the area to be removed. Small areas are removed with small U-shaped or V-shaped gouges. Larger areas are removed with flat gouges or large U-shaped gouges. In cutting an

*Figure 8. Use a bench-hook (left) or an L-stop (right) to hold the block securely on the table.*

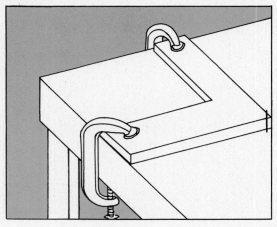
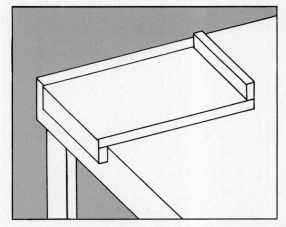

area of line, the angle of the cut should slope away from the image, and the cut should be wider at the base than it is on the surface. This gives the area or line greater support and strength. It is not necessary to cut away all the linoleum — the depth of a cut should never exceed one-eighth of an inch.

Several times during cutting it is good idea to make a trial impression to see how the image is developing. What is removed cannot be re-placed, so when in doubt, experiment with a proof.

## Etching

Another method of preparing a linoleum block (without cutting) is to use a caustic solution to etch the image into the surface. The results are striking and much different from those derived by cutting the block. The procedure involves using sodium hydroxide, which dissolves linoleum, and a wax that resists the action of the caustic in other areas.

Transfer the design either by painting melted wax on the areas which are to remain as surface or by covering the entire surface with wax and scraping away those areas which are to be removed. The wax serves as a resist and keeps the caustic from affecting those areas that remain as surface areas.

The next step is to etch the linoleum. The most practical and available source of caustic is oven cleaner. The variety in a jar is preferable to a spray because, with brush application, more control is possible. The caustic is simply painted liberally over the entire block and allowed to stand. The depth of the bite depends upon the time involved: a light bite takes two to three hours; a medium bite, four to six hours; a deep bite, twelve hours. Since the strength of the caustic is diminished by time, it should be washed off and replaced every few hours. It is advisable to wear gloves.

By controlling the depth of the bite in various areas, many effects can be achieved. If one area is covered with wax and an adjoining area is etched for two hours, the resulting image, when a print is taken, will be a black area and a gray area with a thin white line between. Lightly bitten areas will print as gray areas of grainy dots while deeply bitten areas will not print at all because they are too deep to pick up ink. (If fine white lines are required, a quick-drying varnish instead of wax can be used as a resist, scratched into with a nee-dle, and etched for several hours. This will give remarkable results.) After the image has been bitten sufficiently, remove the block to the sink and scrub with soap, water, and a small scrub brush until no more particles appear. Then melt off the wax with a propane torch and wash with

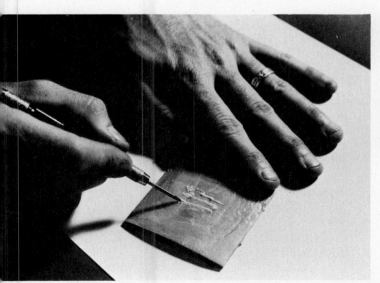

*Figure 9. Scrape the linoleum block to remove appropriate areas (above). Note the difference in the effects obtained by varying the time that the caustic is left on the block (above center and above right). Another means of introducing texture on a linoleum block is to etch thin lines with a fine needle (right).*

mineral spirits to remove the wax residue. Various experimentation in this area will create a variety of effects.

### Miscellaneous Techniques

Aside from the two methods mentioned above, a variety of other methods can be used. Essentially any mark that can be made into the surface of the linoleum will make a representative mark on the print. What would happen if screening were placed on the block and pounded with a hammer? What about a heavy wire brush or an electric drill with a variety of bits? Sandpaper, pounded or rubbed, creates an image. The possibilities are only as limited as the imagination of the craftsman.

## THE WOODCUT

The main advantage of using wood for the block is that the surface is hard and capable of holding more detail. It also has, depending on the variety, natural wood grain texture. Wood is easily repaired if some area is accidentally removed and is adaptable to a variety of techniques for creating images.

There are many varieties of wood which may be used. As mentioned earlier, the best are probably cherry or poplar. They are harder than pine but not nearly as hard or brittle as maple or oak. Both have relatively smooth grains and cut easily and evenly with a minimum of splitting and splintering. Pine, which is inexpensive, is available at almost any lumber yard and often is glued together in planks as wide as 20 inches (if a large print is planned). Clear pine is soft and easy to work. It is very good for rough, textural approaches, such as scratching or denting, as well as for finer more detailed images. Pine is often the beginner's favorite.

Various kinds of plywood are very handy for large prints and, because of its layered construction, the removal of excess material is simplified. One simply cuts through the first layer and peels it off. The type chosen depends upon the surface desired.

*Figure 10. "Bay of Cancer" (below) is a color linoleum cut by the author, Charles Guerin. Also shown is one of the three blocks used to make the print (left).*

*Fiture 11. Many craftsmen like to experiment by printing the grain of wood. These three examples show the variety of effects that can be obtained with wood. Brushing the wood with a wire brush intensifies the grain and adds interest to the print.*

## Cutting the Woodcut

Cutting a woodblock is somewhat different from cutting linoleum because wood has a tendency to split, especially when cut against the grain. To avoid unwanted splitting, cut around the form with an X-acto knife or mat knife. Then, if a split occurs while clearing an area with a gouge, it will be stopped when it reaches the perimeter of one of the permanent areas. If a split does occur in an important area, simply apply white craft glue to the piece, replace it, and weight it down for approximately an hour. Plastic wood can also be used. When dry, sand lightly and the repair will go unnoticed.

## Texture

With many craftsmen, wood is chosen for its grain. When printing grain, there are several methods, depending upon the boldness desired. A very light and subtle grain effect is produced simply by printing the wood surface. To achieve a slightly more vivid reproduction, brush the surface with a wire brush several times. This removes the softer wood fibers, leaving the harder ones in relief. If still more relief is desired, lightly burn the surface with a propane torch before brushing with the wire brush. Grainy wood can be obtained from old weathered barns or fences.

Since wood dents easily, it is possible to create many images, designs, and patterns by ham-mering hard objects into the wood, such as tacks, pins, staples, punches, washers, or screws.

Besides pounding, punching, or denting the surface, scratching, scraping, and buffing also create textures. There are a variety of grinding and scraping bits designed to fit an electric drill which make the work fairly simple and which create new and unique textures at the same time. In working with wood, it should be remembered that almost anything can be used as a tool.

## THE COLLAGRAPH OR THE BUILT UP BLOCK

All the methods previously described involved the cutting or scraping away of material. With the collagraph, the craftsman creates the surface by adding materials and has the advantage of using various textures and shapes. In the easiest collagraph method, shapes made from poster board (compressed cardboard) or mat board are glued with white craft glue to masonite. It is advisable when using any kind of paper or cardboard that the finished block be given a coat of shellac to seal the surface and to prevent it from absorbing ink or turpentine during clean-up.

With the collagraph, virtually any flat object can be mounted to the block to create images. Fabric is frequently used because there is such a large variety of textures. It is often wise to glue the fabric to illustration board (*i.e.,* poster board or mat board) with Elmer's glue and then cut and

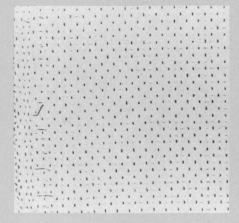

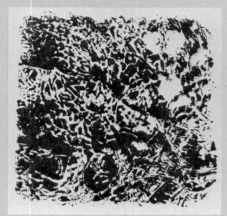

*Figure 12. Interesting effects may be achieved in colla-graphs by experimenting with a variety of textures. Proofs are shown for two: screening (far left) and tinfoil (left).*

mount the shape to the masonite block. Again, shellac should be used to seal the surface.

Another versatile material is modeling paste. This is a mixture of acrylic and powdered marble that dries hard like plaster yet is not breakable. Begin with a sheet of masonite. On the rough side, using a spatula or putty knife, smooth on a layer of modeling paste about one-eighth inch thick. While the paste is wet, the surface texture can be altered with the fingers or a hard tool. It may also be altered by pressing in a texture with such items as leaves or twigs, grass, lace, keys, or coins. After the paste is dry, coat it with shellac and allow it to dry before proofing. Once dry it is possible to go back into the surface with a knife or gouge and remove areas or create lines. Remember to coat the surface again with shellac because turpentine and paint thinners will weaken the paste.

*Figure 13. An interesting texture can be created by printing mat board (below). Modeling paste can be used to create a textured effect on a block, too (below right).*

It should be remembered that many of these various methods can be used together on the same block or separately, depending on the imagination of the craftsman.

## FOUND OBJECTS

Found object printing is often very fascinating because one never knows what to expect. Almost anything that has a relief or a textured surface can be printed: bricks, manhole covers, saw blades, ends of logs, concrete, coins, or keys. Found objects allow for maximum use of the imagination and experimentation.

## COLOR PRINTING

Color printing can be approached in several ways. The first is to make a separate block for each color and print them on the same page by registering the page to each block (see "Registration" below). This method permits a variety of effects because each block can be unique. The

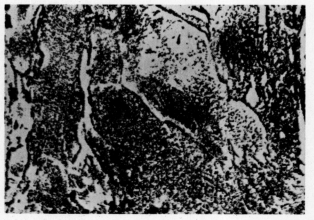

combination of various color blocks on the same page is interesting because the results cannot be completely planned and each new impression is different.

Another method of color printing is the lost block technique, a process which ultimately destroys the block's entire surface by the time the last image is completed. Although this sounds somewhat complex, it is really quite simple.

**1.** Choose the order in which the colors will be printed — usually light to dark.

**2.** Cut away those areas which are to remain white, and print the first color.

**3.** Cut away the areas which are to remain the first color and print the next darkest color.

**4.** Cut away those areas which are to remain the latter color and print the next darkest color. This procedure is continued until the last color is printed; it has the advantage of many colors being printed with only one block.

A third method of color printing is to ink separate areas of the same block with different colors, either for the same impression or for different impressions. Still another very simple, yet very dramatic method is called the split fountain. This method involves rolling up two or more colors on

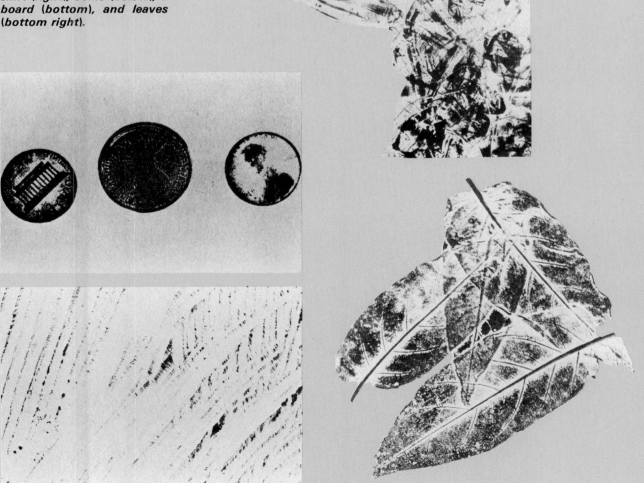

*Figure 14. Printing found objects can yield offbeat effects. Examples shown are a shirt (right), coins (below), a board (bottom), and leaves (bottom right).*

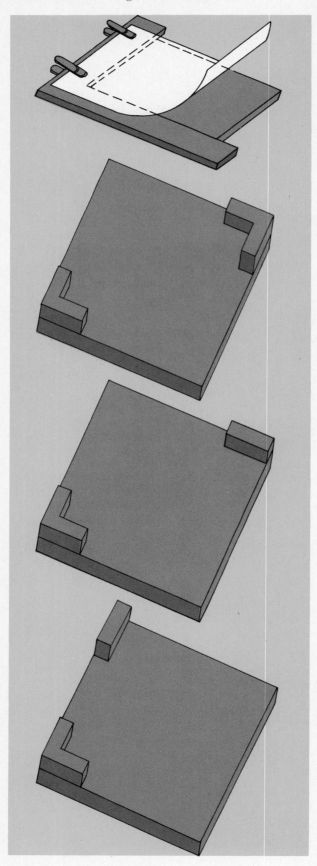

*Figure 15. Registration systems include (from top) the fixed-sheet type and a variety of Kento types. In the fixed-sheet system, clothespins hold the paper to the block. All three Kento systems shown use notches and stops to hold the paper. Two L-shaped, or Kento, notches may be used. Or, one L-shaped notch can be placed diagonally opposite a long flat notch. Still another variation involves placing the L-shaped notch and the long notch on the same side of the rectangular block.*

the same roller at the same time and letting them blend together. The roller, however, must be larger than the area to be covered because the ink is always rolled in the same direction. If the colors were not rolled this way, they would completely mix and defeat the purpose.

## REGISTRATION

Registration refers to any method used to align the paper and the block to assure proper positioning of the image on the paper in relation to a previously printed color. One technique, a Japanese method called *kento,* involves cutting the image into a block that is about two inches larger than the image. This will allow for a two-inch border. At one corner an L-shaped notch is cut, and at the opposite corner a flat notch is cut. On each block of a color print, these notches are positioned in exactly the same place. When printing, one corner of the paper is placed in the L-shaped notch or *kento* and the opposite edge is butted up against the long notch. The impression is then made. There are other variations on this system: if each piece of paper is the same size, two *kentos* at opposite corners can be used; or the long notch can be placed on the same side as the *kento.*

One disadvantage of the *kento* system is that it is only practical where a larger piece of wood is available; it cannot be used with an image that covers the entire block. On the other hand, the *kento* method should always be used for the lost block method.

When printing an image which covers the entire block, the best system is the fixed sheet system. Here, an L-stop is used with the sheet attached with two clips to one end. With this system the paper is raised and each consecutive block is inserted against the L-stop and printed. The paper should only be raised between blocks, never

*Figure 16. This is a famous woodcut by the Japanese artist Hokusai, "Fuji Seen in the Distance Below a Great Breaking Wave of the Sea." (Courtesy, The Art Institute of Chicago.)*

removed, for this destroys the registration. It is not possible to use this system with the lost block techniques because all colors are printed in order.

## PAPER FOR RELIEF PRINTING

The choice of paper for relief printing is important because the printing process involves vigorous rubbing on the back of the paper. The paper most frequently used is handmade Japanese rice paper. This comes in various sizes, textures, colors, and degrees of thickness and absorbency. In choosing paper, keep in mind the nature of the print and the block. If the print is smooth and delicate, use a thin paper with a smooth surface.

One hundred percent rag papers, either handmade or machine made, are especially useful when printing many colors. They are heavier than rice paper and hold more ink without becoming heavy. They are also extremely durable. Experi-

ment with papers until their various effects become familiar.

## INKS AND OILS

There are two basic kinds of ink: water-based and oil-based. Water-based inks are easy to work with and to clean up. They do, however, tend to bleed into the paper and work best when used on slightly dampened rice paper. Oil-based inks are more commonly used because they have a greater versatility in terms of thickness and transparency. These are thick inks which are usually thinned with linseed oil or burnt plate oil to make them less heavy on the paper, more transparent, and more durable.

It is possible and desirable with either type of ink to mix special colors rather than simply using the color right from the can or tube. Place the desired amount of ink from each can on a sheet of heavy glass with a spatula. Mix the colors together thor-

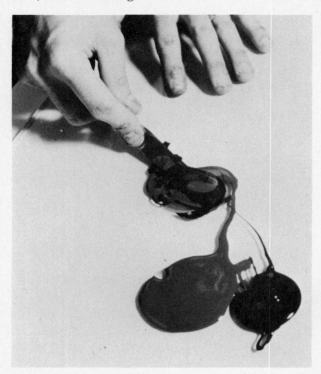

Figure 17. Ink colors can be mixed and blended as desired. Place the inks on a clean surface as shown; then mix thoroughly with a spatula. Experiment with various proportions of basic colors.

oughly with the desired amount of oil before rolling out the color on the glass. This will insure a smooth and uniform color. The exact consistency of the ink will depend on the desired effect. Test print the ink before beginning to print.

## HAND PRINTING

Before beginning, make sure that the table and block are completely free of dust and wood chips. Have the paper handy and a clothes line set up for drying the prints.

The quality of the print will depend upon two things: the choice of the roller or brayer and the choice of the baren (see "Tools"). Make experimental proofs with a soft roller, a hard roller, and one with each baren. Compare these proofs and decide which tools give the desired effect. Clean and put away those not in use to avoid using them accidentally.

## PRINTING

The actual printing is done by placing the paper over the inked block. Be careful not to smudge the paper as it is laid down. Once in position, begin

Figure 18. All materials should be neatly laid out and organized before printing is begun. Be certain that the work surface and the block are free of dust or scraps that could mar the print.

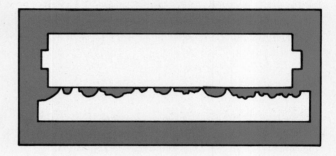

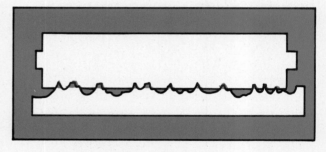

Figure 19. The hard roller (top) hits only the very top of the raised surface on the block. By contrast the soft roller hits both the top and the depressions.

rubbing the block with the wooden spoon or baren. To obtain a uniform print, use the same movement over the entire area, or begin at one corner and rub each area until the image begins to appear on the back of the paper. (More can be seen on rice paper than on 100% rag paper.) Once the image appears uniform, the printing is finished. If the paper used is particularly fragile or if several colors are to be printed, place another piece of smooth paper over the first sheet before beginning to rub. This will protect the print from the friction of the baren. Once printed, gently pull the paper off the block to avoid tearing, and hang it up to dry. Repeat for the next print. If printing a multicolored print, lift the paper, remove the block, insert the next block, and begin printing. Remove paper only when all colors are printed.

It is possible to get various effects by placing some texture over the back of the paper, covering with a second sheet, and rubbing. The ink on the block will pick up that texture.

## Projects You Can Do

The projects described here will allow use of the lost block method of linoleum printing, printing of a black and white woodcut, and making of a collagraph. Choose whichever is desirable — it would be a good idea to read through each one and then decide which to try.

### GREETING CARD

Greeting cards can be made by using the lost block method of linoleum printing. Before beginning, however, review the procedures for the lost block method as described in the section on Color Printing.

**Tools and Materials**

For this project, you will need the following items: (1) blank greeting cards, which can be ordered through any small commercial printer (a wide variety of stocks are available); (2) one linoleum block that is somewhat larger in size than the blank cards; (3) one inexpensive set of gouges; (4) one brayer; (5) a small sheet of glass or a cookie tray on which to roll the ink; (6) a spatula; (7) a wooden spoon; and (8) several colors of ink, either oil- or water-based.

**Procedures**

**1.** Begin by creating a full color drawing of the design for the greeting card on a blank card. Keep in mind that the image as well as any words will be in reverse to print correctly.

**2.** Position the card with the drawing face down on the block and mark the position of the *kento* as well as the boundaries of the card.

**3.** Within the traced boundaries on the block, draw in the design in full color with felt-tip pens.

**4.** Cut away everything outside the boundaries of the image except for the registration grooves.

**5.** Within the image, cut away those areas which are to remain white.

**6.** Mix the lightest color of those to be used, roll it onto the glass, and then onto the block. Make sure the entire surface has a thin uniform film of ink.

**7.** Place the appropriate corner of the blank card into the *kento* and up against the straight notch. Be careful not to smudge the paper when laying it down.

**8.** With the wooden spoon, rub the back of the card until the image begins to be visible from the back of the sheet.

*Figure 20. A small, basic collection of materials is needed for printing greeting cards. A modest set of gouges and a frosting spatula may be used to keep down costs.*

*Figure 21. Begin the greeting card project by making a drawing of the design (above left). Carefully cut away the image on the block (left). Rub the baren over the paper and block (above center). After printing, clean block carefully (above right). The finished greeting card (below) is handsome and cheerful.*

**9.** Carefully remove the sheet and examine the results. If they are satisfactory, hang the card on a clothes lines to dry and repeat steps 7 and 8 until the desired number of cards have been printed. Always print a few extra to allow for errors — five or six extra should do for a three- or four-color print.

**10.** Clean off the ink from the block with a rag moistened with mineral spirits. Try not to remove the drawing.

**11.** Cut away those areas which are to remain the color previously printed.

**12.** Mix up the next darker color and apply it to the block.

**13.** Repeat steps 7 through 12 for each additional color desired. Sometimes it is advisable to let each color dry before proceeding, but it is not absolutely necessary.

**14.** Let cards dry thoroughly.

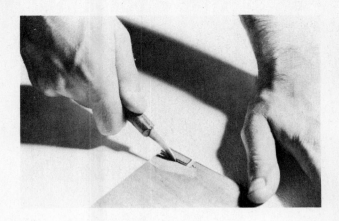

Figure 22. Cutting of the block should begin at the outside edge (above left). When the basic design has been cut away, use a gouge to clean up rough areas that should not print (above). Ink is rolled out onto a glass, then transferred from the glass to the block (left). Rub the baren over the paper carefully and evenly to avoid smudging the image (below).

## BLACK AND WHITE WOODCUT

### Materials and Tools

To do this project, you will need: (1) 15 sheets of medium-weight rice paper; (2) a one-inch thick block of wood of the desired size; (3) pencils, black felt-tip pen, and drawing paper; (4) carbon paper; (5) mat knife; (6) one X-acto knife; (7) a set of fine, good quality gouges; (8) a baren or flat wooden spoon; (9) one tube or can of black oil-based ink; (10) one quart of mineral spirits; (11) a small clothes line; and (12) one brayer or roller about six inches long and two inches in diameter.

### Procedures

**1.** Create the design, keeping in mind the size of the block and of the paper.

**2.** After the drawing is completed, place a piece of carbon paper between the block and the drawing and trace the image from the back of the sheet onto the block.

**3.** Remove the drawing paper and carbon paper and fill in the black areas of the drawing with a felt-tip pen. Once completed, this drawing on the block will look exactly like the finished print in reverse.

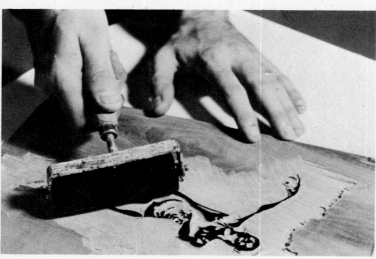

*Figure 23. A drawing of the subject was made for the woodcut (top left). Some of the tools needed for the project are shown (top right). The artist carefully inks the block, preparatory to the printing process (bottom left). The finished print is neat and professional looking (bottom right).*

**4.** Using a mat knife and an X-acto knife for intricate areas, cut around the perimeter of the drawing to prevent the wood from splitting in the wrong places. The angle of the cut should always slope away from the area to be printed.

**5.** With gouges of appropriate size, clear those areas of the design not to be printed.

**6.** Clear away all debris on the table as well as on the block in preparation for taking a proof.

**7.** Roll out a thin layer (it should look like velvet while rolling out) of black ink onto a sheet of glass and then apply it evenly to the block. Recharge the roller with ink several times to assure an even layer of ink.

*Figure 24. "The Crucifixion," by Albrecht Durer. (Courtesy, The Art Institute of Chicago.)*

**8.** While holding a sheet of paper at opposite corners, gently lay it onto the block. Be careful not to move the paper once it is down. In the case of a black and white print, registration methods are not needed because only one printing is involved.

**9.** Gently but firmly rub the back of the paper with a baren or wooden spoon while holding the paper firm with the opposite hand. Rub evenly until the image begins to appear from the back of the paper. To insure a good print, rub as evenly and uniformly as possible.

**10.** Remove the proof and examine it. If the impression is not dark enough, the pressure was not sufficient or not enough ink was applied. If the impression is thick and heavy, too much ink was used. If there appears to be light and dark strokes, the rubbing was not even. If the image is uniform and a crisp black, the impression is good.

**11.** If the impression was not good, repeat steps 8 through 10, using a new sheet of paper.

**12.** Once a good proof is achieved, repeat steps 8 through 10 on all sheets of paper. Compare each print to the first good proof to maintain a uniform quality.

**13.** Hang prints to dry.

## MAKING AND PRINTING A COLLAGRAPH

### Tools and Materials

The following items are needed for this project: (1) 15 sheets of medium-weight rice paper or lightweight 100% rag paper; (2) one piece of masonite; (3) various textures to apply to the

*Figure 25. Materials for a collagraph should be assembled before the work is begun. They include scraps of fabric, modeling paste, a spatula, and one or two brayers.*

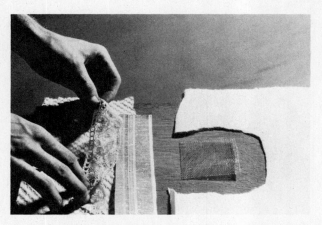

*Figure 26. Begin the collagraph by experimenting with different arrangements of the textured objects on a "dry run" basis. Complete the design in this way before applying modeling paste.*

block such as fabrics, leaves, grass, wire, string, or small found objects; (4) various thick materials to build up the relief — e.g., mat board, illustration board, wood veneer; (5) modeling paste; (6) white craft glue; (7) spatula or putty knife; (8) shellac; (9) an X-acto knife and a mat knife; (10) scissors; (11) various tubes of colored ink; (12) one soft brayer and one hard brayer; (13) linseed or burnt plate oil (optional); (14) a sheet of glass; and (15) a clothes line.

### Procedures

**1.** Begin by doing a rough drawing or by arranging various bits and shapes of cardboard, fabric, buttons, and any other planned articles.

**2.** Once the design has been decided upon, begin applying the shapes to the masonite block with white craft glue.

**3.** Also consider applying a layer of modeling paste and then applying the textures. Note that the paste has its own texture. Continue to use the tools and materials as freely and as imaginatively as possible. To make linear patterns, cut into the dry paste and textures. Remember, the surface is what will print.

**4.** Once the collagraph is thoroughly dry, apply two coats of shellac, three hours apart. Let these dry.

**5.** In printing, there are various approaches to color: using one color only, applying different colors to various sections of the block and printing as many times as desired, starting with

*Figure 27. Four proofs taken from the same block illustrate the subtle differences obtainable in printing. The craftsman should experiment with proofing to insure interesting results.*

the finished collagraph block and following the lost block technique described in the first project, or trying various combinations and approaches.

**6.** The soft brayer will apply ink to more surface than the hard brayer. Decide which to use by experimenting.

**7.** If printing more than once on the same sheet of paper, use the fixed sheet system of registration. (Note: This will not work with the lost block technique unless the sheet is fixed to the L-stop in the same place each time it is printed.)

**8.** Make several proofs to decide what is desir-able. More than one edition can be made from the same block.

**9.** Run the edition, taking notes on the process so it can be repeated for each print.

**10.** Hang and dry.

## *For Additional Reading*

Heller, Jules, **Printmaking Today,** Holt, 1972.

Ross, John, and Romano, Clare, **The Complete Printmaker,** Free Press, 1972.

Rothenstein, Michael, **Relief Printing,** Watson-Guptill, 1970.

# Mask Making

**The ancient art of mask making is still a means of magically transforming oneself into another being for parties, plays, and holidays.**

The rich tradition of mask art can be historically traced through the cultures of every continent: Europe, Asia, Africa, and the Americas. Best known perhaps are the tragic and comic masks of ancient Greek harvest festivals and of the plays during the times of Aristotle. Because Greek amphitheatres were extremely large and the costumes either uniformly alike or nonexistent, the extra large masks were a great help in showing the identity of each character. Furthermore, these masks helped to portray women, since female roles were acted by men.

New identities were given African tribesmen by huge masks which fit down over their shoulders. The masks made them appear superhuman or animal-like and helped them in their invocations to evil demons which seemed to cause illness and bad times. The masks were also used to summon up extra strength with which to meet the enemy in battle, or to thank the gods for showing favors.

Certainly, there were more uses for masks than the giant tasks just mentioned. For centuries, much fun has been derived from simply covering part of one's face at masked balls and at such well-known festivals as Mardi Gras and the Beaux Arts Balls. In palace life of the sixteenth-century French kings, many coy flirtations were carried on by dancing courtesans camouflaged only by small bejeweled eyemasks.

In American folklore, Batman and Robin stepped out of everyday commonness to become — behind their masks — comic book heroes. For years, Emmett Kelly and other circus clowns wore masks when portraying the foibles of people. If they poked fun without their masks, they might very well be considered offensive. By covering their original identities, they each become Everyman, and everyone is able to laugh together at their satire.

Another type of mask is represented by such well-known black-faced minstrels as the late Al Jolson and by such white-faced pantominists as Marcel Marceau. Those entertainers who wear make-up applied directly to their faces are following a tradition that started when prehistoric man smeared berry juice on his face to emphasize the exaggerated shadows thrown by campfires. He became more angry or horrible-looking to ward off evil

*Figure 1. This Senufo mask from the Ivory Coast (opposite) is an excellent example of the artistic expression that can be achieved in mask making. (Courtesy, The Museum of Primitive Art, New York.)*

spirits in the surrounding darkness, or to add more excitement in relating the day's hunting adventures. And as early as the seventh century, the Japanese ceremonial dances of Bugaku used direct facial make-up as well as masks to convey religious meanings.

A mask, of course, is not necessarily applied to the face. Indeed, totem poles are a series of carvings resembling the carved masks worn by Alaskan Indians and those of the Pacific Northwest; the Kachina dolls made by Indians of the Southwest have a similar heritage. The totem, doll, and mask all served the same functions of warding off evil and of appeasing ancestors who had departed from this life. Surely, during the age of armor, the helmeted knight whose face shield was mask-like in its engraved design evoked more fear from those he confronted than a knight wearing an unadorned and purely functional armor piece.

The function of a mask also may be purely utilitarian. For example, the goalie in a hockey game is protected by his mask. And the faces of today's astronauts are always hidden from view as they perform their complicated missions in space.

At one time masks were molded directly from the faces of dead heroes, and then applied to the statuary figures that honored them. Or, they were done in wax, such as those created by the Toussard family and housed today in the Wax Museum in London. As a positive version of the death masks, contemporary potters often take life masks and use the ceramic faces as decoration for plaques and vases.

The masks of today, which are done for whatever special occasions, might well be shown off as part of a wall hanging, attached to the side of a show-off wastepaper basket, or teasingly propped up among the potted plants in one's house. Perhaps such light-hearted fantasy will add humor to today's often over-burdened, logical mind.

*Figure 2. Pericles, leader of the ancient Greeks, wears a mask-like helmet. Armor masks have been an essential part of warfare throughout history. (Courtesy, Vatican Museum; photo, Alinari.)*

## Common Terms Used In Mask Making

**Armature:** the underlying material that gives the mask its structure and stiffness. Such structures may be balloons, wire frames, etc. Often, they give temporary support while the surface material is drying or hardening.

**Contrast:** marked differences in the surface or shape of a mask which provide strong and dramatic effect.

**Embossing:** the process of pressing a pattern or texture into a semistiff material, such as leather or tooling metal foil.

**Enrichment:** any decorations with colors, textures, and shapes that enhance the basic design.

**Foil (Tooling):** a special gauge (thickness) of metal which will hold both its shape and embossed textures without being too heavy to use for mask making. The common metals used are

copper and aluminum, and the gauge most often used is number 32.

**Harmony:** the design quality of all basic parts being alike in some way, such as having similar or related colors.

**Motif:** the main idea in a pattern or a shape that is used repeatedly, with or without variations, to give a unified effect to the design.

**Pattern:** repeated shapes in surface decoration; also a model or template for making things.

**Planes:** surfaces that are basically flat; when two planes meet, the armature or surface must be reinforced at that angle.

**Repoussee:** designs made by embossing lines or punching small holes through a material in decorative patterns.

**Repetition:** using alike things repeatedly to achieve a special total effect; for example, using repeated straight lines to create stripes.

**Symmetry:** a design configuration in which patterns on both sides of a center axis are exactly alike.

## Basic Equipment And Supplies

Materials used in several other crafts may also be used in mask making. However, weight, permanence, and safety must be taken into account. Beware of sharp edges or ends and of substances requiring solvents that might irritate the skin or lungs. Look for materials which will convey ideas in unusual or whimsical ways.

Tools and materials for four types of masks will be described later. However, there are certain common items which fall into specific categories, as listed below.

### TOOLS

1. **For Attaching:** Needles, thread, yarn, fabric glue, modeling paste, casein glue, wheat paste, masking tape, string.

2. **For Cutting:** Scissors and a utility or mat knife.

3. **For Measuring:** Tape measure, ruler, string.

4. **For Marking:** Oil crayons, eye make-up, lipstick, tempera paint.

## MATERIALS

1. **Items From Nature:** Shells, bones, feathers, bark, grass, leaves, husks.

2. **Fibers and Fabrics:** Yarn, string, cloth, rope, nylon stockings, thread.

3. **Papers:** Cardboard, newspaper, magazines, paper bags, wrapping paper.

4. **Metals:** Foil, wire, coat hanger.

*Figure 3. Masks have been used to conceal the individual and, thus, protect his identity. An African dance mask (above) hides a tribesman during funeral rites. (Courtesy, The Seattle Art Museum.) In New Guinea, a ceremonial mask (top right) is a means of disguise in rituals. (Courtesy, The British Museum.) Even the astronauts (below) wore mask-like visors to protect their faces on lunar landings. (Courtesy, NASA.) A wax effigy (bottom right) preserves the image of Lord Nelson. (Courtesy, Madame Tussaud's, London.)*

## Basic Procedures

The first part of a mask-making project is primarily psychological: it sets the stage for the final product.

First, carefully consider the mask's purpose and the mood it is to convey. Second, read the following directions thoroughly to get a feeling of what is to be accomplished. Third, assemble all the necessary materials and set aside a place for working so the mask can be made without clean-up interruptions.

In considering the mood and purpose of a mask, remember these basic guidelines: happy ideas are conveyed by lines and shapes that curve up; violence, anger, and hatred are typified by angular and straight lines; and sadness is shown by drooping shapes and lines. These line variations represent a kind of symbolic language people have learned through the ages, and the so-called reading of them is quite uniform and immediate. Make use of this while planning a mask.

Partially hidden faces are teasing; completely hooded figures are fearsome. Unnatural propor-

tions are usually comical; and painted faces are very mysterious because the face is human but unrecognizable.

Extreme contrasts in texture, made by applying several different materials, are more dramatic and often more frightening. Color changes and color contrasts might also be dramatic; while the use of harmonious, closely related colors can result in gentle and quite elegant effects.

In designing a mask, one might choose a picture to copy or do an original design. If doing an original design, it is fun to go to a large mirror and make faces. Find the expression needed for the purpose of the mask and, while holding the head very still, draw the reflected image on the mirror with lipstick or an oil crayon. Trace all the main lines and features of the facial expression. Then press a piece of typing paper or paper towel to the mirror and rub the back of the paper vigorously. Be careful not to slide the paper while rubbing, as this will smear the image. The drawn image will transfer to the paper. It may be somewhat smaller than expected because of the distance from

*Figure 4. Line variations are used to convey the mood of a mask. Depression (left) and happiness (right) are portrayed on two sides of this four-sided mask titled "All My Faces" by Hede von Nagel. (Courtesy, Hede von Nagel.)*

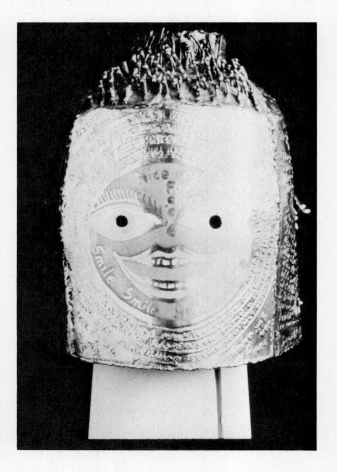

which it was traced, but it will provide a basic form and distinguishing lines. This is a quick way for beginning a design.

Next, read through the procedural steps that follow to get an overview of the approach. Read the part about setting up the armature very carefully. It is the key to the functional success of the total project. These procedural steps are involved in the making of four separate types of masks:

**1.** Rigid paper masks — made with papier-mâché cardboard, and wheat paste).

**2.** Metal foil mask with tooling — made with foil which is embossed and cut.

**3.** Soft fabric mask — a hood enriched with appliqued design and pattern.

**4.** Cosmetic painted mask — an application of the mask directly to the face with cosmetics and stage make-up.

## PROCEDURES FOR BEGINNING ALL MASKS

Each of the following procedures is used in the making of one or more of the four types of masks described above.

### Key Measurements for the Masks or Armatures

Make all of the following measurements *loosely,* otherwise heat and lack of air circulation may make the wearer uncomfortable.

**1.** Measure around the edge of the face — from in front of the ears, following the hairline, and under the jaw. (Use this method to make masks 1, 2, or 3.)

**2.** Measure around the head — above the ears, and across the fullest part of the skull. (Use this method to make masks 1, 2, or 3.)

**3.** Measure the face vertically to locate the placement of eyes, nostrils, mouth, etc. (Use this method to make masks 1, 2, or 3.)

**4.** Measure from the top of the head to the desired bottom length of the hood. (Use this method to make mask 3.)

*Figure 5. Loose measurements should be taken to insure a comfortably fitted mask. Begin by measuring around the outline of the face (A); then, measure around the head at its fullest part (B). Vertical measurements for placement of the features are taken (C), and the length of the mask is determined (D).*

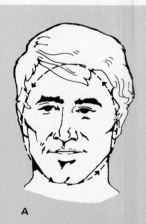

A

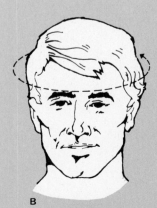

B

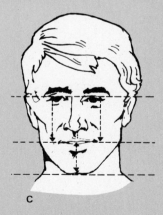

C

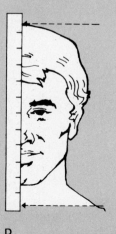

D

## Making the Armature

**1.** Use wire (approximately 10-12 gauge thickness) or coat hangers cleaned with steel wool to make the major planes of the form. Each change of surface direction may need the support of additional wire at its edge. (Use this method to make masks 1 or 2.)

**2.** Attach the wires to each other by tightly bending the ends of one around the other with pliers. (Use this method for masks 1 or 2.)

**3.** If the mask is only frontal, and is not held in place by a top piece, attach rag strips above the ears. Test whether it will stay on the face throughout its development. The rag strips can be replaced later by a more finished elastic band.

**4.** For a hood or any other mask covering the top of the skull, an old wig stand would provide excellent support while working on the mask.

**5.** Use large to medium balloons as support for fabric and paper masks. But double tie them so no air leaks out midway through the project.

**6.** After a bit of hunting in attics and garages, one may discover that some armatures are "ready-made." For instance, a wire armature for a mask with a long, animal "snoot" might come directly from an old lampshade.

## Projects You Can Do

The projects discussed here are simple and inexpensive to do. The important thing to keep in mind is that mask making is fun: the work is enjoyable and creative, and the results are quickly seen.

Remember the basic areas of consideration before undertaking a mask-making project: What is the mask's purpose and mood? Have instructions been read carefully? Are all of the necessary materials assembled?

### RIGID PAPER ANIMAL HEAD

This mask will humorously portray an animal, using a basic and inexpensive form of sculpture. Some distortion, upcurved lines, and happy colors will be used to achieve humorous results. For a temporary armature, paper "sausages" will be made from paper bags and newspaper wrapped together with masking tape.

### Tools and Materials

The tools and materials needed for attaching, cutting, measuring, and marking are masking tape, string, wheat paste or wallpaper paste, casein glue, scissors, utility or mat knife or single-edged razor blade, sandpaper, measuring tape, tempera

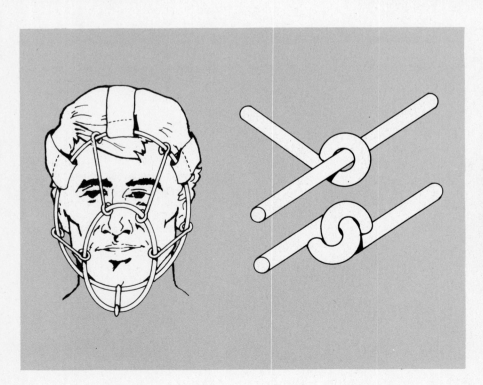

*Figure 6. Wire imparts structure and stiffness to a mask. The ends of the wire must be tightly joined to support the form (right). An old lampshade is an ideal armature for constructing animal-head masks (left).*

or acrylic paints, felt-tip markers, and art brushes in two or three sizes — approximately 2, 5, and 8.

Also needed are buckets for paste and water, pans for paints, and oil of cloves or wintergreen to preserve the paste during the time the mask is being worked on.

The working medium will mostly be two-inch strips of newspaper applied over several brown paper bags.

## Procedures

**1.** Prepare the work area with two or three layers of newspaper and assemble the materials.

**2.** Tear two-inch strips of newspaper, stockpiling at least ten pages for this project. Because newspaper has a grain and will tear more easily one way than another, it is generally best to tear from top to bottom.

**3.** Stir the wheat paste or wallpaper paste in a mixing bowl, using lukewarm water. Stir constantly to avoid lumps. The final consistency should be somewhat like pea soup: not so watery that it is transparent and not so thick that a spoon would stand upright in it. Stir a teaspoon of oil of cloves or wintergreen into the mixture if you wish to keep it for several days. The oil will retard spoiling for a short time.

**4.** Bunch, roll, or bag some shapes that will make up the parts of the mask you wish to make. Run masking tape around them to hold them in shape. Stuff paper bags with dry, loosely crumpled newspaper to make the form desired, then tape the end of the bag shut so the newspaper cannot fall out while the paste strips are being applied.

**5.** Choose one large shopping bag or grocery bag that will fit over the head. This will become the primary armature — that is, several layers of newspaper laminated with wheat paste will, when dry, become a cardboard shell upon which to build the character of the mask. Stuff the bag full of crumpled newspaper and tape it shut. The taped end will eventually become the opening of the mask; the bottom of the bag will become the top of the mask.

**6.** Now begin to apply the newspaper strips to the armature by dragging them through the wheat paste so that they are wet on both sides, and then by laying them across the bag's surface. Crisscross the strips so that they overlap constantly, and apply no less than three complete layers. Then let the form dry, being sure to support the wet sculptural forms while they are drying. Wet paper is heavy and soft, and is very apt to sag and harden into an unwanted shape. Use crumpled newspaper sheets, boxes, or whatever else ingenuity suggests for support. The drying process often takes a day or more.

**7.** Be satisfied with creating only the basic shell on the first session. Three layers of thin newspa-

*Figure 7. Stuff the paper bag with crumpled newspaper to make the desired form and tape the bottom so the newspaper will not fall out while paste strips are applied.*

per, when pasted together, become the stuff that cardboard is made of and are quite as durable. The shell, when dry, can be added to, cut, and otherwise modified as desired.

**8.** Taking the cue from the humorous animal kingdom, tape a small, sausage-like roll of newspaper to the base to make a nose or snout of a pig. Attach tighter rolls to form all of the other shapes of an animal face: cheeks, nostrils, mouth, and eyebrows. Try to be creative. It is not important whether or not the face looks real; rather, it should look imaginative or funny.

**9.** One very useful shape in such sculpture is the cone. Cut a circle, and then cut a line from the edge into the center. When the two cut edges are overlapped slightly, a concave-convex cone is formed. It can be used for eyes, for cheeks, a chin, or any number of possibilities.

**10.** Combine the previous step with another idea. Laminate about four layers of newspaper sheets with paste between each layer. While still wet,

cut the material with scissors to form such shapes as the cone. The result will be a shape that has been formed with scissor precision, but which will dry into cardboard-like stiffness later.

**11.** Every object or shape applied to the base or to another form must be "bandaged" into place by using tiny strips of paper dipped in paste; and finally, by postage stamp sized pieces to make smooth but durable "welds." Failure to do this could result in some parts dropping off when they dry, and it may also present a very difficult surface to paint because of its roughness. Avoid both problems by smoothly applying the bandages, and by graduating from large to tiny paper strips.

**12.** To try the mask on for size, cut the tapes on the opening of the bag and remove all of the newspaper stuffing. The three-to-five-layer shell will not collapse, but will serve as the light, rigid structure upon which all further decoration is to be applied.

**13.** Place the mask on the person to be wearing it

*Figure 8. The base for the pig's nose (below) is easily made by forming a cone with a circle cut from a paper bag. The other forms for the pig's facial features (right) are cut and shaped in a similar manner.*

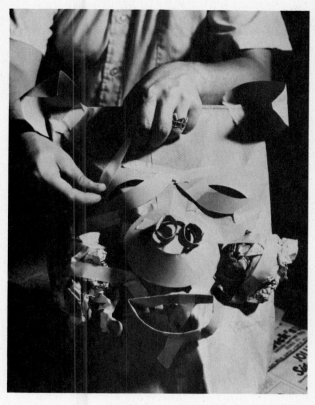

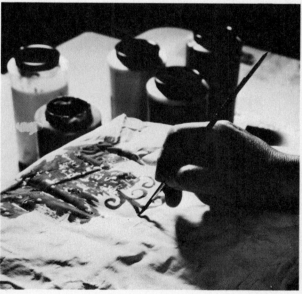

Figure 9. *Use masking tape to attach the cut-out forms to the base* (above). *Newspaper strips that have been dipped in paste are stuck on the bag* (top right). *After the paper has dried, brush the surface with tempera paints* (bottom right).

and find the precise eye level, so the eye holes may be marked. Take the mask off and cut small holes. Try the mask on again and check for accuracy of the holes. Then make them larger. Remember that the farther away the eye holes are from the wearer's eyes, the larger they must be for good vision as well as safety. **Never cut the eye holes or mouth hole while the mask is being worn.**

**14.** Do not build any area up with paper and paste to more than a half-inch thickness before allowing it to dry. Thicker areas may not dry.

**15.** Try the dry mask on and check its weight. If it needs to be lighter, consider cutting open some of the "sausage" areas that were filled with dry crumpled paper for initial support. Pull out the stuffing and patch the surface with more paper bandages. The result will be a series of air pocket shells that will be very strong but quite light.

**16.** When the modeled areas are finished and dry, assemble the paints and brushes. Tempera

paint comes in a powder or as a premixed liquid and is water soluble. The newer acrylic paints are water soluble initially, but harden into a colorful plastic over a short period of time. The latter plastic coating will give the mask a shine and dust-proof durability that could be achieved from tempera only by adding a coat of shellac or clear lacquer.

**17.** Prepare the surface for painting. If there are rough spots, sandpaper them.

**Figure 10. The finished mask is an imaginative representation of a pig.**

**18.** Draw the desired basic features on the mask: curving mouth, nostrils, eyelids, eyelashes, and so forth.

**19.** Using a brush, paint the biggest or solid blocks of color first. Then go on to the edges, lines, and details after the first color has dried.

**20.** Create texture for manes or whiskers by sewing yarn into the mask surface with a heavy-duty tapestry needle. If desired, dip the yarn into casein glue first to provide it with stiffness and a plastic-like durability.

**21.** Finally, give the mask the mirror test. Put it on and stand some 15 or 20 feet away from the mirror. Decide from the view if the desired effect has been achieved. The whole project will have been worthwhile if the magic of visual transformation occurs.

## METAL FOIL MASK FOR TOOLING

The metal foil mask is as old as man's ability to hammer precious metals into sheets which would glitter in the sunlight and cast the sunbeams back at his audience.

### Tools and Materials

Working with metal calls for a few specialized tools and much improvisation. Necessary tools are metal shears or old scissors, nails of various sizes, steelwool, liver of sulphur (obtainable at craft shops or drug stores — sometimes known as potassium sulfide), ballpeen hammer (or any hammer with one round end), ballpoint pen, string, and straightedge ruler.

The metal foil to be used is very thin (number 32 gauge), but very strong. Copper is preferred because it is easily colored chemically and allows for dramatic highlighting. Aluminum foil is acceptable because it has some of the physical characteristics needed in brightness, toughness, and accessibility. Both are easily impressed or embossed, and will hold the shapes forced into the surfaces.

### Procedures

**1.** Begin by cutting a paper pattern the size of the face — a curved sheet should reach from one ear across the face to the other ear. After measuring around the head (above the ears and across the fullest part of the skull) and across the face from ear to ear, add at least one extra inch for a border "hem." The metal will be sharp, and a half-inch border should be turned down on all sides. Crease the metal first, by pressing a ball-point pen into the metal while drawing it along a straightedge ruler. Then fold the border over and firmly press the edges closed.

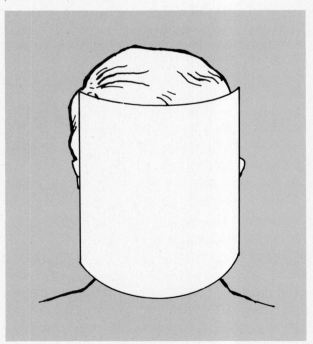

**Figure 11. The first step in making a metal mask is to construct a paper pattern the size of the face. The mask should be large enough to reach from ear to ear.**

*Figure 12. After basic measurements have been made, add at least 1" on the metal for a border hem (A). Using the pattern as a guide, draw the eyes and mouth onto the metal and cut out (B). Cut a U-shape for the nose (C) and fold (D).*

**2.** Now prepare to cut a face into the metal by first drawing the shapes directly onto the metal sheet with a felt-tip pen. Use the paper pattern to locate the eyes and nose and to determine how large the eye and mouth holes should be. Then transfer the shapes to the metal, and cut out the three holes with metal shears.

**3.** Create a nose (first on the paper, then on the metal) by cutting down from one eyebrow, around the bottom of the nose, and up to the other eyebrow in a U-shaped form. This nose can then be bent out to conform to whatever shape is most interesting on the whole face.

**4.** Embossing is done by pressing a ball-point pen or a blunt, rounded nail against the metal. Increase the opportunity for the metal to stretch, both by pressing against the sheet (only when it is supported by a thick pad of soft newspapers) and by pressing from both sides by turning the metal over several times while working it. Use the embossing to create lines under and over the eyes, and over the eyebrows. Cut out or emboss the cheekbones, also.

**5.** When all of the shapes and textures are completed in the mask, cut holes for attachment of an elastic strap to extend from ear to ear behind the head.

**6.** For all practical purposes the aluminum mask will be finished at this point. But if you are working in copper, prepare to color the metal as a final step. First steelwool the entire surface to make sure that it is clean (do not worry about making it shiny at this point).

*Figure 13. A ball-point pen is used to emboss a mask design on metal foil (right). After potassium sulfide has been painted on the surface, burnish the surface lightly with steel wool (below).*

*Figure 14. After the metal has been embossed, cut two holes near each ear, and attach an elastic strap. The strap is worn behind the head to hold the mask in position.*

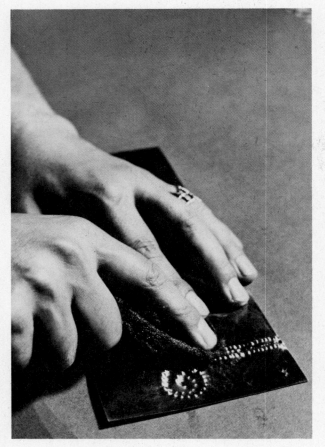

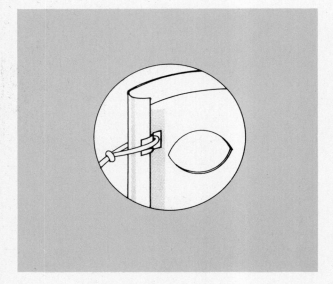

plenty of ventilation: the sulphur fumes are not dangerous but are unpleasant. Cap the container immediately after using it.

**8.** Upon application of the liver of sulphur, the copper will immediately turn black. When it is dry, rub it carefully with fine steel wool. The result should be one of high contrast in color. Do not try to remove all of the black. Merely brush off the top surfaces, which will turn brightly copper-colored in beautiful contrast to the dark sulphur-coated contour areas.

**7.** In a small tin can (about one cup), dissolve a tiny pebble of liver of sulphur (about the size of a pea) in boiling water. Then brush on the liquid with a small paint brush, covering the entire outside surface. Be sure that the working area has

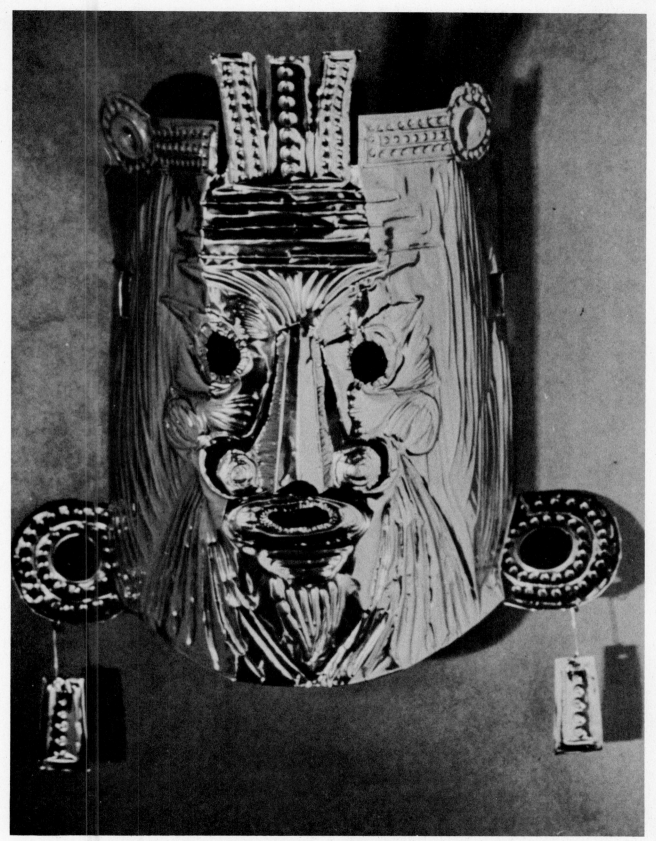

*Figure 15. An interesting effect is created when light is reflected from the face of this mask.*

## SOFT FABRIC HOOD

This hood is not for distorting features, nor for the effects of comedy or fear. Rather, the mood hoped for is one of elegant intrigue. Hiding all facial features except the eyes creates a mood of intrigue; emphasizing the design quality of harmony helps to develop elegance.

Harmony can be used either by duplicating the lines of the hood in a costume's lines, or by matching the main color of a mask to that of a costume — using several similar colors. Very little textural contrast is used, so harmony is not disturbed.

This hooded mask is going to be combined with the cosmetic mask, so harmony is again in play by using the curves of eye and eyebrow shape as secondary mask shapes. No possibility for setting the mood of a mask should be overlooked.

**Figure 16. An intriguing hooded mask can be designed using felt remnants, paint, glue, scissors, and a measuring tape. Old buttons and yarn could be used for additional decoration.**

### Tools and Materials

Necessary tools include fabric glue (flexible), pins and needles, tapestry needle, scissors, measuring tape, string, and tailor's chalk. This mask will be made from felt remnants, yarn and floss remnants, and some medium-sheer, lightweight fabric, such as batiste or dacron and cotton blend.

### Procedures

In addition to the suggestions for measuring described in the section "Basic Procedures," the following measurements should be included:

**1.** Add 8 inches to the line around the fullest part of the skull and across the bridge of the nose, to provide for seams and for air circulation. For example, if the measurement is exactly 16 inches, add 8 inches more, providing a safe total of 24 inches of fabric.

**2.** Divide the total girth established in the pre-

**Figure 17. The fabric is divided into four equal parts (A). An arc, cut from folded paper, serves as a pattern (B). The material is then cut, and the two side panels are sewn to the back panel (C).**

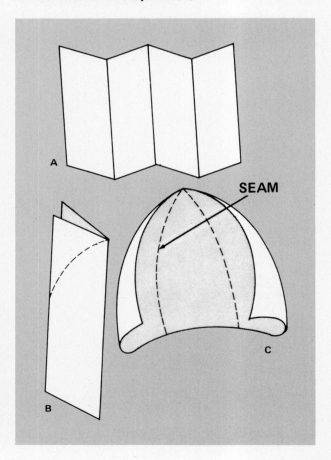

vious step by 4, creating four panels representing the sides of the hood.

**3.** To the length obtained by measuring from the top of the head to wherever the bottom of the hood is desired, add 2 inches. This dimension is the length of each hood panel. Cut out only three sides of the hood. Cut a piece of paper to match the size of one of the hood sides. Fold it in half lengthwise, and cut an arc at the top. Use this as a pattern for cutting curves on all sides.

**4.** Sew three sides together, leaving the front open to develop the face of the mask. Decorate the sides with strips of felt and lengths of yarn. These can either be glued or sewn onto the fabric. Strips with slight variations of color and texture could be used for enrichment. To find the curve motif to use for the facial design of the mask, trace with lipstick or oil crayon on the mirror as described earlier. The eyebrow curve can also be turned

upside down for use as the bottom of each eye-hole and for the bottom curve of the nose shape.

**5.** Measure vertically up and down the face to locate the placement of eyes, nostrils, and mouth. On the fourth piece of vertical material, mark the position of the eyes and nose and the curves below them. This piece of fabric will become the pattern for the features of the mask. It will be called the Face Base.

**6.** Using short lengths of string and yarn, measure from slightly above the eyebrows to the point on the cheekbones where the bottom mask curve seems to fall.

**7.** Using yarn as a guide on the fabric, shape a length of the yarn into the curve of the eyebrow. Trace the line of yarn with tailor's chalk. Then, repeat the curve upside down to complete the drawing of the eye shape.

*Figure 18. Make a pattern to show placement of facial features. Mark and cut the shapes for the eyes (A). Draw a curve at the nose to indicate where the fabric is to be cut; fold pattern in half lengthwise and cut along curve (B). The cut-out mask (C) is now ready for decoration.*

*Figure 19. Four pieces of felt were sewn together to form this hooded mask. Variations of color and shape are added to the face to create an aura of mystery.*

**8.** Connect the upper and lower curves with slightly arching vertical lines. Cut out the eye shapes — making the eyeholes large will allow for intriguing use of cosmetics later.

**9.** Fold the mask front in half and cut off the piece of mask material at the nose, starting with the nose curve and continuing to the outer edges of the mask.

**10.** Lay this cotton lining down on felt remnants and cut out several felt shapes by following the eyeholes and nose line up into the forehead.

**11.** Glue the pieces for nose and forehead onto the Face Base with fabric cement.

**12.** If the mouth and chin are to be covered, cut a piece of medium-sheer, lightweight fabric, following the curve below the nose for the top edge, and make the length half of the top-to-bottom measure of the hood side to allow for hemming. Sew it to the bottom of the curve at the nose line.

**13.** Turn the face and hood inside out, and stitch the side seams together to complete the hood shape.

**14.** Hand stitch extra decoration on the front of the hood if it seems desirable after having tried on the mask. Try to keep the enrichment features in the center and above the eyes to continue the effect of intrigue.

**15.** Because the eyebrow line was the basis for all curves on the mask front, emphasize the eyes and eyebrows with make-up when wearing the mask. Use colors which harmonize with the hood. Don't shy away from colors that you might usually shun — let imagination beneath the mask provide the sense of fantasy.

## COSMETIC PAINTED FACES

Painting the mask directly onto the face has great possibilities because it combines the hint of reality with whatever fantasy one wishes to evoke. Combining the painted face with some disguise for the rest of the head multiplies the effect of mystery or comedy by obscuring more of the reality. Occasionally lining up the edges of the design with the person's facial muscles or features will also help make the design come alive as the person talks. The effect is one that is unique to this type of mask.

### Tools and Materials

Brushes and pads are needed for application of the make-up. Make-up and other accessories include: cream base or petroleum jelly, colored cosmetics, lipstick, eyebrow pencils, eyeshadow, tempera paint, and a wig or headpiece.

### Procedures

**1.** Assemble materials, but do not start more than two hours ahead of the masked event. It is wise to allow at least one hour to work. If not familiar with the procedures, it is a good idea for the beginner to experiment and perfect them several days ahead of time and not the day of the event.

**2.** The hair should be pulled back and the face absolutely clean.

**3.** Then lightly apply a cream make-up base or a very thin layer of petroleum jelly to ease the clean-up later and to protect the face if it is not used to cosmetics.

Figure 20. Ideas for mask-making may be taken from ancient civilizations. This South American mask is designed with bark cloth (top left). A Guatemalan mask (bottom left) from the sixteenth-century conquistadors was carved from wood and realistically painted. (Courtesy, The Museum of Contemporary Crafts of the American Crafts Council, for two pictures at left.) A head covering from Greece (below) is dramatically embellished with paint and beads. (Courtesy, Musée du Louvre; photo, Photographie Giraudon.)

Figure 21. The Yaka mask (opposite) from the Congo is made from grass cloth, raffia, and paint. (Courtesy, The Museum of Primitive Art, New York; photo, Charles Uht.) Silvered copper, shell, and turquoise are the bases for this Peruvian mask (above). This mask of mosaic, turquoise, and limestone on wood (below) was produced in the Mixtec period. Macramé, yarn, and plastic disks are used effectively in a contemporary mask (right). (Courtesy, The Museum of Contemporary Crafts of the American Crafts Council for photos on this page.)

*Figure 22. Before beginning a cosmetic mask, thoroughly clean the face and apply a moisturizer (right). Imaginative designs created with lipstick and eye shadow (bottom left) result in an original disguise (bottom right).*

**4.** Cover the entire face with the lightest possible tone of make-up or the darkest — the idea is to create a contrast with the natural skin color. Pancake make-up applied with a natural sponge and water is best because it is easy to apply and lasts for a long period of time.

**5.** Cover the eyebrows, too, and the outer edge of the lips if these shapes are not in harmony with the intended design.

**6.** Now begin designing the mask. Lipstick, eyebrow pencil, and eyeshadow are locally available in every possible shade. Even nontoxic tempera paint will not harm a face when prepared in the way described, if the skin is healthy. Stage make-up works especially well when the wearer will be seen mainly from a distance. Three sources of professional stage make-up are:

Stagecraft Industries, 615 Bradford, Redwood City, California 94063

Bob Kelly, 151 West 46th Street, New York, New York 10036

New York Costume Company, Inc., 10 West Hubbard, Chicago, Illinois 60610

**7.** To find innovative patterns to use as a mask, one can have another person project a slide with a symmetrical image, such as a butterfly, a flower, or a bird with outstretched wings, onto one's own face, after which the other person can then trace the image onto the face with eyebrow pencil, stick eyeshadow, lipstick, and so forth. The design may be outlined or filled in with sequins or colored with eyeshadow crayons. Adhere sequins to the skin with an adhesive such as used with false eyelashes, or with a dab of clear nail polish applied to back of sequins and pressed onto the design area. Do not use felt-tip pens or food coloring, as they will stain the skin.

**8.** To top off the masking efforts, cover the hair to further conceal identity. Consider making wigs of old, clean nylons cut in strips and glued or sewn to an elastic band that hides under a hat or at the edge of the mask. Wigs that have lost their cap elasticity can be worn as is, or cut and colored with food coloring. Old shower caps or women's heavy net caps for holding hair rollers in place can be used with string, yarn, ribbon, or braid sewn on.

When making the mask, consider extending the forehead (binding material over the top of the head, then teasing or back-coming the hair that sticks out from under the band). Also, a strip of knit fabric from 1 to 2 inches wide and from 2½ to 3½ feet long can be twisted around the head and secured with an old pin or brooch to create a mysterious effect.

In planning the mask, remember to coordinate the costume so that it enhances the illusion being created. All aspects of both the mask and the costume should harmonize. The main thing is to use your imagination.

## For Additional Reading

Baranski, Matthew, **Mask Making,** Davis, 1966.
Grater, Michael, **Paper Faces,** Taplinger, 1968.
Laliberte, Norman, and Mogelon, Alex, **Masks, Face Coverings, and Headgear,** Van Nostrand, 1973.
Shapiro, David, "Faces and Masks and Auxiliary Deceptions," **Craft Horizons,** 30: 36-45 (Dec. 1970).

# Terrariums

**Terrariums, once the province of Victorian parlors, are enjoying a resurgence of popularity. These lilliputian gardens under glass provide delightful green vistas throughout the bleakest months of winter.**

Perhaps the first recorded instance of plants being grown in sealed containers comes from the ancient Phoenician and Greek cultures. During the festival of Adonis, the slain lover of Aphrodite, the youth's death was mourned and then his resurrection celebrated. Quick-flowering plants were sealed in earthenware pots, baskets, or small glass bottles and carefully tended during the eight-day festival. These so-called "Gardens of Adonis" were used to celebrate the perpetual cycle of seasons. At the end of the celebration, the containers of plants, which had begun to fade, were thrown into the Aegean Sea, along with images of Adonis. This represented the completed seasonal cycle of death to life to death again.

**Figure 2. The Wardian case was the original terrarium. Initially, the cases were used for transporting plants from one country to another.**

Further interest in raising plants in small, closed environments for scientific and decorative purposes did not actually evidence itself until the early nineteenth century. As so often happens, the basic principle of growing plants under glass was discovered quite by accident. A London surgeon, Dr. Nathaniel Ward, was an avid student of natural history. During the summer of 1829, while pursuing the careful study of the sphinx moth, he obtained a chrysalis and partially buried it in a small amount of moist garden soil which he placed in a bottle and sealed with a metal lid. Intent upon studying the moth as it emerged from the pupa state, he was astounded, some days later, to discover a small fern and one species of grass growing from the clump of dirt. With the moth completely forgotten, Dr. Ward continued his daily observations of the growing plants and began experimenting with other glass containers and a wide variety of plants. The original terrarium lasted four years, the plants dying eventually only after the lid rusted away, allowing rainwater to seep in and collect in the bottom of the jar.

**Figure 1. Terrariums can be used as the focal point in a room. This floor terrarium, consisting of a covered arrangement of ferns and orchids, can be planted professionally or in the home.**

In 1832, Ward attempted a daring experiment. Filling two large, glazed cases with ferns and grasses, he sent them by ship to Sydney, Australia, a journey of eight months. Lashed to the deck, the compartments were exposed to all extremes of weather and temperature, yet the plants survived the trip. Upon their arrival in Sydney, the cases were filled again, this time with Australian plants, and shipped back to England, around the Cape of Good Hope; again the plants arrived safely. Ward continued his studies, eventually raising over 100 species of ferns normally considered too delicate for cultivation in the polluted air of nineteenth-century London. In 1842, he finally published his research in a study entitled "On the Growth of Plants in Closely Glazed Cases."

By mid-century, Wardian cases, as they became known, were traveling around the world. The profitable Indian tea industry was started when 20,000 young tea plants were shipped to the Himalayas from Shanghai. The Samoan and Fiji Islands received banana trees from China, and Brazilian rubber trees were packed off to Ceylon. Flowering plants and ferns were shipped between Europe and America, and one London nursery reported using over 500 Wardian cases in a seven-year period. The Royal Botanical Gardens in England imported more plants in 15 years than in the previous 100.

Wardian cases as ornamental decoration became very fashionable during the Victorian age. Lavishly designed with many glass panels, a span or domed roof, and special compartments for heating built into the bases, the cases were described by one nineteenth-century author as "... elegant and pleasing additions to the most tasteful and elaborately furnished drawing room ... some being extremely light and graceful and most beautifully finished, with delicate enamel and gilding."

As homes became centrally heated and better insulated, it was possible to grow plants without the glass cases; and by the mid-1920s interest in terrariums had faded. However, in recent years, ecological concerns for saving the environment have brought the contemporary terrarium back into the home, providing once again a small portion of the natural world for man's enjoyment.

## Common Terms Used In Planting Terrariums

**Charcoal:** small amounts of crushed horticultural charcoal, an important feature of the terrarium soil, are generally mixed with drainage material (pebbles) as well as with soil. Charcoal adds porosity and acts as a sweetener by absorbing soil impurities and rank odors.

**Environment:** inside a terrarium, the sum of conditions consisting of available water, humidity, space, temperature, light, atmosphere, and the more subtle effects each plant has on the others.

**Epiphyte:** a plant, such as an orchid, which normally does not grow in soil; usually found in a wild state growing from branches or crotches in trees, deriving most of its nourishment from the air.

**Etiolation:** the stretching of plant cells caused by insufficient light, resulting in weak and drooping stems.

**Featherock:** a form of unusually lightweight, gray stone that makes an attractive, natural-looking addition to a terrarium landscape.

**Habitat:** the conditions necessary for the survival of a particular plant or group of plants; a terrarium

Figure 3. Natural habitats may be recreated in miniature landscapes. Insectivorous plants such as the Venus Fly-Trap are used to duplicate surroundings found in boggy areas.

can be designed to achieve a variety of habitats, including woodland, tropical, marsh or bog, desert, or aquatic.

**Humus:** that material which forms the organic portion of soil.

**Insectivorous Plants:** unusual plants having evolved with a variety of structures enabling them to trap insects, the digestion of which is necessary for the plants to survive in boggy areas, where the supply of nitrates and phosphates is insufficient.

**Lichen:** a nonflowering slow-growing plant that resembles moss but is actually composed of a fungus and an alga.

**Photosynthesis:** the process by which special cells in a green plant manufacture nutrients by using energy from the sun and carbon dioxide in the air, giving off water and oxygen as by-products.

**Porosity:** the state of the soil necessary to prevent sogginess; often achieved by adding sand or vermiculite to topsoil or humus.

**Sheet Moss:** thin layers of moss in large sheets.

**Soil pH:** the acid or alkaline condition of soil; easily measured with a special kit obtained at garden supply shops.

**Species:** those groups of biological organisms that have similar or identical characteristics and that can reproduce amongst themselves but not with individuals of another group.

**Terrarium:** a miniature greenhouse in which the humidity and temperature can be easily controlled and in which a wide variety of small plants may be raised as long as they all thrive on the same conditions of moisture, light, and temperature.

**Vermiculite:** a mica by-product expanded by heat into a spongy, resilient material which, in the form of tiny particles, is often added to soil to make it more porous.

## Basic Equipment And Supplies

Because terrariums are enjoying a tremendous resurgence of popularity, it is no problem to find a wide selection of containers and plants offered for sale. Appropriate glass containers may be found at local department stores, hardware stores, and grocery stores as well as at florists and nurseries. Many varieties of small common plants are sold in general merchandise stores. An excellent source for hard-to-find wild plants, including insectivorous plants and wild orchids, is Arthur Eames Allgrove, North Wilmington, Massachusetts. This mail-order firm ships plants during the fall and winter months and the material arrives well packaged and healthy. Miniature tropical orchids are sold by Hausermann, Inc., P. O. Box 363, Elmhurst, Illinois.

### Containers

Modern terrariums are copied directly after the Victorian Wardian cases. The only basic of sufficient light for healthy plant growth. Often the loveliest bottles are made of tinted glass, and one is tempted to make terrariums from them. However, unless the color is quite muted, the light intensity is reduced and the colored glass tends to transmit its own hue while absorbing other colors in the spectrum. This may cause abnormal growth or stunting in the plants.

Nearly any clear glass or plastic container will do. Various sizes of round, octagonal, and rectangular fish aquariums make pleasing terrariums. Bottles of all sizes and shapes are readily available, including candy jars, large goblets, decanters, gallon-sized mayonnaise jars, apothecary jars, canning jars, large bottles, cider jugs, wide-

mouthed juice and water pitchers, crystal beer mugs, flower vases, scientific laboratory glassware, domes, and bell jars.

The size of the terrarium container is optional. A single, tiny fern set among a few pebbles can look quite charming in a dainty antique perfume bottle, while a fifty-gallon fish tank would be magnificent housing a complete woodland or jungle scene in miniature. In general, the size of the plants should be in keeping with the scale of the container.

### Antique Containers

For a more unusual terrarium, search through antique shops for old curio cabinets. Made with glass sides and a hinged lid set in an oak or mahogany framework, these small cabinets were originally used to display jewelry, china, or collections of miniatures. The cases can be found in a variety of sizes and shapes and make distinc-

*Figure 4. When choosing a container, the primary concern is to select one made of clear glass or plastic. The size and shape are optional but should be in proportion to the plants.*

*Figure 5. One way of displaying a terrarium is to hang it from the ceiling. The design of the container enhances the overall effect of plant arrangements. (Courtesy, Stained Glass City, Chicago.)*

tive terrariums after a sealant is applied to help regulate the environment. Other antique glass containers such as candy, tobacco, apothecary and spice jars, decanters, covered dishes, stemmed goblets, and glass teapots may all be transformed into striking gardens under glass.

## Hanging Containers

Not all terrariums must be set on a surface; they can hang from walls or a ceiling in a variety of ways. Some manufacturers are producing glass bottles with a long neck for hanging and a side opening for ease in planting. Any other bottle or reasonably light container may be hung by using wire, twine, macraméd cords, or leather thongs.

*Figure 6. Terrarium containers made of acrylic plastic are available in a variety of shapes and sizes. (Courtesy, Microscapes, Inc., Chicago.)*

## Commercial Terrarium Containers

A number of acrylic plastic containers made specifically for terrariums are on the market. These come in a variety of shapes, including rounded or flattened domes of all sizes, containers resembling small pagodas or temples, and even ordinary bottles. Most are made with two halves for ease of planting and may or may not contain an opening in the top half. Some plastic containers are cube-shaped or rectangular with a removable base. One company makes a very large plastic globe 20 inches in diameter which rests on a plastic stand, the entire structure measuring three feet in height. Another specialty shops. These are flat on the wall side, rounded on the remaining surface, and again come in a variety of sizes. Some are designed to fit into a corner (with two flat sides and one curved) or structured to hang on an outside corner.

## Handmade Containers

A terrarium container can easily be handmade by using ordinary window glass, masking tape, and cement sealant. Decide upon the size and shape, measure carefully, and have the glass cut by a glazier. Clean and dry each piece of glass, then tape the four sides together with the tape on the

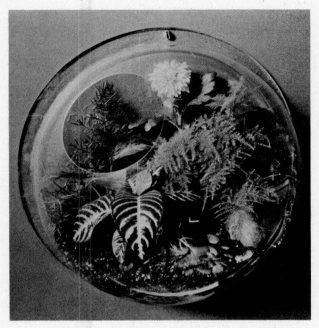

**Figure 7. This terrarium is hung directly against the wall. Its planting of ferns and a zebra plant is brightened by a chrysanthemum blossom. (Courtesy, Microscapes, Inc., Chicago.)**

inside. Join the sides to the bottom with tape and seal all inside seams with the sealant. Immediately wipe off excess sealant with a clean rag. If necessary, a razor blade may be used to scrape off remaining sealant after it hardens. Allow the seams to dry for 48 hours before planting, and either buff all sharp glass edges or cover them with decorative tape to prevent cuts.

## Lids for Containers

Opinions differ on the virtues of sealing a terrarium, although the very term signifies a closed environment. If sealed, the moisture and humidity remain constant and the plants are protected against dust, molds, and household type fungi. An open terrarium is suitable for many plants but must be more carefully watched to prevent excessive drying.

Any number of materials can be used to cover a terrarium opening. The various plastic wraps make unobtrusive seals; but such decorative objects as old perfume bottle stoppers, candy or soap dish lids, crystal dessert dishes, pieces of driftwood, rocks, shells, and large clay or wooden beads can also be used. Corks of all sizes are available at hardware stores, and one can always get glass cut to fit over the larger openings.

## TERRARIUM POTTING MATERIAL

The material going into a terrarium before the plants are added is as important as the plants themselves in assuring the success of a terrarium. The potting material must provide proper nutrition, drainage, support, and room for growth as well as add to the total design and attractiveness of the finished product.

### Moss Lining

The first material to put into a terrarium is a layer of moss. If possible, this should be a thin sheet of living moss that has been gently tugged loose from the forest floor or a damp river bank. Often it will continue to grow within the terrarium. If fresh moss is not available, sheet moss obtained from a florist is acceptable when it has been soaked in water and well drained.

**Figure 8. Careful attention must be given to the selection of plants and potting materials. A proper combination of moss, pebbles, charcoal, and special formulated soil will insure a successful terrarium.**

## Drainage Layer

Providing adequate drainage inside a sealed terrarium is of particular importance. Too much moisture trapped around the root area will quickly lead to rot. For the smallest terrariums, the layer of moss is sufficient; larger containers, however, require a layer of pebbles or broken clay potsherds in addition to the moss.

## Charcoal

Small pieces of horticultural or activated charcoal, sprinkled liberally among the drainage pebbles, serve several purposes. They aid in drainage and absorb excess moisture and soil impurities, keeping the soil "sweet" and free of mold and decay.

## Soil

A general-purpose potting soil obtained from a plant supply store is recommended over soil dug from a garden or woodland. In the first place, the potting soil will be properly formulated, containing a mixture of humus, peat, sand, or vermiculite, and will provide enough nutrients for the average terrarium. Secondly, the soil is sterile and, unlike garden soil, will not contain mold or fungus spores or any "mystery" seeds that may sprout after the terrarium has been planted and sealed.

If soil from the garden or forest is to be used, care must be taken to see that it is well mixed with sand or vermiculite to provide porosity. Vermiculite can be purchased at garden supply centers. If sand is used, it must never be ocean beach sand because the salt contained in such sand is toxic to plants and no amount of washing can remove it. A general formula of one part loam (topsoil), one part humus (leaf mold), and one part sand should be followed when mixing one's own terrarium soil.

## Decorative Materials

Sand, pebbles, rocks or featherock, and pieces of wood all lend an air of naturalness to a terrarium scene. In larger containers the rocks can be used as "boulders" to help bank and hold soil, producing several levels or "hills and valleys" in the landscape. Interesting pieces of driftwood or branches are effective as part of the total design

but are prone to mold after a time. Occasionally, it helps to wash and then sterilize all outside materials by placing them in a warm oven (200 degrees) for several hours.

## PLANTING TOOLS

Some types of terrariums require more planting tools than others. When the opening is large enough, one's own hand is often the only tool needed and the most reliable. Invention is the rule with small containers and narrow-necked bottles.

### Household Tools

Anything around the house that is suitable can be used. Items useful for planting a narrow-necked bottle might be a chopstick, dowel rod, coat hanger, pencil, ruler, tongs, long tweezers, or pieces of an old bamboo fishing pole. A long cardboard tube left over from fancy wrapping paper or a kitchen funnel can be helpful in directing the flow of pebbles, charcoal, and soil into a long-necked bottle. A baby bottle brush might be used to clean

*Figure 9. Although commercial tools are available, adequate planting utensils may be found around the household. Spoons may be used for planting, hooks for arranging, and basters for watering.*

the inside walls of a bottle garden after planting. A turkey baster or a small spray-type bottle make fine tools for adding water to the finished terrarium.

## Commercial Tools

Occasionally, one can find a hand tool called "Flexible Finger" or "Astro Finger" for sale. This device has a grabbing mechanism that aids in planting bottles. Plants can be placed carefully and rocks, twigs, or wood accents added more easily. Also, this tool can help with pruning out dead or unattractive vegetation or cutting back any vigorous growers.

## WATER

Distilled water is highly recommended for all terrariums. Water from the faucet usually contains chlorine, fluoride, salts, and other chemicals that may be harmful to plants. Do not use water from a water softener.

## PLANTS

The proper choice of plants depends upon many factors, including size and shape of the container, whether it is to be left open or sealed, and the amount of light available to the plants. The basic rule is to pick plants requiring similar growing conditions while keeping in mind the total scale of the entire planting.

## House Plants

Most so-called house plants are originally from the tropics and many will thrive in a terrarium. A wonderful variety of small plants are readily available in any number of stores and greenhouses.

## Native Plants

A walk in a nearby woodland will turn up an interesting assortment of mosses, lichens, ferns, and small flowering plants that will add charm to a terrarium setting. Rare or unusual plants such as wild orchids should never be picked, and plants must never be taken from local, state, or national parks. Perhaps the best method of obtaining wild plants is to purchase them from mail-order firms, as mentioned earlier, or from a nursery which handles unusual plants for the wildflower garden.

*Figure 10. Native plants add charm to a terrarium. A selaginella (bottom right) provides ground cover, ferns (top right) enhance fullness and height, and partridge berries (below) add color to the arrangement.*

## Basic Procedures

Terrariums are fun to plant and a continuing source of pleasure afterward. Inexpensive to make and easy to maintain, these gardens under glass are a perfect hobby the year around for all ages, including the very young and very old. Terrariums can bring a special joy to the bedridden or confined person.

Limited only by the size of the container and one's imagination, the miniature landscape may be designed to resemble many habitats found in nature. A damp forest floor, ferny ravine, or mossy rock outcropping is achieved by using native ferns, mosses, lichens, and small flowering woodland plants. Insectivorous plants create the effect of a swampy bog, while various house plants can be chosen to create a rank jungle scene or an open meadow.

Plants can survive in a closed environment when provided with a continuing source of light and sufficient moisture before sealing. Respiration is a complex series of chemical reactions in a plant, but basically the process takes in oxygen from the air and releases carbon dioxide. A second process, photosynthesis, is the manufacture of food by a plant, utilizing sunlight and carbon dioxide and giving off oxygen and water. So, in simple terms, a plant recycles its own oxygen, carbon dioxide, and water; and when all conditions are stable', plants tightly closed up in a bottle or other container can continue to live indefinitely.

### ASSEMBLING MATERIALS

The first step in making a terrarium is to assemble all the materials: container, plants, soil, pebbles, charcoal, sheet moss, decorative rocks or wood, and any necessary tools. Choose a well-lighted work area and an unhurried time of day or evening in order to avoid being rushed.

### THE FIRST LAYER

The glass or plastic container should be absolutely clean and dry before beginning (it is much easier to clean before planting than afterwards). A thin layer of sheet moss goes into the container first, upside down with the green mossy side against the surface. One of the purposes of the moss is to hide the soil, so arrange it as a bowl to hold and disguise the potting materials, letting it come up the sides one-fourth to one-third the height of the container. Determine in advance how the plantings are to lie: whether the terrarium is to have a single level or whether it is to resemble a hilly terrain and have slopes, dips, or rocky outcroppings. The mossy foundation may need to rise higher in one portion than in another. If the terrarium is to have a front and back, the moss may be lower in front and higher in back.

### THE SECOND LAYER

Sprinkle the moss with a small amount of crushed charcoal and add the drainage layer of pebbles or rocks. Plan for one-half inch of pebbles per one inch of soil. It is not generally necessary to have a drainage layer deeper than two inches, even for the largest terrariums. Again, add a scattering of charcoal.

### THE THIRD LAYER

Next, the soil is put in, taking care to keep the sides of the container clean. The soil is more easily handled if somewhat damp — wipe off smudges on the glass as they occur. Before placing the larger rocks, driftwood, and plants, review the design for the terrarium. Are there enough plants for the container? Are there too many? Now that the soil is in, are some plants going to be too tall? Is there too much soil? Remember, for the most pleasing effect, the moss liner and all potting material should not exceed one-third the height of the container. If changes are necessary, now is the time to make them.

### CHOOSING THE PLANTS

Plants should be chosen carefully for variety in height, color, texture, and form. Use tall and medium-sized plants as well as tiny low plants that cover the ground. Leaves may be big, small, broad, narrow, smooth, or hairy, with leaf margins entire, toothed, or greatly dissected and lacy.

*Figure 11. A layer of moss lines the container, and a drainage layer of pebbles and charcoal (a) is added. The soil (b) should be a mixture of humus, peat and vermiculite. Then, plants are arranged from the back to the front (c), beginning with the tallest ones first. The finished terrarium (d) should be carefully watered and covered to allow the plants to recover from the transplant.*

A

B

C

D

Consider the possible colors: some leaves are deep green, some nearly yellow-green, and others variegated white and green or green on the top surface and another color underneath. Plants may stand upright, grow in dense tufts, sprawl along the ground, or may be viny.

After reviewing the selected plants, any rocks needed for banking the soil or for a more naturalistic appearance in the terrarium should be carefully placed. Partially bury each rock or rock grouping if a ledge effect is desired.

## PLACING THE PLANTS

Start with the tallest plants or the ones to be put in the back of the terrarium. Generally, a plant can be loosened from its pot by tapping gently on a hard surface, or by using a hammer. Occasionally, however, one must break the pot in order to free the plant. Remove a plant from its pot immediately before transferring it to the terrarium to avoid exposing the roots to drying conditions. Gently loosen the dirt of the root ball and place in the container. Position the plant at a soil depth equal to that of the plant when potted or when growing in its natural condition. Press the soil firmly around each plant.

Keep in mind the basic elements of good design as well as the basic needs of each plant. Avoid symmetry. Put the tallest or most showy plant to the left or right of center and try to have one or more particular points of interest within the design — whether brightly colored leaves, berries, or an attractive rock. Watch out for the tangled mass look. Moderation in numbers is a good rule of thumb. Each plant needs space in which to grow, so it is better to have too few plants than too many.

## FINISHING THE TERRARIUM

The addition of mosses, lichens, pebbles, rocks, driftwood, or other accessory objects to hide any exposed soil is the final step in completing the design. In addition to improving the appearance of the finished terrarium, such coverings help reduce the rate of evaporation in an open container. If the terrarium is large enough, a reflecting pool may be added: use anything that will hold a few drops or more of water such as a jar lid, transparent ash tray, coaster, soap dish, saucer, or a small bowl or pan. Bury the pool in soil and hide the rim with moss and rocks.

## ADDING THE INITIAL WATER

When everything is firmly in place, the terrarium should be watered sparingly and carefully. Sprinkle water evenly over the entire planted surface, stopping as soon as water seeps through the moss liner on the bottom of the container. Too little water is more easily remedied than too much.

The terrarium can now be sealed, if desired (see *Lids for Containers* under "Basic Equipment and Supplies"), and placed in spot while the plants recover from being transplanted. After a few days, the terrarium may be moved to its permanent location, in indirect or filtered sunlight or under artificial light.

## MAKING A BOTTLE GARDEN

Making a terrarium out of a narrow-necked bottle requires a few tricks and special tools. A straightened coat hanger with a small hook on the end along with one or more long rods or sticks for digging, poking, and probing are sufficient; but a commercially made "mechanical finger," as described in the section "Basic Equipment and Supplies," may be handy.

### Adding Potting Material

Follow the general procedure for planting a terrarium as described previously. The moss liner may be lowered into the bottle in pieces or dispensed with entirely. (The moss is not necessary for healthy plant growth. Its main purpose in both terrariums and bottle gardens is to make the plantings more attractive by hiding the soil.) A funnel or rolled newspaper or a long cardboard tube is helpful in directing the flow of drainage pebbles, charcoal, and soil. Using a stick or dowel rod to mound and firm the dirt, prepare depressions for each plant before placing the first one.

*Figure 12. For a terrarium with a domed cover, begin by placing a shallow clay pot inside a sheet of aluminum foil. This helps to prevent moisture leakage (a). A moss base (b) will hide the soil and drainage layer. Rocks and drift wood are placed; then, the plants are added (c). The finished terrarium, mounted appropriately on a natural wood base, is carefully covered with a glass dome (d).*

A

B

C

D

## Placing the Plants

To be certain each plant will fit through the bottle neck, make a circle with the thumb and forefinger the size of the bottle opening and draw the leafy portion of each plant through. The dirt ball around the roots can be gently washed away in a pan of lukewarm water or under a faucet. Plant immediately after removing the soil.

Lower each plant in the crook of the coat hanger and place inside the bottle; spread the roots if possible and cover with soil, firming gently. After all plants are situated embellish the bare areas with moss pieces, decorative gravel, or whatever other accessories will go through the bottle neck.

## Finishing the Bottle Garden

Clean the inside of the bottle with a bent bottle brush or a piece of sponge attached to a coat hanger. Water well by trickling water slowly over the entire surface with a funnel taped to a drinking straw or narrow tubing. Carefully avoid dislodging any plants. Seal with a cork or lid and follow the general directions given below for maintaining a sealed terrarium.

## MAINTENANCE

Terrariums require some attention beyond admiring glances from time to time. Proper watering and sufficient light are necessary for satisfactory plant growth. Insufficient or excessive moisture and light will cause problems.

## Water

An open terrarium needs water when the plants look wilted, the moss appears dry, or the soil feels dry about one inch below the surface. A closed terrarium needs additional water if condensation fails to appear on the inside of the glass surface for several hours each day. Remember to use distilled water, rainwater, or melted snow.

## Light

Most terrariums require either bright indirect light or filtered sunlight. Never put a closed case containing plants in direct sunshine. The heat of the light will be trapped inside and will cook the plants in a short time. If the light source is not sufficient, the plants will stretch toward the light and grow leggy and stringy. When light always comes from one direction, all the plants will grow toward it, so a container on a window sill should be turned occasionally for more uniform growth.

When natural light is not available or is insufficient, artificial light should be used. This can be in the form of fluorescent light, mercury vapor bulbs, or incandescent lighting. When artificial light is the only source of illumination, color-corrected fluorescent light tubes mounted directly over the terrarium are the best solution. Such tubes produce the full color spectrum necessary for plant growth and do not cast the characteristic purple glow. The length of the light fixture, the number of bulbs, and the distance between the light and the plants are all factors in determining the actual amount of illumination received by the plants. Increasing the length or number of the bulbs or reducing the distance from bulbs to terrarium increases the light intensity. One needs to experiment. The length of time the artificial light remains on should approximate natural sunlight. Plants need a normal period of darkness in each 24-hour period, as do most other living organisms.

## Problems

Probably the trickiest problem common to terrariums is mold. The damp, slightly warm, humid conditions of the terrarium are ideal for the rapid spread of mold; and once this spreading starts, it is difficult to stop. Sometimes overwatering will cause mold to develop and an extended drying out period will clear up the problem. Care must be taken to check an opened terrarium regularly during the airing out process so that over-drying does not occur. A narrow-necked bottle may be left to dry longer than an open fish bowl. When mold first appears on an individual plant or piece of wood, it is best to remove the molding item before the fungus engulfs the entire terrarium. Sometimes a piece of facial tissue tucked into the neck of a bottle garden helps to dry out the bottle faster by absorbing the moisture inside the bottle.

If the mold takes over in spite of precautions, the only remedy is to discard the entire planting, scrub the container well with hot, soapy water, and let it stand in the sunshine for a few days. Then, begin again with all fresh material.

Other problems can be caused by inadequate drainage or the wrong soil pH for the particular plants involved. When stunted growth, abnormal growth, or lack or growth occurs, it is wise to start over.

Terrariums usually need a minimum of care and may survive for years. Often, however, some plants will grow luxuriantly at the expense of others, eventually crowding them out. After a time, any carefully scaled landscape may develop into an unruly, tangled mass. Whenever necessary, one can carefully clean up and remodel a terrarium by removing dead or dying plants, adding new soil and moss, and pruning back the more vigorous growers.

## Projects You Can Do

Probably the ideal terrarium project for the beginner is one utilizing a wide-mouthed bottle, open fish bowl, tank, brandy snifter, or one of the commercial plastic terrarium containers, and a variety of house plants. These containers are easily handled because of the large openings and offer a wide variety of design possibilities incorporating rocks, driftwood, and so forth. House plants, already accustomed to growing inside the home, will thrive with the least amount of care and are most likely to reward the terrarium enthusiast with luxuriant growth.

After experimenting successfully with one or more simple terrariums, a choice among more unusual containers and plants can be made. Planting a bottle garden looks far more difficult than it actually is. The finished effect is even more dramatic once the plants in the bottle garden reach a good size. Having become an enthusiast, the terrarium zealot will find it difficult to look at any clear glass container without mentally planting something in it.

### TROPICAL PLANTS IN A SIMPLE CONTAINER

The following chart lists a variety of tropical plants suitable for the sealed or opened terrarium. Many plants that are large when mature are slow growers and quite satisfactory as terrarium material while in the juvenile state. The important life requirements are listed for each plant. It should be remembered that, when grouping plants in the

*Figure 13. These small covered terrariums were prepared with tropical plants. Small rocks have been added to give a natural appearance to the planned environments.*

same con- among those plants that have similar preferences for light, temperature, and humidity. These characteristics are also given on the accompanying chart. For assembling the terrarium, follow the general steps as outlined in the section "Basic Procedures."

### WILD PLANTS IN A TERRARIUM

A terrarium of wild plants may be particularly fascinating but should not be attempted until one has gained some expertise in raising plants under

**Figure 14. Wild plants may be gathered directly from their natural habitat and transplanted.**

glass. Small woodland plants can either be transplanted from nature or purchased commercially. When moving plants from the wild, however, a few rules should be observed. (1) A number of plants are protected by law in various states and are not to be disturbed unless facing immediate destruction through roadbuilding or some other construction projects. (2) Take only a small portion of any one type of plant from a single site and repair any damage to surrounding vegetation by replacing loose dirt and leaves. (3) Gather only plants which are found abundantly and carry them home in sealed plastic bags with the root balls wrapped in damp paper towels or moss. (4) If traveling some distance by car, do not leave the plants in the hot trunk. (5) Place the material in a terrarium as soon as possible.

Wild plant terrariums should be kept in bright, filtered sunlight with the temperature on the cool side (50 to 70 degrees). Many spring wildflowers will bloom in terrariums but should be transplanted outside again in the late spring or after blooming. The chart on page 202 lists a number of wild plants suitable for terrariums. Follow the basic directions for assembling a terrarium.

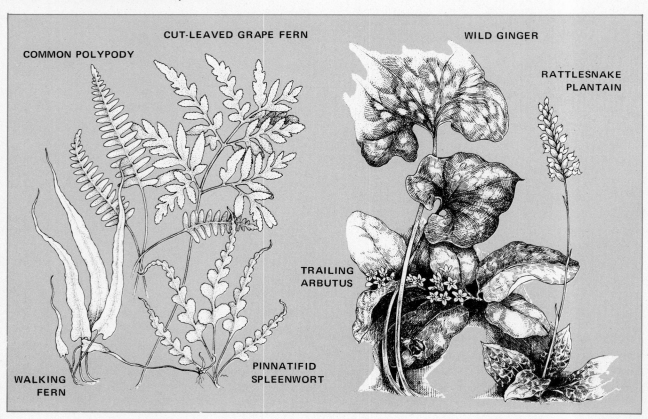

COMMON POLYPODY

CUT-LEAVED GRAPE FERN

WILD GINGER

RATTLESNAKE PLANTAIN

TRAILING ARBUTUS

WALKING FERN

PINNATIFID SPLEENWORT

## INSECTIVOROUS PLANTS IN A TERRARIUM

Some of the most curious and interesting members of the plant world are the insectivorous plants. These small, exotically shaped and brightly colored plant oddities have evolved the means to capture insects and derive from the bodies of their victims some degree of nutrition. Animal-trapping plants have aroused particular interest and speculation among scientists as well as the layman. Science fiction writers have capitalized on this fascination by going one step further and creating vicious man-eating plants. However, the small carnivorous plants are quite harmless to all except the unwary insect and are attractive to observe in their natural habitat or in the specialized terrarium.

### Special Requirements

Insectivorous plants are found naturally in cedar swamps or sphagnum (mossy) bogs and thus make a striking addition to a woodland or bog terrarium. They require an extremely high humidity and a soil that is constantly moist but not waterlogged. They also prefer direct sunshine for a portion of the day, but care must be taken to allow ventilation during those hours. At all other times the terrarium must be sealed. Shredded sphagnum moss should be used as the growing medium for the insectivorous plants. In the absence of moss, sand or vermiculite may be tried. A damp, swampy area can be designed in the front portion of the terrarium and a retaining wall constructed of stones or a hidden layer of aluminum foil incorporated to keep the regular potting soil away from the roots of the insectivorous plants. One may also protect the plant by placing it in a clay pot of sphagnum and sinking the pot in the terrarium soil so that the rim is hidden by moss or stones.

Insectivorous plants may be hand fed sparingly about every two months. Small bugs, flies, or minute pieces of hamburger can be offered by using tweezers. Any excess food will quickly rot, forming bacteria harmful to the plants, so care must be taken to remove any food particles accidentally dropped during the feeding process.

When constructing the terrarium, follow the general steps as outlined in the section on "Basic Procedures," but choose a container that can be sealed. The following plants are recommended for a terrarium of insectivorous plants.

### Venus Fly Trap *(Dionaea muscipula)*

The Venus Fly Trap is the best known of the insectivorous plants and one of the most interesting. It develops from an underground bulb, producing light-green, slender leaves that terminate in two hinged lobes set along the margins with hairlike bristles. This structure is the insect trap. It produces a slightly sweet nectar and is shaded a brilliant red, with both features designed to guarantee close examination by insects. When the insect alights on the leaf, the lobes snap shut in a fraction of a second, trapping and crushing the victim. Digestive juices are secreted by the plant and the leaves remain closed until the insect is absorbed.

The Venus Fly Trap may produce only a few traps or as many as twelve. Generally, the older the bulb, the larger and more numerous the traps. Under terrarium conditions the plant may flower, producing small, undistinguished white blossoms on the end of a long, upright stem. If the flower stalk is removed before maturing, the energy of the plant goes into producing larger traps.

This plant regularly undergoes a normal growth and rest cycle. The traps turn black and eventually all the top growth dies back to the ground. During this dormancy period the plant should be kept moist, in a cool place, and in filtered light. Six to eight weeks later, new growth should appear.

### Northern Pitcher Plant *(Sarracenia purpurea)*

The Northern Pitcher Plant is another interesting insectivorous plant. The leaves are juglike, forming rounded, hollow tubes, generally half-filled with rainwater and digestive enzymes. The lip and hood on each leaf are covered with sharp, downward-facing bristles. Once an insect has landed on the leaf, there is no return from the water trap. The leaves are attractively shaded in green, red, and yellow and turn a bright red in winter, resembling boiled lobster claws. An attractive flower, which looks like an inverted red tulip on a long stem, is produced.

## TABLE OF TROPICAL PLANTS

| Name of Tropical Plant | Non-Flower-ing | Light | | | Nighttime Temperature (F) | | | Terrarium | |
|---|---|---|---|---|---|---|---|---|---|
| | | Low | Med | Bright | 40–50° | 50–60° | 60°+ | Sealed | Open |
| *Achimenes* - Magic Flower | | | X | | | | X | | X |
| *Acorus* - Japanese Sweet Flag | X | | X | | | | X | X | |
| *Aglaonema* - Chinese Evergreen | X | X | | | | | X | X | |
| *Allophytum* - Mexican Foxglove | | | X | | | X | | X | |
| *Anthurium* - Flaming Flower | | | X | | | | X | X | |
| *Aphelandra* | | | X | | | | X | | X |
| *Ardisia* | | | X | | | X | | | X |
| *Beaucarnea* - Mexican Bottle Plant | X | | X | | | X | | | X |
| *Begonia* | | | X | | | X | | X | |
| *Buxus* - Boxwood | X | | X | | | X | | X | |
| *Caladium* | X | | X | | | | X | X | |
| *Calathea* - Peacock Plant | X | | X | | | | X | X | |
| *Calceolaria* - Pocketbook Plant | | | X | | X | | | | X |
| *Callisia* - Stripped Inch Plant | X | | X | | X | | | | X |
| *Capsicum* - Ornamental Pepper | | | | X | | | X | | X |
| *Ceropegia* - Rosary Vine | X | | X | | | X | | | X |
| *Chamaedorea* - Parlor Palm | X | X | | | | | X | X | |
| *Chlorophytum* - Spider Plant | | | X | | | X | | X | |
| *Crassandra* | | | | X | | X | | | X |
| *Cryptanthus* - Earth Star | | | X | | | | X | | X |
| *Cuphea* - Cigar Plant | | | | X | | X | | | X |
| *Cyclamen* | | | X | | X | | | | X |
| *Cyperus* - Umbrella Plant | X | | | X | X | | | X | |
| *Dichorisandra* - Seersucker Plant | X | | X | | | | X | | X |
| *Dracaena* - Dragon Tree | X | X | | | | | X | X | |
| *Episcia* - Flame Violet | | | X | | | | X | X | |
| *Euonymus* - Wintercreeper | X | X | | | X | | | X | |
| *Euphorbia* - Corncob Euphorbia | X | | | X | | X | | | X |
| *Exacum* - Arabian Violet | | | X | | | | X | | X |
| *Fatshedera* - Tree Ivy | X | | | X | X | | | | X |
| *Felicia* - Blue Marguerite | | | | X | | X | | | X |
| Ferns | X | | X | | | X | | X | |
| *Ficus* - Weeping Fig | X | | X | | | | X | X | |
| *Fittonia* - Silver-Nerved Fittonia | X | | X | | | | X | X | |
| *Gazania* - Treasure Flower | | | | X | | X | | | X |
| *Gloxinera* - Rosebells | | | X | | | | X | | X |
| *Hedera* - English Ivy | X | | X | | X | | | X | |
| *Heliotropium* | | | | X | | X | | | X |

## TABLE OF TROPICAL PLANTS

| Name of Tropical Plant | Non-Flowering | Light | | | Nighttime Temperature (F) | | | Terrarium | |
|---|---|---|---|---|---|---|---|---|---|
| | | Low | Med | Bright | 40–50° | 50–60° | 60°+ | Sealed | Open |
| *Hypoestes* | X | | X | | | | X | | X |
| *Impatiens* - **Patient Lucy** | | | | X | | X | | | X |
| *Jacobinia* | | | | X | | | X | | X |
| *Kalanchoe* | | | | X | | X | | | X |
| *Lachenalia* - **Cape Cowslip** | | | | X | X | | | | X |
| *Lobularia* - **Sweet Alyssum** | | | | X | | X | | | X |
| *Maranta* - **Prayer Plant** | X | | X | | | | X | | X |
| *Nicotiana* - **Flowering Tobacco** | | | | X | | X | | | X |
| *Osmanthus* - **Holly Osmanthus** | | | X | | X | | | | X |
| *Oxalis* | | | | X | | X | | | X |
| *Pedilanthus* - **Devil's Backbone** | X | | X | | | X | | | X |
| *Peperomia* | X | | X | | | | X | | X |
| *Philodendron* | X | X | | | | X | | X | |
| *Pilea* - **Aluminum Plant** | X | | X | | | | X | | X |
| *Plectranthus* - **White-Edged Swedish Ivy** | X | | X | | | X | | | X |
| *Podocarpus* - **Chinese Podocarpus** | X | | X | | | X | | X | |
| *Primula* - **Primrose** | | | X | | X | | | | X |
| *Rosa* - **Miniature Rose** | | | X | | | X | | | X |
| *Rosmarinus* - **Rosemary** | | | X | | | X | | | X |
| *Saintpaulia* - **African Violet** | | | X | | | | X | | X |
| *Sansevieria* - **Mother-In-Law Tongue** | X | X | | | | X | | | X |
| *Saxifraga* - **Strawberry Geranium** | | | X | | | X | | | X |
| *Schizocentron* - **Spanish Shawl** | | X | | | | X | | | X |
| *Scilla* - **Siberian Squill** | | | X | | | X | | | X |
| *Scindapsus* - **Devil's Ivy** | X | X | | | | | X | | X |
| *Setcreasea* - **Purple Heart** | X | | | X | | X | | | X |
| *Sinningia* - **Gloxinia** | | | X | | | | X | | X |
| *Smithiantha* - **Templebells** | | | X | | | | X | | X |
| *Solanum* - **Jerusalem Cherry** | | | | X | | X | | | X |
| *Spathiphyllum* - **Mauna Loa** | | X | | | | | X | | X |
| *Streptocarpus* - **Cap Primrose** | | | X | | | | X | X | |
| *Syngonium* - **Arrowhead Vine** | X | X | | | | | X | X | |
| *Tetranema* - **Mexican Foxglove** | | X | | | | X | | | X |
| *Tradescantia* - **Wandering Jew** | | | X | | | X | | X | |
| *Zebrina* - **Four-Colored Wandering Jew** | | | X | | | X | | X | |

## TABLE OF WILD PLANTS

| Name of Wild Plants | Non-Flowering | Height In Inches | General Description |
|---|---|---|---|
| *Anemone quinquefolia* Wood Anemone | | 3—6 | Flowers small, 5-petalled with yellow center; leaves 3-lobed |
| *Anemonella thalictroides* Rue Anemone | | 4—6 | Leaves delicate green, rounded, lobed; flower white |
| *Arisaema triphyllum* Jack-in-the-Pulpit | | 6—8 | Leaves 3-lobed; flowers shaped like hooded pulpit, green and red |
| *Asarum canadense* Wild Ginger | | 4—6 | Leaves elevated on stalks, kidney shaped; flower hugs ground, bell-like, deep maroon |
| *Chimaphila sp.* Pipsissewa, Prince's Pine | | 6—10 | Leaves attractive, green; flowers white |
| *Claytonia virginia* Spring Beauty | | 4—6 | Leaves long, narrow; flowers pink-white, on long arching stem |
| *Coptis groenlandica* Goldthread | | 3—4 | Leaves dainty, clover-like; flowers tiny, white |
| *Cornus canadensis* Bunchberry | | 3—5 | Flowers large, white, 4-petalled |
| *Dicentra canadensis* Squirrel Corn | | 6—10 | Leaves deeply dissected, lacy; flowers white, several on stalk |
| *Dicentra cucullaria* Dutchman's Britches | | 6—12 | Leaves lacy, gray-green; flowers white, resemble inverted pantaloons |
| *Dodecatheon meadia* Shooting Star | | 6—12 | Leaves strap-shaped; flowers star-like, on long stem, white, pink, or lavender |
| *Epigea repens* Trailing Arbutus | | 6—10 | Leaves leathery, evergreen; waxen flowers of creamy white; acid soil |
| *Equisetum sp.* Horsetails | X | 6—12 | Grass-like, stiff; stems joined, smooth or with whorls of needle-like branches |
| *Erythronium sp.* Dog-Tooth Violet | | 5—8 | Leaves 2, mottled green, maroon; flower like dangling lily, white or yellow |
| Ferns | X | 3—12 | Many, wild ferns are small enough for terrariums |
| *Fragaria virginiana* Wild Strawberry | | 4—6 | Typical strawberry leaves, forms new plants on tips of runners; white flowers |
| *Gautheria procumbens* Checkerberry | | 2—4 | Leaves shiny, aromatic; clusters of berries in fall |
| *Goodyera pubescens* Rattlesnake Plantain | | 2—4 | Member of orchid family; leaves unusually attractive, green with white veins |
| *Hepatica sp.* Liverleaf | | 3—4 | Leaves liver-shaped, maroon; flowers pink-purple or white |

## TABLE OF WILD PLANTS

| Name of Wild Plant | Non-Flowering | Height In Inches | General Description |
|---|---|---|---|
| *Juniperus virginiana* **Juniper** | X | 1—6 | Seedling tree |
| **Lichens** | X | 1—3 | Tiny, gray-green scale-like leaves, interesting |
| **Liverworts** | X | ½—1 | Leaves flat, scale-like, form low-lying mats, interesting. |
| *Lycopodium lucidulum* **Club Moss** | X | 2—5 | Leaves deep green, tiny scale-like, many branches. |
| *Lysimachia nummularia* **Moneywort** | | 6—15 | Leaves round; flowers bright yellow; a low vine. |
| *Mitchella repens* **Partridge Berry** | | 6—15 | Creeping vine, leaves small, round; bright red berries in fall. |
| **Mosses** | X | 1—6 | Many species — various textures, colors, sizes; good groundcover |
| *Myosotis laxa* **Forget-Me-Not** | | 6—15 | Flowers tiny, sky-blue with yellow centers. |
| *Oxalis* sp. **Wood Sorrel** | | 4—8 | Leaves clover-like, 3-leaflets, fold at night; flowers white, yellow, pink, red |
| *Pinus* sp. **Pine** | X | 1—6 | Seedling tree |
| *Pyrola elliptica* **Wintergreen** | | 6—8 | Leaves dark green, stiff. |
| *Selaginella* sp. | X | 1 | Dense mat, hugs ground; leaves delicate, lacy, deep green. |
| *Taxus canadensis* **Yew** | X | 1—6 | Seedling tree. |
| *Tiarella cordifolia* **Foam Flower** | | 6—8 | Leaves heart-shaped; spikes of white flowers. |
| *Trillium* sp. | | 6—15 | Leaves 3-lobed, mottled green and red; flower white or deep maroon |
| *Tsuga canadensis* **Eastern Hemlock** | X | 1—6 | Seedling tree. |
| *Uvularia sessilifolia* **Bellwort** | | 6—10 | Flowers drooping, bell-like, yellow |
| *Viola* sp. **Violet** | | 3—12 | Many species; colors from white, cream to blue, violet. |

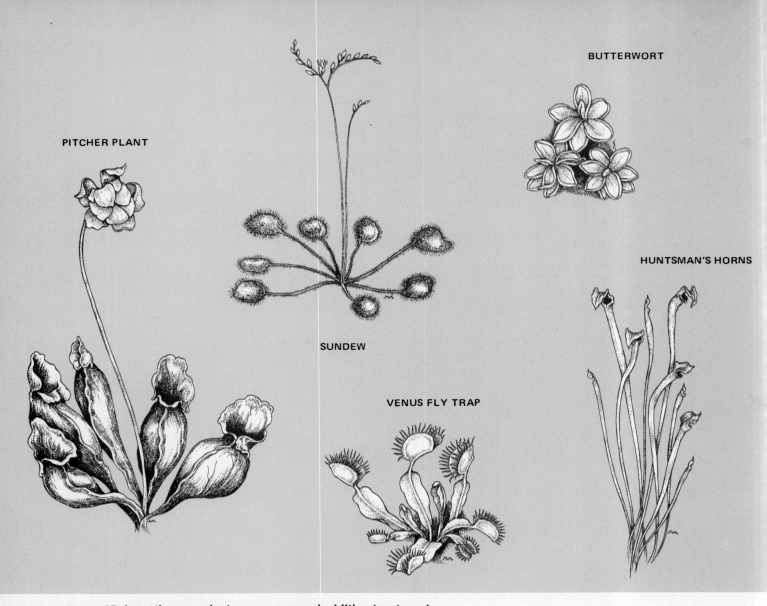

PITCHER PLANT

SUNDEW

BUTTERWORT

HUNTSMAN'S HORNS

VENUS FLY TRAP

*Figure 15. Insectivorous plants are an unusual addition to a terrarium.*

### Huntsman's Horn *(Sarracenia flaval)*

Somewhat less striking than the Pitcher Plant, but related to it, is the Huntsman's Horn. This plant produces long, narrow, hollow leaves that entrap insects in the same manner as the Pitcher Plant. A beautiful but foul-smelling yellow flower occasionally appears among the slender horns.

### Other Insectivorous Plants

Flypaper-type traps are utilized by two other insect-eating plants, the Sundue (*Drosera* species) and Butterwort (*Pinguicula vulgarisis*). The tiny Sundue lures the insect to its doom with slender leaves stretched upright and covered with sticky, glistening red hairs. When an insect touches the leaf, it is caught by the secretions and can not tear its way free before the tentacles close over it.

The Butterwort presents a similar trap, offering shiny, buttery leaf surfaces to the passing insect. The insect lands in the leaf, becomes mired in the sticky surface, and the leaf margins slowly fold over it in a deadly embrace.

## ORCHIDS IN A TERRARIUM

Growing miniature orchids in a terrarium is an exciting challenge for the expert gardener. Orchids are found in the tropical and temperate zones of the world and are either terrestrial or epiphytic in habit. There may be over 30,000 different kinds of orchids with scarcely half of these identified as to species. Hundreds of miniature orchids are offered for sale by orchid growers.

## TABLE OF ORCHIDS

| Name of Orchid | Flower Color | Blooming Time | Height in Inches |
|---|---|---|---|
| *Crastrochillas bellinas* | Cream Brown | Spring | 3-5 |
| *Dendrobium arachnites* | | Spring | |
| *Epidendrum bractescens* | | Spring | |
| *Epidendrum paleaceum* | Yellow | Spring | 6-8 |
| *Ionopsis paniculata* | Blush Lavender | Spring | 4-10 |
| *Laelia pumila* | Rose Purple | Fall Winter | 8 |
| *Lockhartia oersderii* | Yellow Red | | |
| *Lockhartia pallida* | Creamy Yellow | | |
| *Maxillaria fredrickstahlii* | Pale Yellow | | 3-4 |
| *Miltonia cindy* **Kane Waterfall** | Violet-Purple | Spring | 6-12 |
| *Miltonia snohomish* | White Violet | Spring | 6-12 |
| *Miltonia woodlands Suzii × M. roezii* | White | Spring | 6-12 |
| *Mystacidium distichum* | | Summer | 9 |
| *Neofinetia falcata* | White | | 3-6 |
| *Notylia bicolor* | Green White | | |
| *Odontoglossum krameri* | Violet | Winter | 4-8 |
| *Odontoglossum rossii* | White Rose Brown | Winter | 6 |
| *Odontonia dubutante × Oncidium maculatum* | White Maroon | Spring | 8-12 |
| *Oncidium cheirophorum* | Yellow | Fall | 4-8 |
| *Oncidium iridifolium* | Yellow Red | Summer | 3 |
| *Oncidium pulchellum* | Blush Lavender | Spring | 10-12 |
| *Oncidium tetrapetalum* | White Brown | Summer | 3-6 |
| *Oncidium triquetrum* | Yellow White Brown | Winter Spring | 3-5 |
| *Ornithocephalus bicornis* | Green White | Winter | 2 |

| Name of Orchid | Flower Color | Blooming Time | Height in Inches |
|---|---|---|---|
| *Ornithocephalus cohleariformis* | Green White | | |
| *Ornithocephalus iridifolius* | Green White | Spring | 3 |
| *Paphiopedilum bellatulum* | Cream Maroon | | 10 |
| *Paphiopedilum concolor* | Yellow Violet | Fall | 6 |
| *Paphiopedilum fairieanum* | White Purple | Fall Winter | 6 |
| *Phalaenopsis equestris* | White Rose | | 8 |
| *Phalaenopsis intermedia* | White | Spring | 10-12 |
| *Phalaenopsis lueddomammiona* | Violet Maroon | Spring | 6-12 |
| *Phalaenopsis parishii* | White Brown | | |
| *Physosiphon tubatus* | Orange | Winter Spring Summer | 6-8 |
| *Pleurothallis aribuloides* | Red | | |
| *Pleurothallis fulgens* | Red | | |
| *Pleurothallis grobyi* | Yellow Crimson | | |
| *Pleurothallis leptotifolia* | Purple Green | | |
| *Pleurothallis minuthallis* | Green Brown | | |
| *Pleurothallis picta* | Orange | | 2 |
| *Sophronitis coccinea* | Orange Red | Winter | 3-6 |
| *Sophronitis grandiflora* | Red | | |
| *Sophronitis violacea* | Lavender | | |
| *Trichoccentrum pfavii* | White Brown | | |
| *Vanda cristata* | Pink Brown | Spring | 8-12 |
| *Vanda samperiana × Abco curvifolia* | Orange | Spring | 6-10 |
| *Warmingia eugenii* | Cream Brown | Spring | 10-12 |

Figure 16. *Miltonia Snohomish (top) Miltonia Cindy (center), and Phalaenopsis Lueddomammiona (bottom) are just a few of the species recommended for growing orchids in a terrarium.*

Before beginning an orchid terrarium, one should be familiar with the general rules of orchid culture. Species differ as to light, temperature, and water requirements, and it is of utmost importance to group plants that require similar growing conditions in the same container. Unlike other terrarium plants, orchids must be grown in special material — generally osmunda (ferny) fiber or redwood bark — and fed regularly with orchid fertilizer. Care, too, must be taken when watering. Some plants like to be kept evenly moist while others prefer to dry out between waterings. All will quickly die with too much water or poor drainage. Orchid terrariums can never be sealed as these exotic plants need circulating air.

Some miniature orchids will do better than others under terrarium conditions, and the entire subject could use more research and experimentation. The chart on page 207 lists miniature orchids that may do well in a terrarium. Species marked with an asterisk (*) are recommended by Hausermann, Inc., an orchid nursery near Chicago. Complete success is not guaranteed.

## For Additional Reading

Ashberry, Anne, **Bottle Gardens and Fern Cases,** Bonanza Books, 1964.

Baur, Robert C., **Gardens in Glass Containers,** Hearthside Press, 1970.

Budlong, Ware, **Indoor Gardens,** Hawthorn, 1967.

Elbert, Virginia and George B., **Fun With Terrarium Gardening,** Crown, 1973.

Evan, Charles M., **The Terrarium Book,** Random House, 1973.

Grubman, Barbara Joan, **Introduction to Terrariums,** Nash, 1972.

Lewis, Glen, "Terrariums, the World of Nature," **Outdoor World,** 1973.

Wolff, Wendy, **Terrariums and Other Nice Things,** James E. Gick, 1972.